Soviet Influence on
Cuban Culture, 1961–1987

Lexington Studies on Cuba

Series Editors: John M. Kirk, Dalhousie University
and Mervyn Bain, University of Aberdeen

This series will publish texts on all aspects of Cuba, focusing on the post-1959 period. It seeks to be truly interdisciplinary, with studies of all aspects of contemporary Cuba—from foreign policy to culture, sociology, to economics. The series is particularly interested in broad, comprehensive topics (such as women in Cuba, economic challenges, human rights, the role of the media, etc.). All ideological positions are welcomed, with solid academic quality being the defining criterion. In exceptional circumstances edited collections will be considered, but the main focus is on high quality, original, and provocative monographs and innovative scholarship.

Recent Titles in This Series

Soviet Influence on Cuban Culture, 1961–1987: When the Soviets Came to Stay
By Isabel Story
Entangled Terrains: Empire, Identity, and Memory of Guantánamo
By Asa McKercher and Catherine Krull
God and the Nation: A Social History of Cuba's Protestants
By James A. Baer
The People's Professors: How Cuba Achieved Education for All
By Kathryn Moody
Youth and the Cuban Revolution: Youth Culture and Politics in 1960s Cuba
By Anne Luke
Cuba's Forgotten Decade: How the 1970s Shaped the Revolution
Edited by Emily J. Kirk, Anna Clayfield, Isabel Story

Soviet Influence on Cuban Culture, 1961–1987

When the Soviets Came to Stay

Isabel Story

LEXINGTON BOOKS

Lanham • Boulder • New York • London

Published by Lexington Books
An imprint of The Rowman & Littlefield Publishing Group, Inc.
4501 Forbes Boulevard, Suite 200, Lanham, Maryland 20706
www.rowman.com

6 Tinworth Street, London SE11 5AL, United Kingdom

British Library Cataloguing in Publication Information Available

Library of Congress Cataloging-in-Publication Data

Library of Congress Control Number: 2019953563

ISBN: 978-1-4985-8011-3 (cloth)
ISBN: 978-1-4985-8013-7 (pbk.)
ISBN: 978-1-4985-8012-0 (electronic)

Contents

Acknowledgements

A heartfelt thanks to all the many individuals who have helped shape this book, especially Tony and Polly.

Introduction

This book analyzes how Soviet cultural ideas, experiences, and models shaped post-1959 Cuban culture until the period known as *Rectification of Errors and Negative Tendencies* beginning from c.1986. In doing so, this study analyzes a set of circumstances in which the nature of politically engaged art was subject to wide-ranging debate and in which the nature of Soviet "influence" (economic, political, and cultural) was interpreted and re-evaluated. It examines instances of cross-cultural dialogue, showing how notions of culture and internationalism, and the discourse surrounding these, were mutable, flexible, and ambiguous during a period of intense political upheaval in Cuba and internationally.

The research for this book focuses on two key periods, 1960–1963 and 1975–1986. The former was a time when relations between the USSR and Cuba were at their most positive, and outward-looking perspectives were favored in Cuba; the latter was a period during which Cuban-Soviet relations were strained. In investigating these moments, this book examines whether or not what is often described as times of political and economic "Sovietization" were reflected in the cultural evolution of the Revolution or whether the relationship was more complex, as suggested by developments during the late 1970s. More generally, in this study, there is a distinction between Soviet-influenced approaches to culture under socialism, such as the prioritization of certain topics or styles and Cuban admiration for Soviet models for institutions that reflect the value placed on culture, and access to culture, in a socialist society, such as the Palaces of Culture, the Writers' Union, and the Ministry of Culture. This allows for the exploration of how, if indeed at all, the revolutionary government reconciled combatting the residual effects of colonialism and the borrowing of Western cultural norms with the imperative to create authentically Cuban intellectual spaces and to foster organic discourses, and the effect of this reconciliatory process on artists. This book examines how conceptions of the artist's role in revolutionary society changed according to the leadership's prioritization of cultural, political, and economic tasks. This research also sheds light on how Cuban cultural leaders responded to the wave of anti-institutionalism that spread following the sectarian power struggle, dubbed the "mini-Stalinist" affair of 1961–1962, and how they reconciled this impulse with the genuine need to create a cultural infrastructure.

The cultural institutions which form the backbone of this study are the National Council of Culture (Consejo Nacional de Cultura, CNC) created in 1961 to establish the arts as an integral part of the Revolution, replaced in 1976 by the Ministry of Culture (Ministerio de Cultura, MinCult); the Union of Writers and Artists of Cuba (Unión de Escritores y Artistas de Cuba, UNEAC), established in 1961; and the University of the Arts (Instituto Superior de Artes, ISA), established in 1967, but not opened until 1976. The latter two of these institutions played broad roles and were subordinated to the CNC and later MinCult. These umbrella institutions had a significant number of orthodox communists from the pre-revolutionary party, the Popular Socialist Party (Partido Socialista Popular, PSP) and radical *guerrilleros* who supported a third world-oriented socialism within their structures. This made them the most likely institutions within which to find competing approaches toward cultural organization and output.

When analyzing these institutions, I focus on two specific forms of cultural output: theater and the visual arts. The latter is known as the plastic arts (artes plásticas) in Cuba and will henceforth, when discussing Cuba, be referred to in as such. At the center of this body of work are the theater and the plastic arts, because different strategies were adopted in the organization of these two artistic forms and the different resulting relationships with the USSR. Both forms were prized for their educational capacity and inherent mobility, but were also highly valued as revolutionary vehicles with which to combat colonialism and imperialism and defend an emergent national identity.

The plastic arts provide an excellent base from which to analyze the conflicting attitudes toward the USSR that abounded, and continue to abound, in Cuba, shaping cultural approaches and expressions of a certain period. Cultural changes influenced these impressions. Said cultural changes were brought about by leadership changes and shifting political culture in the USSR and the knowledge in Cuba of the internal struggles with ideas about culture within the superpower. Dialogues about the tensions between different types of socialism and different approaches toward internationalism and foreign cultures become particularly apparent when viewed in the context of Soviet debates about the development of the Contemporary Style—a "modern style, embracing all aspects of visual culture" (Reid 2000, 103), modernist influences, and the structural and aesthetic approach of what is known as "socialist realism." Moreover, the close linking of art with pre-revolutionary culturally based opposition groupings and magazines, and the expressive possibilities offered by non-verbal cultural output provide an important standpoint from which to analyze the Soviet-Cuban cultural relationship.

Theater has been chosen as a focus as it provides insights into the Cuban relationship with the USSR in a complementary manner. Theater, along with film, was the most underdeveloped cultural form in Cuba prior to the Revolution. However, unlike film, theater was never totally independent from the broad-based cultural institutions such as the CNC and then MinCult. Internationally, two of the most established theatrical theoretical systems (Stanislavskian and Brechtian) had become closely linked with ideas about socialism and socialist cultural production. In the USSR theater was highly valued and had been intimately linked with the October Revolution from an early stage and was quickly mobilized during the Russian Civil War. The combination in Cuba of theater's underdeveloped state, educative potential, low-skill threshold for participation and lack of other governing body, made theater the ideal site for experiments in the organization, production, and dissemination of a genuinely revolutionary Cuban culture. Finally, theater was the cultural mode which was most seriously affected by the regulatory current of the 1971–1976 period, which has come to be known as the *quinquenio gris*. This period was a phase of institutionalization, which included the implementation of certain structures that borrowed from the USSR and coincided with Cuba gaining full membership of the Council for Mutual Economic Aid (COMECON). The period was also initiated by international outcry about the seemingly Stalinist shift toward culture. The poet/writer Heberto Padilla who had caused polemics in 1968 with his cycle of poetry *Fuera del juego,* was arrested, jailed, and then released upon which he issued a harsh self-criticism which attracted international condemnation (Casal 1971, 462). Perhaps because of all of these factors, it is a period that has become classed as "Soviet" and as evidence of the external and internal "Sovietizing" of the Cuban Revolution (Fornet 2007). Theater, in particular, has become the emblem of this specific moment. Thus, the theater in revolutionary Cuba provides a counterpoint to the plastic arts and an alternative paradigm through which to analyze the Soviet presence in Cuba's cultural arena.

BOOK STRUCTURE

This book is the product of a wide range of sources, and its backbone is formed by a number of trips to Cuba and the Russian Federation to collect primary data. Interviews formed a significant part of this data collection. Some interviews were sought to provide concrete information, for others a range of perspectives on the matter, and in other cases it was for corroboration of events, approaches, and organizational tactics. These interviews were complemented by analyzing discussions and debate regarding cultural production, cultural policy, Soviet culture, and the USSR more generally, in the popular press. Many of the interviews conducted are not quoted here but I remain indebted to the kindness and knowledge of those who shared their time with me.

Chapter 1 traces the Cuban-Soviet relationship generally, setting the subsequent analysis of culture and cultural policy within a wider picture of the evolving alliance between the two countries. Chapter 2 opens with a discussion of socialist realism, providing a succinct overview of its Soviet context, before moving on to discuss the details of both the Cuban approach toward it, and in English-language academia more generally. The chapter also highlights the progression of socialist realism and distinguishes between its different iterations. In establishing the different versions of the concept and their geneses, the chapter provides the Soviet historical context necessary to understand the different ways in which socialist realism could have manifested itself in Cuba, and equally importantly, what element of the Soviet influence Cubans wished to emphasize when discussing the paradigm. The clarifications of these different terms and periods are then used throughout the remainder of the book.

Chapters 3 and 4 conduct an historical analysis of Cuban culture and the evolution of cultural policy between 1961 and 1986. They trace the developments within the field of culture, how policy was applied, and how it related to political and economic revolutionary projects; in doing so, these chapters demonstrate the complex interplay between these spheres. Chapter 3 explores the *quinquenio gris*, establishing that it was a period of intense expression of nationalism, with utopian aims of total inclusion, rather than one of Soviet imposition. Chapter 4 demonstrates the closer linking of culture to economic sovereignty from the 1970s onward and that the 1980s exhibited many more "Soviet" characteristics. Both chapters 3 and 4 explore a number of key features of culture in Cuba: first, the way in which culture was at the center of the government's ideas and approaches toward nation-building and, as such, tended to continue the ideas found in the 1940 constitution, in José Martí's writings, and in the 26th July Movement (Movimiento 26 de Julio, M-26-7) movement; second, the way in which culture afforded a valuable space for debate about models of socialism and about which sectors were best suited to different revolutionary tasks; and, third, that multiple co-existing currents of thought regarding the Revolution, socialism, and Cuba's relationship with the USSR have always existed.

Chapters 5 and 6 examine the impact of cultural policy iterations on theater and the plastic arts, respectively, and explore how and why the two forms might have been treated differently and manifest different characteristics. Each chapter examines the historical evolution of each form, the development of its organization in Cuba and how it expressed different "revolutionary" qualities differently. The conclusion identifies the importance of internationalism in Cuban culture and its external relations.

Finally, a word on style. All translations, unless otherwise indicated, are my own. The transliteration of Russian words follows the Library of Congress system. Embedded terms will be italicized with a translation provided with their first use. The USSR will always be referred to as the USSR when used as a noun and Soviet as an adjective, and, when used as a noun, Revolution will be capitalized.

Chapter 1

The Cuban-Soviet Relationship

Soviet interest in Cuban sugar, and in Cuba itself, dates back to the beginning of the Russian Revolution in 1917.[1] While sugar would for many years come to define the relationship between the two countries, the Russian Revolution is a moment in history which became an enduring point of reference in the evolution of socialism in Cuba and specifically the development of a distinct "Cuban" variant of socialism that drew on many different currents of thought. For Russia, and then the Soviet Union, October 1917 was the beginning of a "systematic" interest in Cuba (Bain 2016, 323). This chapter will briefly trace the development of the Cuban-Soviet relationship, from the beginning of the Cuban Revolution until *Perestroika* and *glasnost*.

The early years of the Russian Revolution and the Soviet Union contained a number of important happenings for the Cuban Revolution and its evolution of cultural policy. These facts include the Civil War, the program of the New Economic Policy, and one of the first declarations of the Soviet cultural policy. During this period of the Bolshevik Revolution (a term used to refer specifically to the period 1917 to c.1925) a culture was born that became known worldwide for its quality, originality, variety, political commitment, and inclusion of the population (discussed in chapter 2).

The Russian Revolution and its aftermath heralded a period of seismic change within the country and its society. Russia was in a state of organizational chaos with widespread food shortages further aggravated by collapsing infrastructure. This was exacerbated by the historical inability of the Tsarist system to reconcile the need to modernize with the autocratic ruling system, and also the fact that the majority of the population were peasants, with high levels of illiteracy among them. Less than a year after the triumph of the Bolshevik Revolution, the country was in a state of civil war that further damaged the national economy which was already weak from the First

World War. However, at the same time that the civil war had destroyed the economy, it had also given the opportunity to ponder the mobilization of culture as an integral weapon of the struggle, and thus, demonstrated its capacity to educate people at all levels of society.

During all those changes within the politics and society of the country, there was a range of attitudes toward the role and duty of culture within a socialist revolution. Those attitudes were often centered on different cultural groups housed in competing cultural institutions (discussed in more detail in chapter 2). In March 1919 the international aspirations of the socialist movement were formally institutionalized with the creation of the Comintern (also known as the Third International or the Communist International). The Comintern was an organization of national Communist Parties which, headed by the Soviet Communist Party, advocated the spread of worldwide Revolution. The Comintern was a paradoxical institution in that it was focused on the international encouragement of socialism and socialist revolution capable of confronting "imperialist globalization" (Martínez Heredia 2017, 30). However, it also "carried the negative traits of great haste, forced homogenization and iron-clad authoritarianism" (Martínez Heredia 2017, 30). In doing so it propagated a particularly rigid and dogmatic type of socialism which positioned the USSR firmly at the vanguard of the global movement.

Indeed, the Soviet Union predated the existence of the Cuban Communist Party which was founded in 1925. Undoubtedly, over the decade following the founding of the Cuban party, communism based on Comintern canons was deeply influential but, like the Anarchist and Syndicalist movements, "never succeeded in understanding sufficiently the nature of the revolutionary Cuban legacy" (Martínez Heredia 2017, 33). In particular, the seventh Congress of the Comintern in 1935 heralded the beginning of a deep misunderstanding of liberalism in Latin America and the beginning of a line of thought which looked to Europe as the guiding model of Marxism and believed it necessary for Latin America to pass through the processes of capitalism before socialism could take hold (González Aróstegui and Martínez Heredia 2010, 31–32). Throughout this time of the First Republic (1902–1934) and then the Second Republic (1934–1958), a distinctively Cuban variant of socialism evolved via thinkers and political activists such as Juan Antonio Mella, (and his founding of the Cuban Communist Party) and Antonio Guiteras Holmes (figure 1.1). Cuba's connectivity to Latin America and the value of armed struggle were central to Cuban socialism (Martinez Heredia 2017, 44) and culture was a key area of struggle in the development of these insurrectionary movements. By the 1930s the culture of, and struggle for, national liberation had become intertwined with the culture and the struggle for social justice and socialism (Martinez Heredia 2017, 44).

Figure 1.1 Monument to Antonio Mella at the Top of Neptuno, Erected in 1975. Photo courtesy of the author.

The presence of Marxist ideas in the development of a Cuban ideology was not limited to Soviet interpretations of Marxism, but included Latin American currents, such as Aprismo, and the ideas of José Carlos Mariátegui and Eneyde Ponce de León which "provided a broad intellectual and political framework from which to view the complex reality of Cuban social relations" (Whitney 2001, 48). Initially, between 1924 and 1929, the emergent Cuban ideology seemed to complement Marxism, and even Soviet Marxism, which was not yet completely orthodox (Whitney 2001, 49). These ideas were mixed with the thought of José Martí and Simón Bolívar, as well as other strains of thought, such as Julio Antonio Mella's conception of a national Cuban Marxism predicated around anti-imperialism, anti-capitalism, and nationalism, and Antonio Guiteras Holmes's ideas about Cuban socialism, insurrectional movements, and societal transformation (Martínez Heredia 2017). As Martínez Heredia has argued, in Cuba, socialism's "presence as both a collective representation and a political discourse has been a constant; however, only at certain moments has it publicly opposed, or stood apart from, other socialisms" (Martínez Heredia 2017, 31).

Despite the growing links with the Comintern, with an affiliated party in Cuba from 1935 (Hallas 2008, 146), it was not until the disbanding of the organization in 1943 that meaningful cultural interaction between Cuba and the USSR began. The Cuban-Soviet Institute for Intercultural Exchange (Instituto de Intercambio Cultural Cubano-Soviético, IICCS) was created in 1945, presided over by the eminent Cuban anthropologist Fernando Ortiz (Bain 2013, 96). The IICCS had an associated publication *Cuba y la URSS*, which was published between 1945 and March 1952 (Bain 2015, 110). The publication showcased scientific, literary, sporting, and artistic work (Figueredo Cabrera 2017, 67). *Cuba y la URSS* is still remembered today by Cubans who grew up with the magazine, and indeed in interviews it has been cited by some as a source of inspiration for ways of practicing culture (López Oliva 2015a). In the opening edition, Ortiz extolled the virtues of greater cultural contact between Havana and Moscow, emphasizing the need for the two to act as united cultural poles at the crossroads of the ebb and flow of cultural contact between what he termed the Union of American States (where the pace of life was dictated by the United States), and the conglomerate that could be termed the Union of Eurasian States and the associated peoples that fell in the orbit of these two "superpowers." Havana and Moscow, he argued were poles in the flow of the "New World" and the "Old World" respectively and performed a "transcendental axial function" when united in their historic task (Ortiz 1945, 1). Through this institute, Moscow was able to exert an element of soft power over Havana prior to the Revolution with the promotion of Soviet culture, society, politics, and general awareness of the superpower. This was arguably further augmented by the system of scholarships to the Soviet Union that began to be offered to Latin Americans in the 1950s (Rupprecht 2015, 196).The IICCS was closed in March 1952, when diplomatic ties between Cuba and the USSR were cut, shortly after Fulgencio Batista came to power, in a demonstration of his pro-US stance (Bain 2013, 112). Cultural interaction, however, continued and was often based around personal links such as those of Cuban ballerina Alicia Alonso and her Soviet counterpart Maia Plisetskaia.

"KUBA" AND THE "URSS"

However, despite these established links, Cuba was perhaps somewhat absent in the collective cultural consciousness of the majority of the inhabitants of the Soviet Union.[2] On January 3, 1959, the newspaper *Pravda* (Truth), official mouthpiece of the Central Committee of the Communist Party of the USSR (KPSS), celebrated the triumph of the Cuban Revolution with an article entitled "Cuba Fights, Cuba Wins!" (Levin 1959). Accompanying the modest coverage of this momentous event was a small map of Cuba, to demonstrate to Soviet citizens where this revolutionary victory had taken place. Inset into this map was a wider map, covering the Gulf of Mexico and the Caribbean Basin, with a large arrow identifying Cuba, and indicating its geographical position in relation to the United States.

To the USSR, the opportunities offered by the Cuban Revolution were practical solutions to a pressing issue of supply. To the Cuban government, the protection the socialist superpower offered was a necessary step for the protection of the nascent independence project in an increasingly polarized world.

However, initially, the Khrushchev administration took great care to give its interaction with the country an essentially economic nature (Lévesque 1978, 15). Moscow made an initial purchase from revolutionary Cuba of 170,000 tons of sugar in April 1959, which was actually less than its order the previous year. The ensuing revolutionary reforms under the Cuban government, particularly the 1959 agrarian reform, fitted "theoretical thinking about the need for land reform throughout Latin America" (Duncan 1985, 32). It also sufficiently encouraged the Soviets to begin to trade with Cuba on a more serious level, due to the political potential that the country presented to the USSR.

Large-scale, official events were also organized, such as the April 1960 Soviet Exhibition of Science, Technology and Culture, which was held a month before the formal reestablishment of diplomatic relations between the two countries. João Felipe Gonçalves considers this event to be an early major contact of the Cuban public with Soviet culture, which ranged from everyday culture (clothing and appliances) to "high" culture (film, music, and literature). Loss (2013) considers that the 1960 Soviet exposition and the "discourse of expansionism, once explained to Cubans through the rhetoric of solidarity" (193), has ultimately shifted to represent the beginning of Cuba's alienation from its true self (185–194).

The exhibition was for many, also, their first interaction with Soviet individuals, as 147 Soviet citizens attended the exhibition. These individuals ranged from the 90 experts who installed the exhibition to the 57 artists, interpreters, journalists, air crew, and security officials who came to the dedication ceremony (2013, 85).

The Soviet exhibition even featured in one of the early revolutionary key cultural publications—*Lunes*. Issue 46, which had contorted typography to spell out "URSS" ("nUmeRo eSpecial de luneS") dealt with Soviet culture in the broadest sense, in celebration of the Soviet Exhibition in the Palacio de Bellas Artes, which showcased the best achievements of the USSR in the fields of science, technology, and culture. The magazine celebrated the USSR's achievements but did so in a way that also asserted Cuba's right to cultural independence and rejected perceived assumptions about small nations' cultural capacities and underdevelopment:

> The presentation of this event is an act of national reaffirmation, of our independence and of our free determination as a people. Until now it has been understood that only the great potentates were capable of establishing exchanges between themselves despite political contradictions. This attitude forms part of the pattern of discrimination towards small countries, whom they not only subjugate but also go as far as wanting to impose their international prohibitions, because they have the intention of also limiting economic relations free from metropolitan interventions. (Cabrera Infante 1960)

On May 8, 1960, shortly after the exhibition the two countries established diplomatic relations. The USSR began to trade with Cuba on a larger scale that year when First Deputy Prime Minister, Anastas Mikoian left Cuba having signed an agreement with Fidel Castro (henceforth Fidel) for the purchase of 425,000 tons of sugar in 1960; one million tons annually for the next four years, and a USD $100 million credit to buy industrial equipment. While this initial agreement was similar to the kind of agreements that Khrushchev had made with other developing countries in Africa and Asia (Miller 1989, 73), it has come to be seen as "a watershed in Soviet-Cuban relations" (Shearman 1987, 8).

Pragmatism was vital to the decision to increase the Soviet sugar order: the Soviet sugar crop had been hit by drought just as the authorities were seeking to increase national sugar consumption. Moreover, Moscow had also recently discovered rich oil deposits and was looking for an outlet to dispose of a crude oil surplus (Miller 1989, 74). By December 1960 the USSR had agreed to supply Cuba with "essential products" if they could not be purchased from other countries (namely the United States) (Lévesque 1978, 22) and by 1961 the Soviet economic aid has expanded into the labor sphere with the arrival of 500 Soviet technicians, 117 of whom were agricultural engineers (Torres Ramírez 1971, 41). Systematic study of Latin America was beginning in the Soviet Union, with the Institut Latinskoi Ameriki (Institute of Latin America, ILA) opening in Moscow in spring 1961. The institute housed over one hundred researchers, across seven departments (economy, foreign policy, workers and social movements, culture, geography, history and agrarian problems of all states and cultures south of the Rio Grande). Cuba was given its own department. The ILA was one of the largest research bodies of its type in the world (Rupprecht 2015, 245). The institute would come to publish many books on Latin America, and this began in 1961 with sending its researchers on series of *komandirovki* (trips/postings) to Cuba (Rupprecht 2015, 247).

However, there were also strong political and ideological reasonings for the swift formation of an alliance between Cuba and the USSR. On July 9, 1960, Soviet economic aid quickly snowballed, as the USSR shouldered the trade deficit left by the United States' 700,000-ton reduction of its sugar quota (Lévesque 1978, 16). That same day, at the All-Russian Congress of Teachers, Khrushchev delivered a speech highlighting US aggressions against the Cuban independence project and underlining that the United States was now within the reach of Soviet artillery should the need arise (Lévesque 1978, 18).

> The socialist states and all the peoples who stand in the positions of peace will support the people of Cuba in its just struggle, and nobody will be able to enslave the Cuban people.
>
> We must not forget that now the United States is not at such an unreachable distance from the Soviet Union as before. Figuratively speaking, if necessary, Soviet artillerymen can support the Cuban people with their missile fire, if aggressive forces in the Pentagon dare to launch an intervention against Cuba. And let the Pentagon not forget that, as recent tests have shown, we have missiles capable of falling exactly to the given square at a distance of 13,000 kilometers. This, if you like, is a warning to those who would like to solve international issues by force, and not by reason. (Khrushchev 1960, 2)

The same summer that a more significant level of trade between the two countries began, the USSR elicited a declaration of solidarity with Cuba from the Latin American communist parties, placing Cuba, and by extension its powerful ally, as the revolutionary figurehead in Latin America (Lévesque 1978, 23). The revolutionary government used the pre-revolutionary Cuban Communist Party, the PSP, as an aggressive negotiating agent, and the PSP, who had swiftly found their policy statements less radical than those of the M-26-7 embraced the role in what some have argued was a means to potentially contain Cuba's radicalization and maintain their influence (Miller 1989, 72; Gonzalez 1968, 39).

Just as the Soviet Union seemed to be moving at an accelerated pace toward Latin America, little over a year after the initial economic agreements, the Cuban Revolution seemed to be moving more definitively toward the Soviet Union. In December 1961, the Cuban revolutionary leadership identified itself as Marxist-Leninist, and this ideological common ground became part of the foundational base of the Cuban-Soviet alliance (Bain 2011, 112). While this moment was of undoubted importance in the political alliance that spanned the next three decades, it was not the first time the Revolution had been classed as socialist. The socialist nature of the Cuban Revolution was first declared on April 16, 1961, at the burial of the victims of the bombings which had occurred across the island the day previously. The following day the failed Bay of Pigs invasion began, catapulting Cuba once more into the attention of the international community.

Days before Fidel's April speech, the Soviet cosmonaut Iurii Gagarin had become the first man in space, swiftly becoming a symbol of the mobility of the 1960s. Gagarin and the space race formed part of the international exploration and imagining of alternative models for society that characterized the decades of the 1960s and 1970s. The 1959 rebel victory and subsequent Revolution confirmed this advent of a hopeful period of seismic global and societal change and, to the average Soviet citizen, Cuba, thousands of kilometers away in the Caribbean, was almost as alien as space itself, perhaps explaining the need for a map in the first report of the Cuban Revolution in the Soviet press. To the USSR, Cuba represented not just a publicity boost but also an unparalleled ideological opportunity. The Revolution, and the young guerrillas who came to form the government in particular, symbolized the power and potential of youth internationally, at a time when the urban population in the USSR surpassed 50% and was disproportionately young (Noack 2013, 172). In this respect, "for some younger people, [the Cuban Revolution] offered a heady opportunity to finally participate, if at a distance, in a revolution of their own. The [Soviet] regime was eager to encourage this perspective" (Gorsuch 2015, 505). By more fully linking itself to the Cuban Revolution, the Communist Party of the USSR (KPSS) could gain prestige on the international stage and demonstrate the vitality of the international socialist movement, at the head of which the Soviet government positioned itself. Moreover, the geographical proximity of a socialist country to the United States in a period of Cold War absolutely presented the very practical advantages of gaining access to new port facilities and potentially increasing the historically superficial Soviet presence in Latin America and the Caribbean basin. The country was arguably also seen as a valuable experiment, in terms of testing out the viability of Soviet theoretical models, such as "revolutionary democracy"[3] (Gorsuch 2015, 501), and in searching for solutions to perceived Soviet problems.

In the polarized environment of the Cold War, which subordinated other national histories to its binary dialogue, the Cuban Revolution's apparently sudden conversion to socialism in December 1961 seemed to demonstrate the hallmark of Soviet meddling and confirmation to external observers of the perception that Cuba had "irrevocably become a communist state closely tied to the Eastern Bloc" (Goldberg 1965, 238). This is an enduring interpretation that has informed understandings of the Cuban Revolution and its policies in academia and beyond.[4] In fact, what was true was that the public declaration of the socialist nature of the Cuban Revolution was the continuation of a Cuban ideology based around national independence, ideas of Cubanness and anti-corruption which had been developing since the nineteenth century, rather than a sudden, imposed, conversion to Soviet communism. Marxism had been inscribed in Cuban ideology from the early twentieth century and the prominence of communists in both the insurrection and governmental infrastructure meant that much of the Cuban population had an awareness of the practical application of communism and its values (Kapcia 2008, 89–99).

Revelations regarding the Stalinist regime in the period immediately after Stalin's death, known as the Thaw, and events such as the 1956 Soviet invasion of Hungary, demanded a more nuanced approach to the USSR as the alliance between the two countries grew. The revelations also highlighted the ideological importance of the period of Bolshevik rule. Fears that a close relationship with the USSR would result in ideological dogmatism, repression, or even a cult of personality abounded in Cuba and Latin America before the Revolution and during it. Evidence of these fears can be found in the outcry from Latin American intellectuals regarding a perceived emergence of Stalinist suppression of artists in the carefully orchestrated public apology of the "Padilla affair" of 1971, or even in Fidel's insistence that no streets or monuments be named after him in a bid to avoid the cult of personality (AP 2016; Ojito 2016). However, for the Cuba of 1961, the USSR was undoubtedly a solution to two pressing internal problems: the need for protection and the need to maintain levels of sugar exports. The rapid deterioration of Cuban-US relations had made it imperative for Cuba to find a new trading ally to support its economy and to secure military protection.

Simultaneously, the presence of Soviet pedagogical materials[5] amongst the Cuban population was already growing: copies of *Panfilov's Men* and the *Volokolamsk Highway* by Aleksander Bek were distributed to Cubans fighting at the Bay of Pigs and at the military schools that were swiftly established in the face of impending attacks from the United States. Considered educational tools for the new Cuban soldiers defending their newly reformed country from imperialist aggression, the books are fondly remembered by some Cubans for the realistic way they spoke of the experience of what it meant to be a guerrilla (León del Rio and Martínez Heredia 2010, 76; Heras León 2015). More generally, the USSR was the model *par excellence* of rapid industrialization, technical progress, economic development, and a culturally educated society. As the Cold War intensified, it was also arguably the easiest, and sometimes, as Cuba's geopolitical isolation intensified,[6] the only, country from which Cuba could receive technical training or appropriate particularly useful or successful organizational and technical artistic techniques. Gorsuch considers the USSR's lack of a "traditional" colonial past to have been particularly important for the revolutionary government (Gorsuch 2015, 502). This view is shared and expanded upon by Bain (2010) and Shearman, the latter highlighting the USSR's lack of historical intervention or colonies in North, Central, and South America (1987, 1–11). From 1962, Cubans were able to study the Russian language and literature at the University of Havana's Escuela de Letras (Cinco Colina 2010, 25), and the first Cyrillic typeface in Latin America, *Ciril*, was created by Cuban graphic designer Felix Beltran in 1974 (Pozuelo 2009, 181). Today the country has an enduring (and unique) Russian-language capability (Bain 2011, 114) that means the country retains strategic value to the Russian Federation.

The Socialist Bloc also quickly opened up its doors to Cuban students, and in May 1961 1,000 Cuban students left for the USSR to train as future technicians and engineers (Torres Ramírez 1971, 41). The Soviet's cooperative attitude was well received in Cuba, with the revolutionary government expressing its satisfaction at the economic relationship that was developing between the USSR and more generally, the Socialist Bloc (Torres Ramírez 1971, 40). Despite this enthusiastic provision of aid, as early as the autumn of 1960 the USSR had felt that the Cuban Revolution was moving too fast. It felt that it was essential that a private sector (such as that encouraged by the New Economic Policy, introduced by the Bolsheviks in the early 1920s to help the ailing Soviet economy to recover) should be preserved for an undefined amount of time, while the state sector and the planning system were established and organized to facilitate the transition to socialism and limit the associated economic imbalances that would occur (Lévesque 1978, 22).

The ideological education of the Cuban population was also progressing apace and was initially entrusted to members of the pre-revolutionary party (the PSP) due to their theoretical knowledge and organizational infrastructure. This area became an early indicator of the nuanced and shifting relationship between Cuba and the USSR. Aníbal Escalante, a leading figure in the PSP, had been entrusted with the construction of the Integrated Revolutionary Organizations (ORIs), which brought together the pre-revolutionary opposition movements the PSP, the 26th of July Movement and the March 13 Revolutionary Directory. However, the PSP also initially dominated the Schools of Revolutionary Instruction (EIRs) which gave Cubans a basic grounding in Marxism. The PSP's domination of the EIRs[7] provided them with the perfect base from which to rapidly politically educate the rebel soldiers. By March 1962, the ORI had been converted into a potent organization which controlled diverse aspects of Cuba's politics and economics (Gallardo Saborido 2009, 87). Because of the fears raised by the prevalence of the PSP in positions of power within the Revolution's institutions, intensified by some members' rigid interpretations of socialism and communism, tensions with other groups and individuals involved in the governance of Cuba swiftly developed. As a result, in 1962 the EIRs were removed from the PSP's instruction, and the ORI ceased activity, pending complete reorganization into the United Party of the Socialist Revolution of Cuba (PURS). On March 26, 1962, Fidel publicly accused Escalante of having "forced Cuba into a sectarian straitjacket" (Karol 1971, 247), and he was denounced as having organized an apparatus which was predisposed toward following his (rather than the government's) orders, and of having created a niche of privileges and a system of favors (Gallardo Saborido 2009, 87). Escalante was sent to be an attaché in the Cuban embassy in Czechoslovakia.

Throughout this period, Marxism in Cuba was becoming an increasingly mass phenomenon, incorporating elements of different strands of thought that were reflective of Cuba's geography and history. This was in part through the political instruction of the EIRs but also reflective of the radicalization of the population after events such as the Bay of Pigs. During this time the Department of Philosophy at the University of Havana was founded, a department that would swiftly come to occupy an important place in the ideological education of the nation and the exploration of versions of socialist ideologies from sources other than the USSR.

The Raúl Cepero Bonilla School, run by the EIR's National Directorate and the University of Havana, was founded to train teachers for university-level teaching. It ran two courses, between 1962 and 1963, and from this school came the teachers who would later form the Department of Philosophy at the University of Havana. The school was directed by Felipe Sánchez Linares and classes were given by Isabel Monal, Pelegrín and Jacinto Torras, Sergio Aguirre and others. Among these, the Hispano-Soviets (from Spain's Civil War) Anastacio Mancilla and Luis Arana particularly stood out.[8] The topics covered included Dialectical and Historical Materialism, Political Economy, History of Philosophy, Universal History, and more focused topics such as Colonialism and Underdevelopment (Díaz Sosa 2006).

By 1963, there was already theoretical distancing among some sectors, such as the University of Havana's Department of Philosophy, from Soviet Marxism (and its manuals) and a concerted move toward the positions adopted by the Bolsheviks in the October Revolution (León del Rio and

Martínez Heredia 2010). Soviet manuals continued to be used in the EIR, in part due to the intensive nature of the courses, which made deeper study of the original texts impossible, and also due to the lack of teaching personnel equipped to deal with more in-depth study (Soto 1965). In 1964 the first national Meeting of University Professors of Marxism was held. Presided over by José Antonio Portuondo it included Lionel Soto—head of the Basic Schools of Revolutionary Instruction, EIBR—on the panel. However, after the Third Meeting of University Professors of Marxism (the Second National Meeting) held in September 1966, the Department of Philosophy formally broke with the Soviet conception of Marxism in the midst of the "crisis del manualismo." The resultant course was called "history of Marxist thought" and lasted until 1971, with the course text-book, the "Yellow Book" (*Lecturas de Filosofía*), compiled by members of the faculty and later adopted by the University of Oriente and the University of Las Villas. The Yellow Book contained works by Aleksei Leont'ev, Amílcar Cabral, Che Guevara, Antonio Gramsci, Manuel Sacristan, Louis Althusser, and Fidel, among others (León del Rio and Martínez Heredia 2010). However, although the Department of Philosophy had broken with Soviet Marxism, the Revolution was still ideologically heterodox and numerous currents were still in circulation, under the uniting banner of the Revolution.

After the Cuban Missile Crisis, the Cuban government was able to capitalize tactically on the country's strategic geographic and propagandistic value in maximizing Soviet economic support. The ensuing Soviet support of the Cuban Revolution may have initially been an opportunity to show the superiority of one of the two antagonistic systems vying for global power. However, Cuba, and the type of socialism practiced by the revolutionary government, became a site of competition with, and dispute, of the Soviet projection of itself as the leader of the global socialist movement. The Cuban and the Soviet leadership had fundamentally different opinions of the global political situation and the best method to pursue socialism at an international level. While at first this resulted in economic maneuverings on the part of the USSR to gain influence in Cuba during the 1960s and 1970s, by the late 1970s and early 1980s, the two countries ultimately adopted a more pragmatic approach. They worked together to achieve mutually beneficial goals, and the balance of influence shifted as Cuba cemented its reputation as vanguard of Third World socialism.

Between 1964 and 1965 Cuba briefly introduced the Soviet system of work quotas and wage scales (Mesa-Lago 1981, 30). Then in 1965 the Great Debate ended with rejection of the Soviet-style policies favored by Carlos Rafael Rodríguez and other former members of the PSP, and the adoption in 1966 of strategies propounded by Che Guevara (Miller 1989, 104), namely: a more radical political approach; the implementation of the "moral economy" with incentives as the most effective way of increasing production; centralized planning; large scale mobilization; and a budgetary system of financing state enterprise (rather than the self-management system used in the USSR and Eastern Europe). Furthermore, the decision-making power remained with Fidel himself or in his close advisors rather than in specialists at the middle and lower levels of decision-making (Duncan 1985, 98; Miller 1989, 104; Mesa-Lago 1981, 28). Fundamentally, there was little change in Cuba's economic relationship with the USSR and, from the mid-late 1960s onward the two countries entered a phase of "mutual accommodation" (Gonzalez 1971, 90). This accommodation was, in part, thanks to growing ideological distance between China and Cuba, and therefore Cuba's increased strategic importance to the USSR. This distance stemmed from China cutting its rice supply to Cuba from the 250,000 tons it had sent in 1964 to 135,000 tons in 1965 (Lévesque 1971, 118).

As the chill of the Cold War set in and the Cuban government became increasingly geopolitically isolated, the Revolution moved toward greater definition of what it stood for. This united the competing ideological currents under the (radicalized) banner of "Marxist-Leninist socialism" with the formation of the Partido Comunista de Cuba (PCC) in October 1965. The PCC was founded at a low-point in Cuban-Soviet relations and signaled a departure from traditional "Soviet" socialist models and a decline in the influential positioning of members of the former PSP, some of whom, like Edith García Buchaca, had already been removed from positions of power (in Buchaca's case from a position of considerable power in the National Culture Council, the CNC). Although it might be expected that members of the former PSP would be particularly prevalent in the PCC, it was in fact dominated by the M-26-7 movement (Gordon-Nesbitt 2015, 314), who formed the majority of the Central Committee. Throughout the mid-1960s the ideological differences between Cuba and the USSR became increasingly apparent, most obviously in the field of armed struggle; yet, the USSR continued to provide aid to Cuba in the hope that its economy would become more efficiently organized (Lévesque 1978, 167) and by 1966 the Soviet-Cuban relations had become seriously strained.

In January 1966, the first meeting of the Organization of Solidarity with the Peoples of Africa, Asia and Latin America (OSPAAAL)—the Tricontinental Conference—was held in Havana and attended by over 500 delegates from eighty-two countries.[9] Kapcia (2008, 117) asserts that the conference was organized by the USSR in a tactical move to present itself as the ideological ally to Latin America rather than China. However, while the organization may have been Soviet, the focus on armed revolution and the implicit rejection of peaceful coexistence (more forcefully articulated in the open letter sent to Pablo Neruda by Cuban intellectuals after he attended the PEN club in New York) were distinctly Cuban. The Cuban delegation presented resolutions on topics that included imperialism's cultural and ideological penetration, cultural Revolution in countries free from the yoke of imperialism, cultural and scientific patrimony, and the national formation of cadres (Soto 1966, 78).

Concurrently with these developments, the Revolution's leadership had tried to establish a greater level of economic and political independence from the Soviet Union, which had begun to bring economic pressures to bear on Cuba from late 1967 onward (Pérez-Stable 1993, 99). The USSR had begun to exert economic pressures on Cuba for several key reasons: to gain greater levels of cooperation with foreign policy and ideological goals (Shearman 1987, 20) and to combat the isolationist tendency that had extended into ideology and now saw Cuba pitting its definition of "revolution" against that of Moscow and Washington. Soviet frustration began to be expressed in the economic sphere, and, the USSR began to slow the supplies it sent Cuba and refused to increase oil deliveries by more than 2 percent. This has historically been interpreted as the expression of Soviet dissatisfaction regarding the Cuban domestic economy, its radical foreign policy, and the USSR's associated humiliation at the 1966 Tricontinental (Lévesque 1978, 135). However, these measures may also have been "making a virtue out of necessity" (Miller 1989, 108–9), due to a slowdown in domestic oil production and the knock-on effect on the USSR's international export program (Miller 1989, 108–9).

Cuba's challenges to the Soviet Union's ideological leadership intensified between 1966 (with the Tricontinental) and 1968 (Shearman 1987, 18), and definitions of socialism and Marxism on the island had become increasingly "Cubanized" as Marxism became an increasingly mass phenomenon and the leadership's focus had shifted to the Third World. In January 1968 the Cuban government held the Cultural Congress of Havana, an event which was uniquely positioned to continue advancing the international aspirations of the Cuban Revolution. It brought over 400 intellectuals together from both industrialized and less economically developed countries. The conference considered the role of the intellectual in the revolutionary context, with Roberto Fernández Retamar drawing on Italian Marxist Antonio Gramsci's thinking regarding the social function of the intellectual as a starting point for the discussion (Gordon-Nesbitt 2012, 58). Havana challenged the norms and practices of the Socialist Bloc, emerged as the clear winner of the debates, and became *the* authority on anti-colonialism.

The 1968 Cultural Congress of Havana occurred at the same time as the discovery of a "micro-faction," seemingly indicative of a shift away from the USSR (although perhaps an adoption of some of its tactics). The uncovering of the micro-faction, led by disgraced Aníbal Escalante and comprising thirty-five members of the former PSP, coincided with the announcement of strict fuel rationing, due to a dispute with the USSR. The micro-faction was accused of denigrating the PCC's line and of having engaged in unauthorized relations with members of the Soviet embassy. As a result of this collaboration the embassy had received negative reports and recommendations that the USSR should impose economic sanctions (Lévesque 1978, 135). Escalante was sentenced to thirty years in prison for working against the Revolution.

Set against growing cooperation (and dissatisfaction) between the two countries throughout the 1960s, Cuba had become increasingly present in the Soviet popular and academic press. *Kuba* a Russian-language general magazine about the country for international consumption had been in publication in Russian, translated and published by Progress, since August 1964 and regularly showcased the links between the countries and explored Cuban everyday culture. Explorations of popular everyday culture were complemented by *Latinskaia Amerika* (Latin America), an academic publication on the region, which had been founded in 1969 in celebration of the first decade of the Cuban Revolution. *Latinskaia Amerika* was published by the Soviet Academy of Sciences and featured contributions from Soviet and Latin American individuals working in the fields of culture, politics, and journalism. The journal was one of the few Soviet publications that focused on Latin American culture, which it placed in the context of sociopolitical developments. Particular attention was paid to Cuba and, in order to help Soviet readers understand Cuba's "originality," the developments in Cuban culture were presented systematically across the different fields of culture: literature, science, education, theater, cinema, and architecture (Shatunovskaia 1979, 306).

The shift in the relationship between the two countries during the first decade of their alliance, and beyond, was reflected in a way the other was presented in their respective national presses. As the Cuban variant of socialism diverged from that of the USSR, from the mid-1960s onward, the country was increasingly presented to Soviet citizens as a "little brother" and the Revolution was positioned as a national liberation movement—some ideological steps behind socialist revolution as it did not consider class revolution as a decisive factor. Conversely, in Cuba during the 1960s, ideas about the USSR's superiority were rejected and the country was presented as an equal; the popular press focused on the USSR's history and national traditions, while efforts were made to demarcate the basis and bounds of cooperation between the two countries. This was in contrast to the "romanticism" of the 1960s, which saw the relationship between the two countries "characterized in both the Soviet and Cuban media as a parent-child relationship, a friendship, a brotherhood, a business partnership, and a military alliance" (Gorsuch 2015, 501).

1970s

As the Revolution entered its second decade there was an increasingly systematized and institutionalized interaction between the two countries. Soviet-Cuban economic collaboration became coordinated through the Intergovernmental Soviet-Cuban Commission for Economic, Scientific, and Technological Cooperation, established in December 1970 (Packenham 1986, 72), and was further bolstered in 1972 by Cuba joining the Council for Mutual Economic Aid (COMECON) and then by the creation of the System of Economic Planning and Direction in 1976/7. The aid that the USSR provided Cuba totaled around USD $65 billion between 1960 and 1990 and proved to be the "golden handcuffs" that locked both countries into a relationship of mutual dependency (Leogrande and Thomas 2002, 342). The Cuban government found itself unable to move the country away from sugar exports destined for the Eastern bloc and COMECON, due to the enforced focus on sugar production, the low international price for sugar on the open market, and the underdevelopment of other sectors of the Cuban economy (Leogrande and Thomas 2002, 342). On the other hand, the USSR itself was dependent on Cuba's prestige in the Third World and, by the mid-1970s, had become so financially committed to the Cuban Revolution that, were it to fail, there would be nothing to show for the investment (Bain 2005, 771). After the 1978 rise in global sugar prices, Cuba swiftly returned to trade with COMECON and into an "even closer and more exclusive economic relationship with the Soviet bloc" (Leogrande and Thomas 2002, 333). Over the next decades, Cuba continued to benefit from Soviet economic aid and technical assistance, including a space mission (MID and MinRex 2004, 356) and, by the 1980s, power stations built with Soviet cooperation were supplying 42 percent of the country's generation capacity (Blasier 1993, 84). The year 1985 marked the high point in trade between the two countries at almost 10 billion roubles (Bain 2005, 774).

Soviet material culture in Cuba escalated after Cuba gained full membership of COMECON in 1972. Soviet goods such as radios, washing machines, and fridges, many of which were given to the best workers as rewards in the 1970s, became a regular fixture in everyday Cuban life. This was in some way reflective of the wider increased presence of the USSR, and the other "brother" socialist countries, in the Cuban consciousness by this stage, but this was largely performative or informative. The anniversary of the October Revolution was regularly celebrated in the cultural press, with whole magazine issues dedicated to the USSR and the culture of the October Revolution every October/November; these tended to showcase the best of Soviet (specifically Bolshevik) culture and promote greater knowledge of the country and its constituent republics. Outside these significant months, regular informative articles appeared in cultural magazines, showcasing culture in other socialist countries. Lenin Park, after four years of construction, was inaugurated in 1972, the same year that the first Day of Soviet Culture was held. The first iteration of the Day was held in Havana (inaugurated by the Soviet Minister of Culture, Ekaterina Furtseva) and Santiago de Cuba (inaugurated by the Moldavian Minister of Culture, Leonid Culiuc). It was held between November 1 and November 12 to celebrate the fifty-fifth anniversary of the October Revolution and saw the introduction of the Weeks of Soviet Cinema (Oramas 1972a; Pavón 1972; Furtseva 1972; Camacho Albert 1972; Vázquez 1972; Oramas 1972b; López Oliva 1972). From this year onward regular Days of Soviet Culture were held in Cuba. The Day of Cuban Culture in the USSR began in 1973, in celebration of the Moncada Assault's twentieth anniversary (Shatunovskaia 1979, 306). Similarly, the Revolution's twentieth year was celebrated with a book *The Culture of Cuba: 20 Years of the Cuban Revolution* published by Nauka. This was an edited book with chapters from Cuban and Soviet cultural figures, covering each form of artistic expression, cultural education, and the ideological importance of culture and education.

Interest in Latin America and its cultural production continued to grow in the USSR evidenced by the publication of a number of books dealing with Cuba and, more widely, Latin America, in addition to the already existing publication of the works of Cuban poets and novelists. For example, in 1977 *Socialist Realism in Its Current State of Development* (Rodionovich Shcherbina 1977) was published by the publishing house Nauka. The book contained a chapter on "the reality of people's struggle and the reality of national consciousness in the modern Latin American novel" (Kuteishchikova 1977). The majority of the discussion in the chapter was about Manuel Cofiño's 1971 novel *The Last Woman and the Next Combat*, which he had consciously defined as socialist realist. Earlier in the year Progress publishing house had also published the collection of poems *Moscú-La Habana, La Habana-Moscú*, which was celebrated in Cuba for covering both sides of the relationship "in this book two voices are heard: that of the Cubans who sing to the motherland of October and that of the Russian poets who aggrandise the isle of liberty" (Kuteishchikova and Terterian 1979, 67).

The Soviet-Cuban tie was further strengthened between 1974 and 1975. Brezhnev visited Cuba from January 28 to February 3 in 1974, and took the opportunity to emphasize that the USSR was not a pacifist country and was not in favor of peace at any price (Lévesque 1978, 181). Then, in December 1975 the First Congress of the Cuban Communist Party was held, interpreted by the USSR as the "culmination of the formative process of the Cuban Marxist-Leninist vanguard" (Lévesque 1978, 184). However, the First Congress of the PCC rather than codifying the hierarchical nature of the Cuban-Soviet relationship actually asserted the independence of the Cuban

Revolution from the Soviet Union. In part this was due to the timing of the event, at a low point in Cuban-Soviet relations, and through the make-up of the Party's members, dominated by the members of the 26 July Movement. It clarified the nature of the relationship between the two and where it sat in the larger picture of Cuba's national independence and socialist internationalism. In doing so, the focus was firmly placed on the Bolshevik Revolution, the early years of the Soviet Union and the rapid education of a predominantly uneducated population. The experience of the USSR (post-1930 onward) in cultivating a culture that was aimed at combating man's exploitation of man and the establishing of a state that encouraged the national expression of its constituent peoples was hailed as a particularly valuable example from which to learn (PCC 1976c, 473). In order to achieve an educated citizenship that was both capable of understanding vanguard art movements and producing an art that reflected the new societal values, the PCC committed itself to holding days of culture and fostering co-productions with socialist, Caribbean and Latin American countries, in addition to incorporating art education into citizens' basic instruction (PCC 1976b, 111–13). Books and translations that would deepen the Cuban population's knowledge about the other socialist countries were also identified as an educative cultural tool (PCC 1976c, 473).

Other institutions were created or reorganized along more Leninist lines: the 1975 Congress of the PCC established a new Political Bureau, Secretariat and Central Committee, creating a ruling institution built on a Leninist model. The political system was also substantially reorganized, with the implementation of the pyramidal structured Soviet-styled Poder Popular (popular power) in 1976, with ex-PSP member Blas Roca as the first president of the single-chamber parliament (Kapcia 2005, 123). A Council of State was introduced into the institutional landscape and membership in the PCC grew significantly, from 100,000 members in 1970 to 202,807 members in 1975 and then to 434,143 members in 1982 (Duncan 1985, 108).

The 1976 Constitution, which was not dissimilar to the Soviet Charter, possibly because of the important role played by Blas Roca, activist of the former-PSP, in its drafting (Kapcia 2014, 140), also made explicit mention of the USSR. It affirmed Marxism-Leninism as the Revolution's ideological lodestar, socialist internationalism as its supporting framework and cooperation, mutual aid, and solidarity as its preferred method. The Constitution, while acknowledging the close relationship with the USSR, did so in terms that emphasized the equality of the relationship, whilst also recognizing the Revolution's Latin American, Caribbean, and Third World focus (PCC 1976a). As the Revolution's international scope and focus was confirmed, Cuba's historic links with Latin America, the Caribbean, and Africa were more systematically explored and their expressions encouraged. Cultural links between these renewed areas of focus were strengthened. Foreign policy also clearly reflected the renewed interest in these regions, reflecting the "increased emphasis that Cuba began to place in the 1970s on its political role in Third World affairs, especially within the Nonaligned Movement" (Erisman 2018, 50). Involvement in Africa grew significantly during the 1970s and, as Cuba positioned itself as the leader of the Third World independence movement, became an arena in which it was able to exert pressure on the USSR. Cuba had long-standing historical and cultural links with the continent and had been actively involved in guerrilla movements there since the early 1960s, complemented by medical internationalism in Mali, Congo, Tanzania, and Guinea-Conakry, during the same period (Erisman 2018, 49).

Africa was also a key area in Soviet foreign policy, and frequently became an area of ideological contention. By the mid-1970s the conditions and opportunities were idea for Cuba to become more deeply involved in Africa. Full membership of COMECON had created a degree of economic security which allowed for a more wide-ranging foreign policy, and the collapse of the Salazar regime in Portugal provided precisely this opportunity (Bain 2018, 32). In November 1975 Cuban troops were sent to Angola to fight alongside Agostinho Neto's radical left-wing government, the Popular Movement for the Liberation of Angola (Movimento Popular de Libertação de Angola) (MPLA). Cuban military personnel and civilian internationalists remained in Angola until 1991, helping to reconstruct the country after independence from Portugal and the subsequent civil war. Outside of Angola, Cuban military involvement in Africa included Guinea/Cape Verde Islands, Mozambique, Congo, and Ethiopia (Erisman 2018, 49).

Angola, in particular, Ribeiro argues, formed an "alternative narrative" to the growing presence of the Soviet Union in Cuban everyday consciousness and instigated "a nationwide reflection about history, identity, race, and heroism in Cuba" (Ribeiro 2018, 210). From the beginning of Cuban military involvement in Angola, and beyond, there was also an intensified drive to assimilate the best of universal culture, deepen understanding of Latin American culture and articulate Cuban national culture within a socialist international framework. This period was characterized by the systematic effort to remedy the technical shortcomings that inhibited the coherent expression of national characteristics and perpetuated Cuba's state of economic dependency. Ideologically, Cuba and the USSR still differed, but there was clearly defined common ground, specifically the idea that socialism was a path through which to achieve communism. Pragmatically speaking, this served both parties well: the USSR remained the leading light of communism and was able to play the role of "big brother," guiding Cuba through the transition and helping the island's technical development by educating Cubans in all subjects in the USSR (which would also demonstrate the prowess of the Soviet educational system), while Cuba was able to take advantage of the technical knowledge that it lacked. This indeed implied looking to the USSR and the Socialist Bloc for useful cultural aspects, organizational or technical. Armed struggle still remained a point of contention between the USSR and Cuba, and toward the mid-1970s foreign policy progressively became the key area in which Cuba and the USSR fought out their differences.

At the end of the 1970s the tables were turned and Cuba was drawn into Soviet actions abroad. After a period of détente relations between the United States and the USSR progressively deteriorated, resulting in the Soviet invasion of Afghanistan in December 1979. The subsequent re-ignition of Cold War tensions presented the Cuban government with, once more, the sense that the country was under attack, a feeling only heightened by subsequent events of the early 1980s, such as the Mariel boatlift, the tightening of the embargo under Ronald Reagan's presidency, the invasion of Grenada, and the *contras* in Nicaragua. When the USSR invaded Afghanistan, Fidel Castro was the president of the Nonaligned Movement, and his failure to condemn Soviet actions led to questions about the extent of Cuba's impartiality (Bain 2018, 27). However, supporting the invasion of Afghanistan provided the Cuban government with some leverage against Moscow, exerting pressure on the USSR to commit to taking similar action in the Caribbean if socialism in Cuba was ever threatened (Bain 2018, 32). Cuba never gained membership of the Warsaw Pact and was also at the forefront of the renewed superpower tensions, and so a track record of supporting Soviet military maneuvering in Czechoslovakia and Afghanistan, both of which were justified by the Brezhnev Doctrine, to the detriment of Cuba's international standing was a valuable bargaining chip (Bain 2018, 28–32).

Against this backdrop of rising international tensions, throughout this latter half of the 1970s and onward, perhaps reflective of the growing cultural presence of each country in the other, tourism became an increasingly important point of Soviet contact with Cuba. This led to the propagation of certain stereotypes regarding the two countries. Interactions between Cuba and the USSR were tempered and informed by these popular stereotypes, many of which remain today and were arguably reinforced by each country in the promotion of their externalized image. To the Soviet citizen, Cuba was seen as an ideologically friendly tropical island, located in the "West," full of beaches, beautiful women, and rum. In her analysis of the Cuban imaginary in the Soviet population, Gorsuch argues that the emergent Soviet "romantic passion for Cuba was often accompanied by a concomitant nostalgia for an idealised Soviet past" from the pre-Stalin years (Gorsuch 2015, 497). *Kuba*, the Russian-language edition of Cuba's general magazine for international consumption, reinforced this ideal: from the mid-1970s onward the back matter was frequently a cocktail recipe involving Havana Club and young women, often in bikinis, frequently appeared on the front matter.

1980s

Twenty-six years after the beginning of the Cuban-Soviet alliance, Cuban and Soviet populations were a more familiar presence in each other's cultural-political lives. In 1985 the physical idea of the Soviet Union was cemented with the construction of the monumental building, the USSR's embassy, on Quinta Avenida, between streets 62 and 66. The building, dubbed the *torre de control* (control tower), was built to a design by Aleksandr Rochegov and still remains a dominant feature on the Havana skyline, as the embassy of the Russian Federation (Figure 1.2).

Figure 1.2 Soviet/Russian Embassy Designed by Aleksandr Rochegov. Photo courtesy of the author.

Somewhat like the *torre de control*'s unavoidable presence on the city's vista the Soviet presence and the idea of the Soviet Union loomed large but was static and mostly ignored by the majority of Cubans through-out the 1980s. The terms as General Secretary of the KPSS of Iurii Andropov (November 1982–February 1984) and then Konstantin Ustinov-ich Chernenko (February 1984–March 1985) brought little change to the Soviet-Cuban relationship on the surface. However, under the surface the relationship had begun to shift irrevocably, while Andropov was the Gen-eral Secretary of the CPUS, it had been made clear to Raúl Castro, while visiting the USSR that Moscow would not step in and militarily defend Cuba should the United States invade (Leonov 2015, 201–204). Such non-interventionist sentiment was alluded to in Andropov's 1983 address to the KPSS:

> The correlation of forces in the world arena has substantially changed. An unprecedented sharpening of the struggle between the two world social systems has taken place. Meanwhile, an attempt to solve the historical dispute between the two systems through a military clash would be disastrous to humankind. The character of the further development of mutual relations between them - i.e. in essence, the question of the preservation of peace on earth - is both today and in the foreseeable future the pivotal problem of the foreign policy of our party. (Andropov 1983, 2)

Perhaps the Cuban government had sensed an imminent change in the rela-tionship because defensive preparations had already begun in response to a rising sense of siege and fear of imminent attack. In 1980 the War of All the People was launched, creating the volunteer force, the Milicias de Tro-pas Territoriales (Territorial Troops Militias). The priority of the nation, as Fidel argued the following year at the closing of the Second Congress of the Committees for the Defence of the Revolution, was self-sufficiency in this respect:

> There are those who wonder what will happen in the world. And I ask myself this also. What will happen in the world if they make an open attack on Cuba? Because, well, in the first place what we should learn, and have as a philosophy, is to not wait for someone else to defend us. Rather, in the first place, we should be ready to defend ourselves. What class of revolutionaries would we be, if we uphold our principles, because we are waiting for others to defend us. We defend our principles, first of all, against our own shield. And we respond with our principles and our attitude, first of all with our own skin. (Castro 1981)

Despite this cooling of Cuba and the Soviet Union's military links, trade with COMECON grew to account for between 79 and 83 percent of Cuba's total trade between 1979 and 1985 (LeoGrande and Thomas 2002, 334–35). It was not until Mikhail Sergeevich Gorbachev came to power in October 1985 that there was a change in the two-decade relationship. At the heart of this evolution was the common goal of the improvement of socialism.

When Gorbachev came to power, the Soviet economy was ailing, with the gap between the USSR and the West in terms of scientific and technological advances widening. Domestic growth rates were falling and social issues such as alcoholism were pressing. The interlinked policies of *glasnost'* (openness) and *perstroika* (restructuring) were designed to address these issues and improve socialism within the Soviet Union. *Perestroika* was aimed at rebuilding the Soviet economic and political system for greater efficiency, while *glasnost'* was geared toward tackling the secrecy that characterized Soviet society, part of which was the greater communication and open debate about the errors and corruption of the Soviet system. *Perestroika* was implemented in April 1985, and the partner policy of *glasnost'* was announced at the 27th Congress of the Communist Party of the Soviet Union (February 25 to March 6, 1986) and was initially seemingly limited to "a new and livelier style of presentation" and encouraged the media to probe the deficiencies of corrupt officials (Hoskins 1985, 459). However, the extremely limited public communication about the extent and gravity of the Chernobyl explosion in April 1986 was a watershed moment for *glasnost,'* its aftermath marking the beginning of a period of public discussion of the problems in society (Bartlett 2005, 279–280). The seeming "wave" of bad news, from which the public had previously been kept, gave rise to a new type of cultural output, for example the dark and pessimistic film style the *chernukha* (a slang name derived from the Russian for black, *chernyi*). The reformism of *perestroika* and *glasnost'* were accompanied with a "new thinking" in foreign and military policy, which included a reworking of the Warsaw Pact and improvements to the bureaucracy of COMECON. The impetus moved away from ideological dogmatism and military strength as a means of guaranteeing security (Hosking 1985, 464).

As the processes of *perestroika* and *glasnost'* were beginning to take more shape, another process, also aimed at the improvement of socialism, was initiated in Cuba. *Rectification of Past Errors and Negative Tendencies*, begun in 1986, was an attempt to find a collective solution to the problems that had become undeniably evident in Cuba by the mid-1980s. These problems included economic stagnation and "numerous perceived social problems that had arisen from the focus on the material rather than

moral benefits after 1975" (Clayfield 2018, 127). However, the suggested
solution to these problems was very different to Gorbachev's, and instead
championed a return to the more idealistic models of the 1960s, which
became a point of tension in Cuban-Soviet relations (Bain 2005, 769).
In part, *Rectification* meant a revival of the spirit of the 1960s (Kapcia
2008, 107). Implicit in this idea of rectification was the identification of
the problem—the "past errors and negative tendencies"—which were the
"pro-Soviet policies and dogmatic and even imported ideological interpretations" (Kapcia 2008, 107). Explorations of national identity, culture, and
historiography went hand in hand with this process and the elaboration of a
new identity which fitted this process. It also marked a return to ideas and
values of *guerrillerismo*, which had declined, although never disappeared,
during the late 1970s and early 1980s (Clayfield 2018). Throughout this
period, the leadership was very clear that the socialism practiced in Cuba
was distinct from other socialisms, and specifically that of the USSR, as
Cuba "had always interpreted socialism in its own way in order to meet the
country's specific needs, and would continue to do so in the coming months
and years" (Clayfield 2018, 130).

Once *Rectification* was introduced in Cuba the focus was placed by some
sectors of society on the similarities between rectification and glasnost and
the common ideological goal—the improvement of socialism (Bain 2005,
776). However, Gorbachev wished to remove the ideological impetus from
Moscow's relationship with Havana. The Soviet relationship with Cuba
"became closely linked to the larger national debate over the character of the
Soviet regime or that of its successor" (Blasier 1993, 68) and as such Soviet
policy toward Cuba became dependent on the outcome of the larger political
question (Blasier 1993, 68–9).

A further blow was struck to Soviet-Cuban relations in 1987 when superpower relations began to improve which decreased the strategic importance
of Cuba. From 1989 onward Cuba made its objection to *perestroika* and
glasnost' clear through key events such as the banning of key Soviet publications—such as *Tiempos Nuevos* and *Sputnik* (Puñales-Alpízar 2012,
30)—and ambiguous reporting of key Soviet events (Bain 2005, 783–90).[10]
Trade between Cuba and the Soviet Union was renegotiated in 1990 with a
one-year treaty, as opposed to another five-year treaty which had tended to
be the norm thus far. This was a reflection of the gradual changing of terms
in the Cuban-Soviet trade relationship. In 1985 Moscow had paid over five
times the world price for Cuban sugar; however, this slightly reduced to three
times the world price by 1989 (Bain 2005, 777). On September 11, 1991
Gorbachev announced that the remaining Soviet soldiers in Cuba were to
be recalled, reflecting the improving relationship between the Soviet Union

and the United States of America. While these changes under Gorbachev marked a shift in the relationship between the two countries, an established relationship continued to exist. However, the Soviet Union ceased to exist on December 25, 1991, leading to a decrease in Cuba's GDP by 35% between 1989 and 1993 (Brundenius 2002, 365). Contact and interaction between the Soviet Union and Cuba suddenly disappeared until the mid-1990s, when they began to gradually return in the form of pragmatic commercial exchange (Bain 2008, 65).

Since the mid-1990s, relations between the two countries have continued to grow, and the links that extend beyond the Russian Revolution have been emphasized (Bain 2013). In 2008 the Russian Orthodox Church *Our Lady of Kazan* was built in Havana Vieja, and in 2010 Russia was the guest of honor at the Feria del Libro, and in 2014 Vladimir Putin wrote off $32 billion USD of Cuba's historic debt to the Soviet Union in a gesture of solidarity. In 2016 65,386 Russian tourists visited Cuba (ONdE 2016, 9).

LOS BOLOS

To the Cuban citizen, the USSR was monumental, brusque, and homogenous, the latter earning its citizens the nickname *"bolos"* (bowling pins).[11] Soviets, or *rusos*, which was the blanket term frequently used by Cubans, were perceived as cold and insular, and their culture as removed from that of the Cubans; indeed, initially, the Soviet citizens actually present in Cuba were physically kept apart from Cubans in separate residential areas. One of these former "Soviet" settlements, with a statue of a globe that speaks of internationalism at its center, now forms part of Alamar, in Habana del Este. At an everyday level, these stereotypes are reflected in the popular tales about the Cuban streets being at their busiest when Soviet films were played on state TV, or children being threatened with Soviet children's cartoons, dubbed *muñequitos rusos* (Russian dolls), as a punishment for bad behavior.

The idea of the "'Soviet" lingers in Cuba today and is, in Damaris Puñales-Alpízar's opinion, "one of the most important cultural imaginaries" (2012, 362),[12] representing a country and an associated world order that no longer exists and whose remains form an important part of the Cuban national cultural imaginary (Figure 1.3). However, the impact of the USSR on Cuba and on Cuban culture during its existence "awaits an examination of the complexities of the actual exchanges without the burden of defending their national terrains" (Loss and Prieto 2012, 3). It is these actual exchanges between Cuba and the USSR that this work explores.

Figure 1.3   Old Havana and the Russian Orthodox Church. Photo courtesy of the author.

NOTES

1. Some publications go even further, however, in the joint publication *Rossiia-Kuba. 1902–2002: Dokumenty i materialy* (2004) the Cuban and Russian foreign ministries trace links between the two countries back to 1902. Meanwhile in *SSSR-Kuba: Al'manakh* the intertwined history of the two countries is traced back to 1530 (Progress and Martí 1990: 527).

2. Reflected by the lack of Soviet presence in Latin America generally during this period. Between 1953 and 1957 exchanges between the USSR and Latin American countries "accounted for less than 10 percent of all reported exchanges between the Soviet Union and non-communist countries" (Barghoorn 1960: 219).

3. In the International Conference of Communist and Workers' parties in November 1960 the USSR adopted the concept of "the national democratic state," a radical government from the Third World between socialism and capitalism, and cited Cuba as an example (Lévesque 1978: 24).

4. Some individuals consider that the Cuban revolution rapidly descended into communism (Patterson 1986); others consider the first half of the 1970s to be particularly Soviet (Horowitz 2008, 214–215; Fitzgerald 1987/88), and yet, more that the Sovietization of the 1970s has endured (Franco 2002). These approaches mean that at a pervasive, everyday level the Cuban-Soviet relationship, and the Revolution more generally continues to be understood in Cold War binaries.

5. Loss (2015, 65) discusses the proliferation of Soviet pedagogical manuals during this period.

6. The period of increasing Cold War absolutes, and growing focus on proxies after the lessons learned from the Cuban Missile Crisis meant that Cuba was systematically isolated. This was particularly true between 1962 and 1975 when Cuba was excluded from the Organisation of American States, leaving the USSR the country's only recourse to technology and skills. Its Third World allies unable to provide the training that Cuba needed to pursue its ambitious developmental goals.

7. The system of EIRs was made up of three levels, the Basic Schools of Revolutionary Instruction (EIBR), the Provincial Schools of Revolutionary Instruction (EPIR) and the National School of Revolutionary Instruction (EIR—the Raúl Cepero Bonilla school) (Díaz Sosa 2000)

8. The USSR provided refuge for some of those exiled in the October 1934 Revolution and also to many Spanish children between 1936 and 1937 (Caballero 2009). Anastacio Mancilla, a Hispano-Soviet was a professor in political economy at Moscow State University, the USSR sent him, and others, to Cuba to provide the revolutionary leadership with lessons in Marxism (Yaffe 2009, 49). For more information about Mancilla's views on the political and economic views of his former students see "From the Diary of Ye. I. Pronskiy, Record of a Conversation with University of Havana Instructor, Anastacio Cruz Mancilla, 29 May 1964," June 22, 1962, History and Public Policy Program Digital Archive, TsKhSD, f. 5, op. 49, d. 757, ll. 121–123, r. 9125. Translated for CWIHP by Gary Goldberg. https://digitalarchive.wilsoncenter.org/document/117087

9. Anne Garland Mahler (2019) has examined the Tricontinental and its legacy in detail, contributing to a much-understudied area of post-colonial and Cold War scholarship. Mahler examines the movement's ideological roots, its relation to China and the Soviet Union, as well as detailed analyses of the aesthetics of various key practitioners.

10. The popularity of these publications before 1985 has been discussed by Juan Carlos Betancourt (2012, 83n.15), who argues that before 1985 "no one in Cuba, save a few curious readers, were interested in the inoffensive newspaper, *Novedades de Moscú* (News from Moscow) or the magazine, *Sputnik*. Stacks of these publications collected dust. Nevertheless, when news of the shift arrived, they gained a cult readership among Havana's intellectuals and artists. From then on it was only possible to get them at black-market prices, until the officials quickly banned their circulation." This discussion is further developed by Loss (2013, 73), who argues that when after 1990 Cuba no longer received Soviet newspapers and magazines "many were left stranded without the Soviet publications—*Novedades de Moscú, Tiempos Nuevos,* and *Sputnik*—that had begun to serve them as guides in navigating their own difficulties and hopefully emerging on the other side, not necessarily on a path to democracy or capitalism, but to a reformed socialism."

11. This epithet provides the name of a 2008 documentary, *Los bolos en Cuba*, by Enrique Colina, which examines the Cuban-Soviet relationship within the Cuban everyday existence.

12. For more discussions about the Cuban, and particularly the Cuban-Soviet imaginary see Jacqueline Loss (2004, 2012, 2013).

Chapter 2

The Conception and Trajectory of Socialist Realism in the Soviet Union

SOCIALIST REALISM IS NOT AN ISLAND

The Cuban Revolution occurred at a time when cultural production in the USSR was undergoing a period of reassessment as part of a process that has been dubbed the "Thaw." Although the Cuban Revolution "from its inception, emerged thawed," the cautionary study of the experiences of the USSR and its relationship to culture was considered essential by some cultural practitioners (García Espinosa 1963, 10). Julio García Espinosa's article from which the previous quote is taken began an intense cycle of debates which continued, very publicly, throughout the 1960s. Throughout these debates the specter of socialist realism in socialist cultural production and its relationship to Cuban culture was heatedly debated among intellectuals and artists.[1]

The debates unfolded over the course of the decade and continued throughout the 1970s and 1980s with varying levels of visibility and public participation. Within these debates what is clear is that there was a widespread and deeply nuanced understanding of what "socialist realism" had the potential to be, but also of what it had become under Stalin. However, outside Cuba the concept of what socialist realism had ultimately become in many ways came to represent the perceived power dynamic between Cuba and the USSR. Thus, assumptions about the Cuban Revolution have frequently been informed by Cold War biases and perceptions of a wholesale imposition of Soviet models and styles. The most emblematic of these styles is socialist realism, which, it is sometimes argued, was systematically implemented in Cuba, particularly in the early 1970s, by certain pro-Soviet sectors of Cuban society (Toledano Redongo 2002, 422–24; Buckwalter-Arias 2005, 367; Fornet 2007, 19; Yoss 2012, 65). Debates about the role of culture in a socialist system with international aspirations, and about the type of culture within socialism were a constant feature of the Cuban Revolution. Socialist realism, as the most dominant approach toward culture under socialism, was therefore a constant specter within these debates in and about culture.

Socialist realism is undoubtedly the clearest, most prolonged, cultural approach immediately identifiable with the USSR. The paradigm had two branches, one concerned with the organization of culture and the conditioning of the interactions between society, politics, and culture (Robin 1992, 43). The other branch was focused on differentiating the culture produced within the USSR from that created in capitalist societies and in harnessing the culture's potential to transform society. These two different approaches could theoretically either exist separately from one another or work together. Thus, politics and culture were formally inextricably linked by the term. Furthermore, as a cultural product that was completely specific to the USSR (particularly from the late 1930s to the mid-1950s), socialist realism was closely linked to the USSR's international prestige, particularly when it tried to position itself as the theoretical leader of the global communist movement.

Socialist realism is also one of the USSR's most contentious cultural products and processes due to the specific way in which the idea manifested itself in the late Stalinist years (1946–1953). It has come to be the metonym for the restriction and repression of society experienced under the Stalinist regime, when culture was viewed in a binary manner (Gardiner 2014, 55). Because of this, perhaps, combined with the enduring perception of socialist realism as a uniform, inflexible approach, designed to dictate and not innovate, it is only recently that the approach has undergone a period of reassessment. However, the idea of socialist realism was always driven by debate. Initially, when the term was officially introduced in 1934 at the First Congress of the Union of Soviet Writers, at a practical level, it ended a prolonged period of in-fighting between literary groups and was the working result of an ongoing process of the reconciliation with Russia's and the USSR's cultural history and its new historic direction (Robin 1992, 11). The debate about appropriate cultural approaches, facilitated by socialist realism's amorphous nature, continued throughout the USSR's existence and occurred at all levels.

Internationalism is also central to understanding the approach. Socialist realism demanded that the best of world culture, including cultures within the new nation (Russian literature before 1917/1934 and literature from non-Russian republics), be suitably critically assimilated and articulated within a union-wide context. The international element of socialist realism also existed outside of the paradigm's artistic content: the method could also be easily exported to help foster a greater revolutionary consciousness and popular mobilization. It also could consolidate the steps already made toward socialism. Socialist realism's potential for export, if utilized correctly, could provide a valuable tool for establishing the USSR as the vanguard of the international socialist movement. Furthermore, as the USSR's cultural figurehead it had weight and international prestige and was a potential point of conflict for socialist countries—such as China—that did not always support Soviet approaches and models. These inherently international aspects of socialist realism, and socialist Soviet culture, were closely related to its discursive qualities regarding form, content, and approach.

Such aforementioned qualities of socialist realism meant that understanding the surrounding debate is also central to the academic understanding of socialist realism in the USSR. Among non-specialists, it has come to be understood as best exemplified in the visual arts. However, socialist realism was an approach based on narrative, both in terms of cultural production, and the organization of the mechanisms of cultural production. Socialist realism as a narrative form within the organization of the mechanisms of cultural production refers to the idea of a system of cultural apparatus organized to aid the coherent mass articulation of an emergent socialist culture in all artistic forms that reflected the revolutionary reality.

Socialist realism had distinct phases, which responded to the charged political atmospheres in which it operated. The inclusive and dynamic socialist realism(s) of the early 1930s were informed by the cultural dynamism of late imperial Russian culture. It was also influenced by the cultural experimentations and innovations of both the October Revolution and early Bolshevik rule as Soviet culture created its own traditions (Dobrenko 2007, 25). Gradually, the concept drew more and more on ideas and approaches from a small pool of works that became identified as the canon of socialist realism and were therefore safe from criticism and attack (Clark 2000, 4). Ultimately the approach resulted in a clear "hierarchy of genres" (Gardiner 2014, 327), and the didactic, verisimilar, uncritical, aesthetic, narrative of culture during the period, 1947–1953, which has commonly been termed by academics as Late Stalinism (Clark 2000, 215; Fürst 2002; Gorsuch 2003). During the periods that are known as the Thaw and Stagnation, efforts were made among some sectors of the cultural sphere to broaden the term and recover the dynamism of earlier cultural production. Concurrently, however, there were reactions against the pushing of boundaries of cultural policy, creating confusing and conflicting approaches toward cultural production.

Finally, in the late socialist period of the USSR (mid-1970s–1991), socialist realism became a source of parody and of kitsch through *sots-art's* reworking of the paradigm's perceived tenets and values (Cullerne Bown 1998, 456; Condee 2000, vi). This last phase occurred at the same time that a current in Cuban art was also consciously parodying perceived official tenets, values, and visuals.

In theory, socialist realism could include many different methods and many different genres. It provided both a new way of seeing and a conceptual framework for the development of society and upon which to hang policies. The approach was therefore necessarily future-gazing in its outlook: "able to glimpse [the USSR's] tomorrow" through the planned work of its today (Zhdanov 1977, 22). As such, it allowed the real and the phantom to exist side by side (Petrov 2011), reworking reality into "an ideologically consumable product" (Dobrenko 2007, 14). Through externalizing the essence of the immanent state of being, socialist realism was theoretically able to call these new realities to life (Petrov 2011, 880). Thus writers became revolutionaries at the "front ranks of those fighting for a classless socialist society," actively helping to "remould the mentality of people in the spirit of socialism" (Zhdanov 1977, 24).

Socialist realism, in all its different incarnations, still looms large in the Cuban cultural imaginary, and its potential introduction into the Cuban setting formed a basis for many of the heated public debates of the 1960s. Cultural figures interviewed in Cuba for this research were aware of the debates of the Thaw, and of the existence of socialist realism as an organizational and aesthetic approach. There was also widespread awareness of the most commonly understood iteration of socialist realism, referred to here as "high Stalinist socialist realism," and the damaging effects of this cultural approach. However, there was also an awareness of the different manifestations of socialist realism among cultural figures (Cano 2015, Pérez 2015, Rafael Rodriguez 2015). Such an awareness was also present during the cycles of debates, with some cultural figures arguing that socialist realism could be something inclusive, dynamic, and diverse, in addition to recognizing the fluid nature of the paradigm (Aguirre 1963, 1981).

THE BOLSHEVIK REVOLUTION

The October Revolution was a continued point of reference for the Cuban revolutionary government. This included the different approaches toward culture that were adopted during this initial period. Discussion of these approaches, and the development of socialist realism, formed an integral part of the cultural debates of the 1960s in Cuba. Therefore, it is important to identify the essential discussions and approaches during these years.

Just as the revolutionary government in Cuba refused to favor one particular artistic approach, in the 1920s, the KPSS also initially refrained from promoting a specific style or approach. The social commitment, plurality, and prolific nature of cultural production in the first decade of the October Revolution had its roots in the cultural effervescence of the Silver Age of Russian culture, the romantic anticapitalists' rejection of Western bourgeois civilization in Central Europe and the cultural impetuses that grew out of the failed 1905–1907 Revolution against Tsar Nicholas II. In the wake of the Revolutions of 1917, intellectuals responded to the call to transform an underdeveloped Russia into a society that would become an international beacon in the political, economic, and cultural spheres. Throughout the 1920s, no one group or approach was privileged over the other, as the state sought to keep all cultural practitioners within the Revolution. Free competition between groups was permitted, while none of them were allowed to speak on behalf of the Party. Artists, and particularly writers, were co-opted into supporting the new government and were allowed to write in any style they pleased, provided it was not counter-revolutionary (Maguire 1968, 20). While the potential methods to facilitate cultural and societal transformation were disparate and often hostile to one another they were united by shared goals, such as a hatred of capitalism and its perceived effects on culture. Moreover, the coexistence of various rival factions stimulated a great outpouring of cultural works (Frolova-Walker 2012). Initially, the ritualization of space, a common denominator among different approaches, was at the core of attempts to realize a culture with transformative powers and, during the 1910s and 1920s, visual art, architecture, theater, and the performing arts emerged as the sites and spaces most commonly chosen for creation of this new socialist culture. Thus, cultural forms and their associated spaces became "factories of the perfect" (Clark 1996, 23).

Performing arts were particularly important, as they provided participants with a way to enter the public sphere and stake a claim in the new community in which they were to have a voice. There was a veritable explosion of theatrical activity in the early years of the Revolution, creating a popular and participatory movement of previously unimagined scale. Proletkul't, the explicitly proletarian cultural institute, its name a portmanteau of the words *proletarskii* (proletarian) and *kul'tura* (culture), had hundreds of theater groups performing agitational plays across the country, alongside which there were independent groups attached to factories, villages, and social clubs (Steinberg 2002). The Proletkul't movement did not necessarily reject all ties to the past, as is sometimes assumed; rather, a significant portion of its work involved training and cultural education, which were rooted in the country's pre-revolutionary history (Mally 1990).

Amateur theater blossomed in the 1920s, due to heartfelt revolutionary euphoria and spontaneity, but was ultimately quashed by pressures from

above (Mally 2000). One of the early revolutionary theater groups spring-
ing from the October Revolution was the Theater of Revolutionary Satire,
Terevsat, the invention of Mikhail Pustynin, the director of the local branch
of the Russian telegraph service—Rosta—in Vitebsk, in North-East Belarus.
Teversat's activities began as a means of spreading news and propaganda
to those unable to read the newspapers, in a type of "living newspaper."
As Leach describes it "in a collage of brief, unconnected items, structured
according to the format of a revue, these 'living newspapers' kept their audience informed about and engaged with the issues of the day" (1999, 303–04).
The group went on a tour in the countryside and at the Civil War Front before
moving to Moscow permanently in April (Leach 1999, 304).

Narkompros (the People's Commissariat for Education), responsible for
educational and cultural administration, also set up a theater division in June
1919, Tsenoteatr, which "awarded 'academic' status, large subsidies and
artistic freedom to the major theaters, and a lesser position, with smaller
subsidies and less freedom, to the others" (Leach 1999, 303). Tsenoteatr was
then dissolved in 1920 and replaced with the Theater Department, which was
headed by Veselovod Meierkhol'd (Leach 1999, 306). The academic theaters
were broadly the "best" of the Imperial theaters (the Malyi, the Moscow Arts
Theater, the Bolshoi, the Vakhtangov, and the Jewish Theater), and they continued to function under the aegis of Narkompros. These theaters faced competition from other, more revolutionary, theaters such as the Moscow Trade
Union and Proletkul't theaters, and the Theater of Working Class Youth,
TRAM (Fitzpatrick 1971, 238–39).

The visual arts also experienced a period of creative outpouring in the
wake of the Revolution. The avant-garde, which, prior to the Revolution,
had made its mark fighting bourgeois aesthetics and values, now found itself
able to begin to realize what its adherents saw as their public role (Kelly
and Milner-Gulland 1998, 140–41). Pre-revolutionary institutes were closed
down and new art institutes were established, such as the Free State Art Stu-
dios (SVOMAS). During this time other institutions also proliferated, such as
the Institute of Artistic Culture, (INKhUK) in Moscow, and later Leningrad.
SVOMAS was focused on helping the underprivileged (workers and peasants) become aware of, and create, art (Clark 1996, 50–51). This was not necessarily a rupture with pre-revolutionary culture, but rather the practicing of
ideas that had existed prior to the October Revolution, as part of the Romantic Anticapitalistic school of thought. Artistic production remained diverse
and included both avant-garde and more traditional approaches. However,
between 1921 and 1923, constructivism was particularly celebrated, possibly
due to the close relationship between Constructivists and Narkompros (Kelly
and Milner-Gulland 1998, 143–44). Constructivism's close links to economic

productivity and clarity of expression, at a time when the focus was on economic recovery and greater involvement from the previously marginalized peasants, may also have contributed to its promotion. Not only an aesthetic movement, but also a way of perceiving the world and living in a manner appropriate to the new age, constructivism considered art and design to be a political means to be used in the construction of the new society (Figures 2.1 and 2.2). As such, they had a very clear, very direct social utility which should be prioritized over artificial style (Kaier 2005).

Once the Civil War ended in 1921, the Bolshevik government found itself in charge of a country in which peasants made up the majority of the population with an economy ravaged both by World War I, the Civil War itself, and the policy of War Communism (1918–1921). The government desperately needed to rebuild the economy and moved to do so by introducing a variant of capitalism in the New Economic Policy (NEP). NEP was a type of state-controlled capitalism, which, it was thought, would help to gradually establish socialism though returning to a limited market system, in which market mechanisms would gradually strengthen the state sector at the expense of a private sector over several decades. The hybrid system would create a changed political atmosphere in the country that would eventually allow Russia to reach socialism, driven by Cultural Revolution and the expansion of cooperatives among the peasantry. The NEP was also a tacit admission that the Bolshevik Revolution had thus far failed to bring about

Figure 2.1 Mossel'prom Building, Example of Avant-Garde Architecture and Constructivism. Photo courtesy of the author.

Figure 2.2   Detail from Mossel'prom Building—Panels Painted by Alexander Rodchenko and Varvara Stepanova. Photo courtesy of the author.

the desired dictatorship of workers and peasants. NEP permitted small-scale private enterprises, established taxes on harvests, brought in labor reforms and incentivization to promote productivity, sought foreign investments, and began to advocate an early version of peaceful coexistence. The policy improved the life of the peasantry and parts of the intelligentsia, but many urban workers experienced worsened conditions as industry was subsidized at the cost of investment in housing and urban wages. Under the NEP, social relations were fluid, and there were many opportunities for self-advancement. The fastest growing group was the service workers, who (theoretically speaking) were an unproductive layer that formed part of the petit-bourgeoisie. The Bolsheviks thus tried to control this seemingly spontaneous proliferation of social groups, which they saw as having no place in a socialist society, by imposing old class categories. Society was classified into exploiters/disenfranchised—those who had actually benefited from the NEP, but also those perceived to have done so, such as kulaks (rich peasants), NEPmen (small traders), spetsy (technical specialists)—and toilers (poor and middle peasants) (Ball 1997). The NEP also gave considerable liberty to intellectuals and their cultural practices. Nationalities that formed part of Soviet Russia and then the USSR were allowed to reinstate customs and use of their language, which had previously been banned under imperial rule. Cultural production during the NEP was characterised by fierce competition between proletarian artists and their dedicated institutions, with alternative artistic movements from the avant-garde (such as constructivism, utopian projects, suprematism, futurism, experimental theater).

This diversity was reflected in the cultural policy of the 1920s, which became concerned with obtaining and maintaining the intelligentsia's support rather than antagonizing it, and official cultural policies were generally carried out by government agencies rather than the Party itself (Fitzpatrick 1974, 267–268). Lenin's death in 1924 and the subsequent power struggle signaled the beginning of the decline of the international aspirations of the October Revolution and also heralded a more significant change in cultural policy.

Toward the end of the 1920s, the inclusive culture that thus far had existed began to be limited by the increasing militancy of proletarian cultural organizations in the search for an authentic Soviet revolutionary culture. These proletarian organizations were often completely opposed to the trends of the avant-garde and equated revolutionary aesthetics with a return to the realism of the nineteenth century (Clark 1996, 183–200). However, the Party still did not yet favor any one single approach and, in July 1925, the Central Committee responded to (rather than pre-empted) the mounting tensions in the increasingly factionalized cultural world with its resolution "On the Policy of the Party in the Sphere of Artistic Literature." In the drive to assimilate cultural achievements, a guarded variant of internationalism was propounded in the assimilation of Soviet constituent national and ethnic cultures into the expression of a Union-wide culture. The resolution set the tone for a broadly inclusive cultural policy, which allowed for plurality in both terms of cultural output and cultural institutions and associations, lessened the power of the proletarian movements and established the position of the *poputchiki* (fellow travelers). *Poputchiki* was the term given to artists and intellectuals who did not join the Communist Party but who were sympathetic to the Revolution; during the Cultural Revolution they were more derogatorily referred to as *burzhuanye spetsialisty* (bourgeois specialists)—linked to the term *spetsy*.

In setting an inclusive tone, the 1925 resolution also contributed to the debate on social positions within revolutionary Russia, which were becoming increasingly linked to political and ideological positions. The resolution highlighted the existence of a Cultural Revolution within the Revolution and emphasized the ongoing class struggle, which in turn meant that no art could be neutral. It also reoriented the proletariat's goal as one of affirmative construction and focused on the involvement of wider sectors of society than ever before. It called for the proletariat to immediately move toward the take-over of positions in the cultural world. However, it also recognized that the occupation of the cultural world was trickier than in other areas, as a culturally repressed class could not work out its own literature, art, or style. In order to overcome this obstacle, the Party argued that its job was therefore to help the proletariat win its right to hegemony, whilst recognizing the differences with *poputchiki* and facilitating their transition as rapidly as possible to communist ideology. Criticism was a key educational tool in this battle. Yet it drew the line at establishing a unitary style and organization and refused to support any one literary faction and therefore any one literary style or form. Instead the Party stated that it supported free competition among groups and movements, as they were at the core of the development of proletarian literature and an eventual style appropriate to the epoch. It promised to streamline literary administration, combat uninformed meddling in literary affairs, and emphasized the different roles of the artist and the critic. The resolution ended with a call to arms, stressing the importance of the assimilation of the technical accomplishments of the old masters for the eventual creation of an appropriate form that could be comprehended by millions (KPSS 1925).

As mentioned, the assimilation of characteristics specific to the constituent Soviet nationalities and ethnicities was also encouraged. In a speech made by Stalin to students of the Communist University of the Toilers of the East (Far East University/Stalin School) on May 18, 1925, the inclusiveness of socialist culture was emphasized:

> Proletarian culture, socialist in its content, takes different forms and means of expression among different peoples drawn into socialist construction, depending on differences of language, ways of life, etc. Proletarian in content, national

in form – such is the universal culture towards which socialism is heading. Proletarian culture does not annul national culture, but gives it content. And conversely, national culture does not annihilate proletarian culture, but gives it form. (Stalin 1952, 137)

However, between 1921 and 1927, there was a fundamental redefinition of what Revolution in Russia and the USSR meant, which included reassessing the country's viable path to socialism. The subsequent politics of class warfare, the offensive against all perceived backwardness, unleashed by Stalin and his supporters, the resultant climate of fear, and the increasing international and intellectual isolation changed the development and implementation of socialist cultural policy. In 1928, the NEP ended and the First Five Year Plan was introduced; there was a return to central planning, a focus on rapid industrialization, the collectivization of agriculture, and the elimination of class enemies. The change in structure of the means of production, toward greater collectivization and industrialization, was symptomatic of the move away from a mixed economy. Industrialization enthroned the proletarian agenda and weakened the arguments of the *poputchiki* who seemed increasingly anachronous with the emergent social order, as the Party increasingly favored the proletariat and the State remained neutral. The pluralistic and vibrant cultural competition that had characterized culture under NEP gave rise to the Cultural Revolution, a period of intense cultural upheaval (1928 to 1932), caused by a drive to create a proletarian intelligentsia. During this period, the Red Army was demobilized and the Komsomol (the Communist Party's youth wing) began to mobilize, which created an aggressive anti-intelligentsia sentiment. The permissive attitude and artistic experimentation of the NEP, along with the positions of the pre-revolutionary intelligentsia, so far tolerated by the government, came under relentless attack. Collectivization and forced industrialization swiftly ended the mixed economy, and workers and peasants received preferential treatment in areas such as education, providing a previously unmatched opportunity for social mobility. (Fitzpatrick 1979)

In 1928, a group of engineers in Shakhty (North Caucasus) were arrested and accused of having conspired with the former owners of nationalized coal mines in a bid to sabotage the Soviet economy. The engineers were brought to trial; the majority were sent to prison and some were executed. This was the first of what would become a long series of high-profile show trials that would ultimately color the international perception of the Soviet Union. It was precisely this type of event, and the political shift that it meant, that foreign intellectuals who had been supportive of the Cuban Revolution began to fear and to voice their concerns about in the early 1970s, particularly concerning the "Padilla Affair."

The Shakhty engineers were held up as proof that the bourgeoisie were now using sabotage as a means of class struggle. The *Shakhtinskoe delo* (Shakhty Affair) was emblematic of a type of binary discourse that would come to dominate during the Cultural Revolution, as the Party's conflicts with the intelligentsia became conceptualized in terms of all-out class struggle between the "exploiters" and "toilers." The process of class war also reflected the grievances of the younger generation, with powerful roots in social mobility and the fight against established authority, and these pre-existing tensions shaped the form that the Cultural Revolution took in different cultural areas (Fitzpatrick 1992, 118). One particularly extreme movement that thrived during the Cultural Revolution was the magazine *New Left Front of the Arts*, (*New LEF*), the second run of the *Left Front of the Arts*, in circulation from 1923 to 1925, which advocated a literature of fact, factography. Factography was the idea of the active transformation of reality through work. The boundaries between style and genre were fluid and at the core was the idea of dialectical revolt and of moving artistic practice toward information, production, and discourse (Tupitsyn 1996, 7). *New LEF* believed that fact was something that was made and signification was a labor process, not a process of reflection (Fore 2006, 6). The editorial board's argument was that contemporary reality contained such a variety of conflict and characters that fictional renderings of reality, particularly those that looked to the nineteenth century and its literary techniques, were entirely unnecessary (Kenez and Shepherd 1998, 40).

Within the visual arts, the standing of the Association of Artists of Revolutionary Russia (AKhRR) was initially boosted by the Cultural Revolution until in-fighting weakened the leadership. During this period of "repressive anarchy and institutional improvisation," government activity in the arts declined and Party activity increased (Fitzpatrick 1971, 253). The class-war nature of the Cultural Revolution saw aggressive, but unsuccessful, competition between groups for hegemony in the arts. Here too, the Shakhty Affair had ramifications within the cultural world, as Narkompros's policies of cooperating with the *burzhuaznye spetsialisty* and discouraging iconoclasm were questioned by cultural figures and bodies (Fitzpatrick 1971, 242–243). Narkompros began to fall from favor but did not disappear; however, due to in-fighting neither did the Russian Association of Proletarian Writers (Rossiiskaia assotsiatsiia proletarskikh pisatelei, RAPP) and other proletarian organizations establish dominion. Despite lacking an official mandate they assumed leadership, exercising "a repressive and cliquish dictatorship over literary publication and criticism" but also engaging in intense competition with Communist radicals from other institutes (Fitzpatrick 1992, 137–38). The intense competition between groups reflected the divisions by questions of taste in wider society. Undoubtedly, some sectors of society embraced, and were empowered by, the avant-garde ideas that were closely linked to production and utility. However, others found these ideas alienating. The majority of Soviet citizens were grounded in a nineteenth-century concept of art that favored realist narrative paintings, sentimentality, melodrama, and ornamentation (Bowlt 2002, 39–40). The increased social mobility begun by the NEP meant that individuals whose backgrounds would previously have excluded them from cultural practices took up positions within culture and cultural administration. This change in the composition of the cultural administration began to contribute to the gradual promotion of realist narratives in cultural production, reflective of the popular tastes of the Soviet population.

Proletarian organizations such as RAPP were closed in April 1932 by the Party Central Committee's decree *"On the Reformation of Literary-Artistic Organisations,"* as part of a concerted effort to bring cultural production together in a unified, but diverse, socialist front (Fitzpatrick 1992, 243). Specifically proletarian organizations, with their aggressive policies, seemed increasingly out of step with the atmosphere and rationale of the 1930s; theoretically, the inequalities caused by the NEP had been addressed, creating a more unified Soviet society. Cultural institutions were beginning to reflect this new equality; meanwhile, the way was being made ready for a single cultural entity to replace the existing multiple organizations, each with its own disparate aim. As Andrei Zhdanov, then Secretary of the All-Union Communist Party (Bolsheviks), argued at the 1934 Soviet Writers' Congress, "the main difficulties confronting [the nation] in the work of socialist construction [had] already been overcome" (Zhdanov 1977, 15).

The enforced unification of cultural institutions, which sought to reflect the unity of collectivized, industrialized Soviet society, severely limited the available artistic affiliations and compelled many diverse practitioners onto a common ground, thereby creating an artificial sense of unity (Tupitsyn 1996, 127). Old factional divisions remained however, and loaded terms such as "formalism," "naturalism," and "socialist realism" began to be used to score points and settle conflicts.

UNIFYING TERM

With the creation of a superficial sense of unity and the overcoming of the challenges of socialist construction an important point of focus of the authorities of the USSR in the early 1930s was the happening/embedding of socialism. This was pursued rather than the *post hoc* creation of the right theoretical conditions for socialism to flourish. This process was also socialist realism's focus.

At the same time as the disbanding of RAPP and the creation of the Soviet Writers' Union in 1932, the concept of socialist realism as both an "institutional formation and artistic practice" surfaced and was the subject of great debate, which became formally articulated in 1934 at the Writers' Congress (Petrov 2011, 873). The idea for a Soviet Artists' Union also arose in 1932, but it was slow to form and it was not until 1936 that the All-Union Committee on Artistic Affairs of the Government of the USSR, which included the Main Administration for Visual Arts Institutions and the Main Administration for Supervision of Performances and Repertoires, was founded. The Cultural Revolution of the previous years, it was argued, had raised the cultural awareness of the people to such a level that it was no longer necessary to decree specific organizations for distinct sectors of society.

Initially, socialist realism served as a loose rhetorical framework within which policy could be built. It also functioned as a convenient empty term that would help to unify the factionalized cultural community and provide a democratic style that would ensure that culture was understood by all sectors of society, regardless of their class origin or educational level (Robin 1992). The term arose out of the need to support diversity and rule out exclusivity in culture and was an early attempt at crossover between elite and mass culture (Ivashkin 2014, 447). As such, it both defined and was defined by the theories and practices of high and low culture (Kenez and Shepherd 1998, 47–48).

As revolutionaries, socialist realist writers were also called upon to continue to defend the USSR from the attack, obvious or insidious, of Western bourgeois values. The focal point of this was the anti-*formalizm* drive that criticized art for showing excessive influence from the West and overtly avant-garde approaches. The drive began in the 1920s, with Russian Association of Proletarian Musicians (RAPM) and the attack on works such as Shostakovich's *Lady Macbeth of the Mtsensk District* gained considerable force in the 1930s and ended in the restrictive period known as the *Zhdanovshchina* of late 1940s (Fitzpatrick 1992, 189). This defensive capacity was to eventually play a heightened role in the late 1940s, as perceived foreign influences became increasingly undesirable. The socialist realist model, therefore, actually supported the internationalism of the 1920s and called for writers to subsume all that was good from world literature and art. In doing so, it should gather up the best of the squandered literary heritage of the bourgeoisie, study it, critically assimilate it, and take it further deploying these new weapons (genres, styles, forms, and methods of literary creation) in the engineering of the new Soviet soul (Zhdanov 1977, 22). Thus, socialist realism also helped to form a "cultural quarantine" against foreign modernism (*formalizm*), seen as a product of the late stages of capitalism (Fitzpatrick 1992: 197–214).

In addition to highlighting the inexorable path toward socialism in their work, the socialist realist artist had the task of educating and inspiring the consumer of culture through the propagation of appropriate myths and images. This necessarily differentiated socialist realism from bourgeois culture and society, which according to Gor'kii had "completely lost the capacity for invention in art" (1977, 44). Within the terms of socialist realism, myth making involved extracting the cardinal idea of reality, embodying it in imagery, and adding the desired and the possible with the aim of provoking a revolutionary attitude (for example, a desire to change for the better, for the ideal) toward reality (Gor'kii 1977, 44). Gor'kii's argument can be understood as the application of what the art critic John Berger would later term "glamour," but within a Marxist framework, rather than the capitalist, consumer framework Berger discusses (1973). With the commercial drive removed, publicity is replaced by the idea of Revolution—the arrival of full communism—, the fruition of which promises happiness. By buying into the promise of the artwork toward which the viewer looks for affirmation, encouragement, and inspiration for the tasks they aim to solve, the viewer imagines themselves transformed by the product—Revolution—into an object of envy for others who have not yet been liberated from the capitalist system. The burgeoning industry of copying artworks in the Stalinist era contributed to "glamour" in Soviet society by turning art into a culturally and socially loaded consumer good that denoted success (Yankovskaya and Mitchell 2006). This complements Dobrenko's argument that socialist realism created socialism and also Clark's argument that socialist realism was the USSR's myth repository (2000). Socialist realism thus became not only a style but also the foundation for cultural state-building, and, within this "myth bank" the October Revolution became the foundational myth of the contemporary USSR (Clark 2000; Frame 2012, 289). Internationalism was, therefore, a necessary element of the construction, and evolution, of the constituent myths contained within socialist realism, as was the appropriation of potentially useful cultural tropes and practices from other countries. Clark terms the revival of pre-Soviet Russian culture in the 1930s part of a "Great Appropriation":

> In building up its own image, Moscow appropriated both laterally (absorbing contemporary trends in other countries, primarily western European, but also American) and also diachronically (appropriating Great Russian and European culture of the past). (Clark 2011, 8)

The Great Appropriation was to some extent tempered by conflicting interpretations of cultural policy. Increasingly the Party had final authority; it set forth a list of vague cultural aesthetic labels and an idea of functionality, but left debates about specific artistic form and content to the professional community of established individuals within cultural institutions (Rolfe 2009). Cultural policy was legitimized often by reference to individuals already hailed in their own profession, rather than through party doctrine or official announcements. Socialist realism was no different; its framework was established early in the 1930s but the detail was never glossed, and because of that, it never became completely clear if socialist realism was the only method, a style, or one of a number of equally acceptable methods, and if realism could refer to a realistic style or a certain perception of the moment (Robin 1992).

Therefore, in theory, socialist realism could take any number of forms in any number of genres, but once it was hailed as the official method of Soviet literature, writers were urged to follow novels that had been identified as exemplars of the nascent system. In literature this included figures such as Gor'kii, who swiftly became the standard figure to evoke when the intelligentsia sought the safety of unfailing reliability in literature as the world around them became increasingly unreliable (Fitzpatrick 1976, 223). The avant-garde progressively came under attack and the classics were reinstated (Solovyova 1999, 329). This move toward the classics was arguably part of the wider idea of *kul'turnost,'* of being "cultured," promoted in the 1930s, which entailed the rise of traditionally middle-class values such as propriety, culture, and good taste. *Kul'turnost'* was a state to be aspired toward and came to symbolize both individual achievement and industrial efficiency (Kelly and Volkov 1998, 297).

By the end of the second decade of the October Revolution, socialist realism had therefore changed from an approach for the potential construction of international socialism to one for the construction of intranational—Soviet—socialism, as the Party's focus shifted inwards. Perhaps the best known result of the drive to construct "socialism in one country" was the systematic rooting out of those deemed to be damaging or dangerous to Soviet society. The Great Purges between 1936 and 1938, which saw millions of Soviet citizens sent to their deaths in the Main Camp Management (GULAG) prison camp network, left an indelible mark on Soviet culture. Socialist realism began to become a more restrictive term as the vague cultural edicts of the Party and the culture of fear and instability created a self-reinforcing set of culturally acceptable aesthetic labels which were ruthlessly policed, often by critics with little or no interest in culture whatsoever (Rolfe 2009). The once open and inclusive term became condensed into a set of catchphrases or keywords: *narodnost'* (national character), *partiinost'* (party spirit), *dostupnost'* (accessibility), *opora na klassiku* (support of the classics). The catchphrases highlighted the need for a socialist realist work to contain elements of folk or national music and culture, reflecting the ideology of the KPSS, ensuring that the work was accessible to everyone and open to popular demands, and finally based on past classical models. The net result was that writers began to draw from this small, celebrated repertoire of works and "socialist realism became so intensely citational that, by the mid-1930s, a single, conventionalized system of signs was already evident in virtually all novelistic depictions of positive heroes" (Clark 1997, 31). Paradigmatic literary works from which inspiration was drawn included; in the 1930s, Nikolai Ostrovskii's *How the Steel Was Tempered*, the story of Pavel Korchagin's (the archetypical positive hero) journey toward socialism and the sacrifices he made for society. Maksim Fadeev's *The Young Guard*, which focuses on the activities of the antifascist underground Komsomol organization, active during the Second World War (WW2), seemed to be the chosen paradigm of socialist realism for the forties, although it was never clarified (Clark 2000, 160). Other post-factum models of socialist realism included: Gor'kii, Vladimir Maiakovskii, Vesevolod Ivanov—*Partisan Tales*, Dimitri Furmanov—*Chapaev*, Alexander Fadeev—*The Rout*, Sergei Eisenstein—*Battleship Potemkin*, Anton Makarenko—*Pedagogical poem*, Fedor Gladkov—*Cement*, and Marietta Shaginian—*Miss-Mend, or the Yankees in Petrograd*.

The Stalin Prize, established in 1941, further reinforced the bounds of acceptability and cemented the nascent hierarchy of artistic forms. The process for approving the award (which involved six stages of oversight going through the *Komitet po Stalinskim premiiam* through to Stalin himself) became more obscure over time (Frolova-Walker 2016, 19). The Prize, and the exclusion of certain artists from its consideration, served to establish a hierarchy of authority, but the long process of selecting recipients and the surrounding debate also reflected the ongoing arguments between those promoting "high" art and those aiming to promote mass popular culture (Frolova-Walker 2016, 55–56). The Prize, which included different classes of award and categories for film, literature, the visual arts and music, was in turns both tolerant and restrictive, particularly when it came to music. Within the visual arts, Oliver Johnson argues that the Stalin Prize was intimately linked to the re-establishment of the Academy of Fine Arts, its emphasis on traditional realism, and the bid to centralize power (Johnson 2011).

Within theater, Konstantin Stanislavskii became the legitimizing figure and the founding paragon of socialist realist theatrical production. Stanislavskii, with Vladimir Nemirovich-Danchenko, had founded the joint-stock company, the Moscow Art Theater, (MKhAT) in 1898. The theater focused on realism in its productions and Stanislavskii pioneered an acting system that would facilitate heightened psychological and emotional realism in actors' portrayals of characters. Stanislavskii's system, which has become a world-wide institution, is based on a series of linked techniques that are used to help actors communicate believable emotions from three-dimensional characters in their performances. A holistic system, it drew on currents from the Russian avant-garde, in addition to incorporating elements of psychology and physical fitness.[2]

An alternative theatrical figure who eventually became a high-profile victim of the "hard left," and an indication of which styles and approaches might not be acceptable, was Vsevolod Meierkhol'd. A former student of Nemirovich Danchenko at the MKhAT, Meierkhol'd had been active in the Theatrical Department of Narkompros, of which he was appointed the head in 1920. Before he founded his own theater in 1923, Meierkhol'd and other avant-garde artists led the "Theatrical October" campaign, a campaign focused on creating a revolutionary style of theater that would render obsolete the academic theaters and their style. Like Stanislavskii, he argued that an actor's emotional state was linked to their physical state; however, his style was a significant departure from the realism of Stanislavskii. Meierkhol'd strongly advocated the use of ideas of symbolism and constructivism in theater, devising the biomechanics acting technique, which advocated that every movement of the actor must demonstrate an inner reaction to an emotion and combined elements of circusesque styles and ideas about mechanics and efficiency. Meierkhol'd also emphasized the artificiality of theater, rejected the idea of a "fourth wall" and had earlier sought to reject "traditional" theater in the search for a more radical variant that would be capable of expressing the new reality. A victim of the anti-*formalizm* campaign, Meierkhol'd was convicted of anti-Soviet activity and shot in 1940. He was rehabilitated in 1955.

In the climate of fear and paranoia directors became increasingly unwilling to take risks or experiment with theatrical forms that could be interpreted as a departure from the officially sanctioned, stunted version of the Stanislavskian system. This narrow reading of Stanislavskian "stage realism" (psychological realism and emotional authenticity), which traced a genealogy from the System back to the nineteenth-century realist school of Aleksandr Fedotov and Mikhail Shchepkin, consequently became popularized (Gardiner 2014, 49–50). By the 1940s the naturalistic focus on detail of the sets of the MKhAT and the Malyi (two of the "academic" theaters against which Meierkhol'd had rallied) became the unfailingly reliable approach against which all other theater productions' set designs and aesthetics were measured. This saw the widespread implementation of naturalist three-walled sets, which maintained the fourth wall, the use of real props and mass choreography alongside avoidance of theatrical stylizing and devices or techniques that emphasized the artificiality of theater such as Meierkhol'd's biomechanics method. Dramatic plots did not differ wildly from the emergent format of the Soviet socialist realist novel that followed the masterplot and dramatized journeys of heroes and heroines from class ignorance to ideological enlightenment (Gardiner

2014, 51). By 1950 the number of theaters had fallen from 900 to 545 (Deza and Matthews 1975, 718–19).

Socialist realism was slower to become enshrined within the visual arts, perhaps in part because the nebulous nature of the term, and the erratic enforcement of its perceived boundaries, meant that art forms with a less clear narrative, such as the visual arts, were more flexible. An emphasis was placed on realism in paintings, and the *kartinka*—a large, oil-on-canvas, labor-intensive composition featuring multiple figures and dealing with a significant theme—became a promoted style (Reid 2001, 164). This trend notwithstanding, alternative approaches that drew on impressionism and other figurative trends were also given space for expression. Until Anatolii Lunacharskii's departure from being Commissar of Enlightenment in 1929, realism made little headway compared to other artistic forms such as literature and cinema, despite efforts from Proletkul't or AKhRR. The association's works tended to be neo-realist treatments of workers and soldiers or mythologizations of Soviet history, and clearly looked up to Il'ia Repin as the figurehead of Russian realism (Kelly and Milner-Gulland 1998, 145). Repin had been a member of the *Peredvizhniki* (itinerant wanderers), a group of Russian realist artists who, in the mid-nineteenth century, broke away from the Imperial Academy of Arts and formed an independent artistic cooperative. The cooperative began life based in St. Petersburg but then travelled around the Russian provinces in an effort to bring art to the people. The *Peredvizhniki* eschewed high society and focused on popular themes, including inequality and injustice, folk customs, and landscapes. The group was strongly influenced by literary critics such as Vissarion Belinskii and Chernyshevskii, and also brought together artists from diverse geographical locations. Elizabeth Valkener (1989) charts the development of the tradition of realist art from a sociopolitical perspective, which necessarily deals with the influence of Chernyshevskii's generation of thinkers on Russian art.

The year 1932 was also a key year in the organization of the visual arts; all existing artistic groups were dissolved and the Union of Soviet Artists, a "loose co-ordinating body for the various regional and republican Unions," was founded (Kelly and Milner-Gulland 1998, 146). Vsekhudozhnik, (the All-Russian Union of Artists' Cooperatives), founded in 1929, became a key player in the maneuverings of power after 1932. It unified conflicting groups and promoted artistic production on a mass scale and worked out the economic system of the Soviet art world. Cooperatives such as Vsekhudozhnik were the principal producers of socialist realist visual media for everyday life, offering artists thematic plans and advance contracts: "the artists would sign a contract with an enterprise, institution, or the cooperative itself and would then deliver the work, which was based on an assigned theme, within a predefined period of time" (Yankovskaya and Mitchell 2006, 776). However, a significant proportion of Soviet painters did not participate within this system (Yankovskaya and Mitchell 2006, 776). The first regional sections of Vsekhudozhnik were in Rostov-on-Don, Nizhnii Novgorod, Samara, and Sverdlovsk. Eventually nearly all regional capitals, from Leningrad in the West to Khabarovsk in the Far East, had a cooperative section. When Vsekhudozhnik was closed down in 1953 it had a total of sixty-seven societies (Yankovskaya and Mitchell 2006, 780). Landscapes, still lives, and other nature scenes that, due to the demands of the style, could not offer the clear narrative demanded by socialist realism, offered nonconforming artists a protective space within which they could avoid ideological commissions with clear socialist themes (Swanson 1994).

From 1932 to 1933, a milestone exhibition, *Artists of the Russian Federation after Fifteen Years*, was held. This exhibition presented the main players in the competition for socialist realism, consigning the avant-garde to history. Reid argues that the contenders could, broadly speaking, be separated into two camps, adaptations of the Russian realist tradition versus more expressive abstract tendencies (Reid 2001, 155). There was considerable room for differing interpretations of the new directives of socialist realism; orders from "above" were contradictory and inconsistent but were also interpreted and implemented against the backdrop of factional conflicts between both artistic factions and the bureaucracies that patronized them. Such heterogeneous approaches can be found in the differences between the treatment of Kuz'ma Petrov-Vodkin who died in 1939 and whose work was infrequently shown from then until the Thaw, and Aleksandr Gerasimov whose work was regularly shown in exhibitions and who received numerous honors. The treatment of Pavel Kuznetsov or Aleksandr Deineka, the latter of whom became a key figure once more during the Thaw, also demonstrate these irregularities. Such competing currents prevented socialist realism from achieving a clear, established ontology (Reid 2001, 154). Greater regulation and centralization of the art world came in 1938, with the establishment of the Organizational Committee of the Union of Soviet Artists. Aleksandr Gerasimov, protégé of the Commissar of Defence Kliment Voroshilov (Reid 2001, 159), and president of the Moscow Union of Artists in 1932, was the Organizational Committee's first president, and then the first director of the Academy of Arts (Kelly and Milner-Gulland 1998, 146). The Organizational Committee specified that, to be a member of the new system of local artists' unions, an individual should have specialized education, produce independent original works of high quality, and exhibit regularly; independently stage theater productions; be a critic or scholar publishing in the Soviet press regularly; or be a master of folk art and create independent, original, high-quality products (Yankovskaya and Mitchell 2006, 783). These requirements made a significant portion of artists ineligible to join the Union.

Visual arts were closely linked to the idea of, and drive for, *kul'turnost.'* In the context of a changing value system and the popularization of certain desired practices, "art provided, not only a space for the visualisation of ideas, but also a marker of belonging to a socially successful group" (Yankovskaya and Mitchell 2006, 770). It was perhaps in this context that the paradigmatic exhibition *The Industry of Socialism,* the first All-Union art exhibition was conceived. Preparations began in 1935; the exhibition, which would involve 700 artists, was to be held in 1937, although in the end it did not take place until March 1939. The exhibition's purpose was twofold: it would be the first public display of socialist realism, and would enact the integration of artists into useful, planned, socialist production (Reid 2001). A brainchild of the Commissar for heavy industry, "Sergo" Ordzhonikidze, the exhibition was closely linked to the industrializing drive of the 1930s. As such, the problems of the art world therefore took on a political tone and complaints about short-ages of materials, spontaneous or orchestrated, could be used as evidence, against the supplier, of criminal dereliction of duty (Reid 2001). The exhibi-tion "identified socialist realism with the forms of 'high' art canonised in the pre-revolutionary academy, oil painting and sculpture" (Reid 2001, 157). Reid also points out that in commissioning work according to a written script, it privileged, "from the outset, narrative painting, identifying socialist real-ist art almost exclusively with the *kartinka*" (Reid 2001, 164). Nevertheless, within this remit, it was still able to maintain a guarded diversity of styles within the boundaries of acceptability; the *kartinka* dominated but still life and impressionist-inspired pieces still abounded (Reid 2001, 169). The public reaction to, and subsequent "serious, comprehensive discussion," of the exhi-bition was to help guide artists in the synthesis and improvement of a national art form (Grigor'ev 1939).

The guarded diversity of *The Industry of Socialism* was already anach-ronistic by the time it opened in 1939. Clear hierarchies of style had been established during this time and the labels "formalism" and "naturalism" now implied a willful inaccessibility to the wider population. In discussing the exhibition Grigor'ev used loaded language to criticize the perceived short-comings of some of the artists:

> We dwelled on the main creative achievements of our masters. However, it would be a mistake to turn a blind eye to the many weaknesses of the artists. Socialist realism does not tolerate the sentimentality, falsehood, varnishing and belching of naturalism. (Grigor'ev 1939)

Within *The Industry of Socialism*, and the types of art and artistic production it privileged, there was a return to neoclassical canvas painting and sculpture, the privileging of novelistic realism over modernism and the identification of these forms as the most appropriate to depict proletarian subjects. There had been plans to incorporate an abridged and revised version of *The Industry of Socialism* into a Museum of Soviet Art as the core collection that would constitute the canon of socialist realism, but these were put on hold with the advent of WW2 in the USSR in 1941 and "the definitive statement of the nature and scope of socialist realism was deferred once more" (Reid 2001, 183). However, while a once-and-for-all official definition remained elusive, institutional reforms that had taken place between 1936 and 1940 were reinstated and legitimized social and cultural hierarchies, and these dictated the direction that socialist realism would take in the late Stalinist period.

DOGMATIZATION

Socialist realism was understood in Cuba in a variety of iterations and contexts, and this understanding changed over the course of the Cuban Revolution as new generations of Cubans were brought up within the Revolution. Initially, the group that had the strongest understanding of the paradigm was, understandably, the PSP and therefore to some extent, Sociedad Cultural Nuestro Tiempo (henceforth Nuestro Tiempo). However, as struggles for power intensified within both the budding infrastructure and the differing interpretations of culture under socialism, socialist realism became synonymous with enduring prejudices about the PSP and the type of cultural production (it was assumed) some of their more "orthodox" members wished to promote. Discussion about the paradigm in the 1960s was, therefore, particularly heated and attention focused on the high Stalinist variant of socialist realism.

During the late Stalinist period, the backward-looking approach toward socialist realism, which had developed between 1936 and 1940, became progressively internalized. What is referred to here as "high Stalinist socialist realism" has come to be understood generally as the only variant of socialist realism. This is perhaps because of the lasting damaging effect that the application of this manifestation of the approach had on cultural expression and promotion, creating an easily identifiable, homogenous narrative style across the visual arts, literature, theater, and the cinema that remains emblematic of the period. The approach, in both aesthetic and organizational applications, moved from inclusive to exclusive as experimentation became increasingly dangerous. This stunting of culture, by which socialist realism has come to be characterized, was only partially addressed in the wake of Stalin's death and the ensuing institutional readjustments.

The need to mobilize the population during WW2 opened up the boundaries of acceptability within Soviet culture. The fight against fascism became synonymous with the national struggle for survival: ideological controls were relaxed and the use of pre-revolutionary imagery was encouraged. The Orthodox Church was allowed to re-establish the Patriarchate and the secret police had its activities curbed. To many citizens, this liberalization created hope that a victory would ignite more widespread reforms (Fuller 2002, 334). However, after the war, against the increasingly hostile backdrop of the Cold War, the artistic and the political became even more inextricably linked. In the post-war USSR, reconstruction of the economy was once more a priority, along with a greater imposition of domestic political controls (Fuller 2002). There was more intense regulation of culture, a rise in national chauvinism and a significant narrowing of the parameters of acceptability. Within approved socialist realist works there was a greater interest in the true and the false, rather than focusing on an individual journey toward enlightenment. In keeping with the trend of rising nationalism more symbols relating to the native land were used in art and the heroism of socialist realist works of the late 1930s faded away (Clark 2000, 192–98). In a further acknowledgement of the realist agenda, the space that had been the Imperial Academy of Arts in Leningrad was made into the Il'ia Repin Leningrad Institute for Painting, Sculpture and Architecture in 1944.

The effect on cultural production was twofold; the scope of socialist realism contracted, and the importance of an artist's legitimizing biography, giving them the right or the experience to embark upon the creation of a realistic socialist cultural product, increased. In 1946 a campaign that became known as the *Zhdanovshchina*—after Andrei Zhdanov, Commissar of Culture in 1946 and Chairman of the USSR between 1946 and 1947—was initiated. The *Zhdanovshchina* marked a reactionary, conservative period that saw a drive to remove all Western, bourgeois influences from Soviet intellectual and cultural life and artists. The Zhdanov Doctrine divided the world into two spheres, imperialistic (with the United States at its head) and democratic (with the USSR at its head). It advocated significant anti-Western sentiment in all spheres of Soviet life, including science. Artists had to ensure that their creative works conformed to the party line or face persecution. During this period intellectuals deemed to have Western leanings were persecuted and their work banned. The period began in August 1946 with two resolutions from the Central Committee. One criticized the publication by the Leningrad-based journals *Zvezda* (Star) and *Leningrad* of works by satirical writer Mikhail Zoshchenko and the Silver-age poet Anna Akhmatova. Zoshchenko and Akhmatova were expelled from the Soviet Writers' Union and the journal editors were replaced. These developments also reinforced the idea of Moscow as the center of authoritarian culture. St Petersburg had been the more liberal center of culture in the USSR and the attack on their only "thick" (serious) cultural journal *Leningrad* signaled that the liberalization of culture which some members of the intelligentsia had hoped for would not be forthcoming. The second resolution was "Concerning the repertoires of dramatic theaters and measures to improve them." The resolution, issued on August 26, 1946, lamented the direction of Soviet theater and lack of plays that dealt with contemporary themes (according to the resolution, only twenty-five of 115 productions) and opined that too many artists were removed from or avoided dealing with contemporary issues and that this rendered theater's educative potential ineffective (Anon 1946, 593).

The resolution denounced the focus on bourgeois foreign works, called for an increase in new plays that dealt with Soviet contemporaneity, emphasized the need for theatrical critics, less bureaucracy, and a union-wide competition for the best contemporary Soviet plays. Gardiner identifies three playwrights who were particularly promoted by the Writers' Union during the *Zhdanovshchina*, Anatolii Sofronov, Anatolii Surov, and Nikolai Virta (2014, 61–70). Their plays dealt with contemporary topics, such as municipal government and Party leadership, good and bad workers, and the *kolkhoz* (collective farm). The theory of *beskonfliktnost'* (conflictness) was also promoted in theater during the late Stalinist period: it proclaimed that plays should not depict any real conflict because society was now free of all class-based antagonism. This theory led to a glossing-over of the negative and promotion of unrealistically high individual moral standards in theatrical works, subsequently criticized as *lakirovka* (varnishing).

Within the visual arts, realist works, drawing on the nineteenth century, national-populist ideas of the *peredvizhniki* tradition were increasingly privileged from the mid-to-late 1930s. Three types were particularly favored: the portrait, above all of political or military leaders; the historical painting; and the genre painting (depicting scenes of everyday life) (Kelly and Milner-Gulland 1998, 146). These styles and genres became further enshrined with the re-establishing of the pre-revolutionary Academy of Arts in 1947. Previously in Leningrad but now in Moscow, the new Academy was led by Aleksandr Gerasimov, who remained its director until 1957. However, while the *Zhdanovshchina* provided clear guidelines for composers, writers, filmmakers, and theater producers, visual art did not suffer from the same degree of intervention from the Central Committee. Within this context, the Stalin Prize became an important site of negotiation rather than a space for reinforcement (Johnson 2011, 821). Gerasimov's circle dominated the selection process for the Stalin Prize, attempting to promote the criteria determined by the Academy of Fine Arts and thereby consolidating its hegemony. Artistic works were assessed by their ideological, political, and productive criteria. The net result of this was that the prize was increasingly seen by younger artists as a closed system, awarded on nepotistic grounds rather than merit (Johnson 2011, 842–843). The production of original artworks diminished and copying increased. The copying of sanctioned artworks helped to guarantee a comfortable existence during the late Stalinist period, without the danger of political repercussions. It also helped to turn art into a regular, accessible consumer product that ensured artistic education on a mass scale and the standardization of audience reception (Yankovskaya and Mitchell 2006, 785–88). Yankovskaya and Mitchell also argue that late Stalinist paintings were characterized by their monumental size, attention to detail, and group nature, possibly due to the way that works were priced after the war (Yankovskaya and Mitchell 2006, 789).

In this increasingly regulated atmosphere, a further decree, this time directed at the music world but symptomatic of the wider approach to culture, was issued in August of 1948, cementing the drive against perceived non-Soviet trends. Georgian composer Vano Muradeli and his opera *Velikaia druzhba* (The Great Friendship) were accused of *formalizm* (formalism). Other composers, such as Prokofiev and Shostakovich, were also accused of formalist tendencies and their work was banned. This heralded the beginning of the campaign against *formalizm*. The *Zhdanovshchina* and the anti-*formalizm* campaign reignited the type of binary division that had characterized the Bolsheviks' early thinking about bourgeois specialists and the proletarian intelligentsia in the early 1920. In politics the division was between Western–imperialist/Soviet-democratic; in culture the division was between formalist and socialist realist. Socialist realism thus became a term used by those in power to indicate approval or bestow a value on a cultural production, although it could equally be co-opted to legitimize works that would otherwise be viewed askance, in the same way the label "*formalizm*" could be used to condemn a work and its author (Gardiner 2014, 51).

As the chill of the Cold War set in, foreign influence on culture became conflated with anti-patriotic sentiments and, on January 28, 1949, the campaign against *kosmopolitizm* (cosmopolitanism) began. As Gardiner discusses (2014, 87–93), the editorial "Ob odnoi antipatriot007icheskoi gruppe teatral'nykh kritikov (On one Antipatriotic Group of Theater Critics) in *Pravda* denounced a group of theater critics, who had found the quality of some plays that dealt with Soviet contemporaneity lacking. The critics in question were deemed to be Western-oriented, and harshly criticised for holding up the development of Soviet literature and potentially distracting the youth because of their 'rootless cosmopolitanism" (Anon 1949a). This article was then re-used and applied to the visual arts on February 10 of the same year, clearly linking *kosmopolitanizm* to *formalism* and willful meddling in the creative work of realist artists (Anon 1949b).

The anti-*kosmopolitizm* campaign was further complicated by the puzzling appearance of a clear anti-Semitic drive. This prejudice saw the closure of the Moscow State Jewish Theater (GOSET) and the Kamernyi Theater run by

Aleksandr Tairov—which in 1932 had incorporated the Realistic Theater's company into its troupe (Beumers 1998, 92–95).

THAW(S)

After Stalin's death on March 5, 1953, and the ensuing power struggle until Khrushchev's departure from power in 1964, there was a period of frenetic reformism across all spheres of Soviet life, known as the Thaw. During this period the government sought political change through the reform, and in some cases rebuilding, of institutions of Party and State. This included addressing the cult of Stalin, which after Nikita Khrushchev's "Secret Speech" in 1956, began to be more systematically dismantled. Il'ia Erenburg's novel *Ottepel'* (Thaw) gave the period its name, Erenburg's novel addressed subjects, such as the Purges and anti-Semitism, which had previously been taboo in Soviet society. The novel is loosely based around two painters, a Party hack and a talented artist who does not paint in the socialist realist style.

The Thaw was "a time of rapid change, of moving back—though not eliminating—barriers, of asking new questions, raising new subjects, and to some extent experimenting with new techniques" (Hosking 1980, 19). As such, it was a hopeful, yet disorienting, period (Dobson 2009, 15), that was not actually a continuous process of relaxation and liberalization but a series of several "thaws" that were almost immediately followed by reactionary clampdowns by the Party (Jones 2006b, 11). These "thaws" occurred in 1954 (following the September 1953 Central Committee Plenum), 1956 (following the twentieth Party Congress) and from 1961–1962 (following the twenty-second Party Congress), while periods of reactionary policy are identified from 1954–55, late 1956–1957 and 1962–1963 (Clark 2000, 211). For example, Garaudy's *D'un réalisme sans rivages*, published in 1963 was placed on a black list in the USSR, due to his "revisionism" (Reid 2012).

During the Thaw artists were no longer obliged to give primacy to the party and social issues at the exclusion of the personal and could enjoy greater freedom of artistic expression (Woll 2000, 4). Socialist realism remained the dominant cultural paradigm during the Thaw, and, however, was actually strengthened by the re-opening of discussions about what the creation of a socialist art form could include. The cautious openness in the cultural world was first (publicly) ushered in by Vladimir Pomerantsev's essay "On Sincerity in Literature" (December 1953). The essay attacked the rigid, reductive Stalinist, canons of socialist realism that had prevailed since the 1930s (Pomerantsev 1953). This included an attack on the tendency to varnish reality (*lakirova deistvitelnosti*)—through false descriptions of prosperity, avoidance of extremes and the ignoring of potentially problematic topics

(Freeze 2002, 353). *Lakirovka*, and the overly romanticized, embellished view of Soviet reality that it implied became a particularly resonant term (Pomerantsev 1953). Between the *Industriia Sotsialisma* exhibition and the Thaw, the master narrative of socialist realism had become one of affirmation, the enactment of Soviet myths, and the inexorable move toward full communism. Set against the environment of mass repression and totalitarian politics, the efforts to produce "glamour" within a socialist system turned into what Pomerantsev considered *lakirovka*.

Pomerantsev's approach did not mean a rejection of socialist realism, but it rather, in its argument for a synthesis of unflinching representation of reality and socialist commitment, sat neatly within the earlier boundaries of the approach, and even earlier traditions in Russian intellectual thought. This expansion of the limits of socialist realism was at the heart of cultural discourses within the Thaw, as cultural practitioners made a concerted effort to broaden the term into a paradigm that "could embody a multiplicity of styles, genres and forms" while retaining its didactic message (Gardiner 2014, 22). The idea of *beskonfliktnost'* was debunked in 1952 in an official campaign against the movement. In 1953, the Ministry of Culture took over the responsibility of repertoire control and delegated the responsibility for municipal theaters to Moscow City Council. The canonized Stanislavskii system was attacked and Meierkhol'd was rehabilitated (Beumers 1998, 95). New appointments to theaters were made, which included Anatolii Efros to the Theater of the Lenin Komsomol (1963) and Iurii Liubimov to the Taganka Theater (1964). New theaters were also founded: Oleg Efremov, along with young graduates from the Moscow Art School, founded the Sovremennik Studio which became an official theater in 1965 (Beumers 1998, 95). The Sovremennik "reflected a new atmosphere in the Soviet theatrical sphere and aimed to speak to a younger generation with its modern choice of repertoire and progressive stage aesthetic" (Gardiner 2014, 262).

As part of the periods of reassessment and debate ushered in by the Thaw(s), debates about internationalism re-entered the public sphere. Initially, the concept of socialist realism, as *the* socialist art form and cultural approach, had had a strong international element to it. For, just as the USSR's model for the transition to communism, via the late stages of capitalism and then socialism, came to be viewed as the de facto political and economic model to emulate (above all by the USSR), socialist realism had the potential to become the principal cultural approach for international communism and its constituent cultures. This international dynamic began to be rediscovered by artists from the mid-1950s onward, particularly within the context of debates about modernism and the Soviet Contemporary Style.

This rediscovered internationalism permitted an opening-up to external influences in the theater and the dramatist, Bertolt Brecht played a significant role in the revitalization of Soviet theater. Brecht was awarded a Stalin prize in 1954,[3] the same year as future Cuban national poet and future head of UNEAC, Nicolás Guillén. In May and June of 1957, the Berliner Ensemble toured Moscow and Leningrad for the first time since its creation in 1949. This was also the first time that Brecht's work had been staged in Russia since the playwright relocated to the German Democratic Republic (GDR). The tour was important and influential in both the cultural and political spheres. Brecht's international reputation, ardent support of communism and the USSR and public opposition to war and increased armament meant that the USSR had a figurehead for its nuclear disarmament campaign. In the Soviet press, an image of Brecht which emphasized his Marxist ideals and his opposition to American imperialism was constructed. This also consolidated Brecht's position and influence within the cultural politics of the GDR, and the Ensemble's staging of the work of an artist previously considered "formalist" by Soviet critics helped to contribute to the reassessment of appropriate forms of socialist realism (Gardiner 2014, 196–209). In 1959, two years after the tour of the Berliner Ensemble, an anonymous Soviet writer published a critique of socialist realism in the French press. The writer is widely thought to be Abram Tertz, the pseudonym under which the dissident writer Andrei Siniavskii wrote. Siniavskii and fellow writer Iulii Daniel were placed on show trial between September 1965 and February 1966, accused and convicted of publishing anti-Soviet work in the foreign press. The article which sparked the trial drew parallels between socialist realism and religious thought and doctrine. It also underlined how socialist realism had become hermetic and rooted in the past. However, the essay did also hint that socialist realism—if, in its new permutation, it could still be called that—had the potential to evolve further into something altogether broader (Tertz 1960).

The concept of socialist realism was also broadened in the visual arts prior to, and concurrent with, the periods of crisis and clampdown during the Thaw(s). Within painting, the paradigm evolved though efforts to define and contest the "Contemporary Style," a style that reflected the artist's awareness of the momentous changes occurring in Soviet society (Bown 2012, 99–101). Bown identifies Nina Dimitrieva's 1958 article "Towards the Question of a Contemporary Style in Painting" as the keystone of the debate about the Contemporary Style. This debate was fundamentally about the modernization of Soviet art and its opening up to international influence, such as Mexican muralists. At issue was the legitimacy of selectively assimilating modernism—Russian, Western and, increasingly, postcolonial—which for so long had been anathematized as formalist decadence and *kozmopolitizm*, into a modern, civic, social art; and the question of whether this art could be considered "realist" (Reid 2006, 209–12). The question of modernism arose during the Thaw and was "embraced by reformist elements within the art establishment as a means to strengthen and reinvigorate the art of social-ism" (Reid 2009, 89). Reid argues that a Soviet variant of modernism (the Contemporary Style)—frequently considered anathema to Soviet culture and more widely, socialist culture—came into existence in the 1950s and 1960s (Reid 2000). Garaudy, in the face of strong criticism for *D'un réalisme sans rivages*, was also particularly vocal in the defense of modernism and its place within Marxist culture.

This emergent modernism was an assimilated, re-elaborated variant, a socialist hybrid of modernism and a way of moving past the late Stalinist period and reinvigorating socialism (Reid 2009). Abstract art was still odious to conservative movements; however, complete quarantine was no longer a viable method, given the resurgence of the internationalist project and its Soviet leadership (Reid 2012). The new focus on internationalism in the USSR meant the necessary interaction of Soviet culture with other national (socialist) experiences (Reid 2000). International cultural exchanges "were recognized as a means to reduce international tension as well as to glean use-ful models for selective imitation" (Reid 2012, 262). Back in the USSR, exhi-bitions featuring French impressionist and post-impressionist artists, such as Paul Cézanne helped to broaden the idea of socialist realism, stimulated the artistic world, and inspired debate. The inventory of subjects that fell under the remit of socialist realism was opened up, socially critical paintings were encouraged and family breakdown, sexual politics, conflicts with the Party and poor work practices all became acceptable subjects (Bown 2012, 97).

However, in the face of foreign affair failures, such as the Cuban Mis-sile Crisis, and mounting economic inefficiencies, dissatisfaction with the Khrushchev administration began to mount. Disgruntlement with Khrush-chev's government reached a head in October 1964 and, after an extraordi-nary session of the Central Committee, he was removed from power. The initial artistic freedom and opportunities presented by the Thaw dissipated and were soon replaced by a policy that became progressively stricter and more alienating. These were implemented within a cultural apparatus—the "interlocking system of censorship, unions and patronage which had taken form and had always been present in the Stalin era" that had remained imper-vious to de-Stalinization (Jones 2006b, 13).

STAGNATION (1964–1986)

In Cuba in the 1970s, as the cultural authorities focused on educating and including the Cuban population in cultural production, socialist realism became a point of entry for discussions about the USSR in cultural maga-zines. This coincided with the promotion of cultural administrators who had grown up within the Revolution and who had been politically educated via the USSR's Marxism manuals. The subsequent greater regulation of culture during this decade, particularly 1971–1975, has come to be taken by some academics as evidence of the existence of what has been termed high Stalinist socialist realism—organizational and aesthetic—in Cuba (Farber 2011, 23; Puñales-Alpízar 2012, 54).

Shortly before this period in Cuba, socialist realism underwent a further period of reassessment in the USSR. The change in leadership sought to establish political and economic stability but was ultimately restorationist, halting institutional reforms, avoiding wide-sweeping change, and to some extent rehabilitating Stalin. The discursive spaces that the Thaw had opened up began to close. Explorations of the meaning of socialist realism decreased and instead the period was characterized by a reactionary approach toward culture, particularly after 1966 (Beumers 1999, 370–371). A host of cultural figures known for their liberalizing approaches were removed from positions of influence or had their membership of official cultural organs, such as the Writers' Union, withdrawn. At the Twenty-Third Party Congress, held in 1966, a number of controversial theatrical productions were banned and posts were reshuffled—Anatolii Efros was dismissed from the Lenin Komsomol Theater and placed in the Malaia Bronnaia Theater (Moscow Drama Theater) as staff director in 1967. Party membership and the location of the theater that was being considered, along with key political or public events, played a role in censorship decisions (Beumers 1998, 95–96).

However, a number of trials of creative figures with links abroad/foreign links (such as Siniavskii and Daniel, poet Iurii Galanskov and fellow poet Aleksandr Ginzburg) resulted in significant international criticism of the USSR. The following furor formed part of the basis for the adoption of a guardedly more flexible cultural policy. It allowed for a degree of experimentation within the boundaries of socialist realism and access to a greater range of discourses within which the intelligentsia could frame its discussions. This more flexible approach included the selective and small-scale publication of some outstanding and controversial works, including pre-revolutionary and early post-revolutionary literature, such as Osip Mandel'shtam's poetry, the 1979 edition of Andrei Belyi's novel *Petersburg*, or the 1973 editions of Mikhail Bulgakov's novels, including *The Master and Margarita*. Foreign literature in translation was also published, including selections of a trinity of writers—Kafka, Proust, and Joyce—who had previously been particularly singled out as clear example of the decadence of Western modernism. A similar approach was taken within the visual arts and, after the infamous bulldozed exhibition at Beliaevo Park in 1974,[4] and the ensuing international outcry, a second exhibition was successfully held in 1975 at Izmailovo Park (Lovell and Marsh 1998, 62).

As the boundaries of socialist realism continued to be questioned by artists and intellectuals cautious currents still circulated underneath the surface of the seemingly stagnating cultural world. One such individual was Dmitrii Markov, director of the Institute of Slavic and Balkan Studies of the Academy of Sciences (later the Institute for Slavic Studies), who argued that socialist realism was always an open, aesthetical broad concept, unlimited by expressive style or subject matter and capable of expressing the various truths of contemporary life (Markov 1977). From the 1960s onward the continuing reassessment of socialist realism and art and culture under socialism also saw some artists consciously and directly confront and parody the tenets of socialist realism and tradition of realism in Soviet culture through *Sots-art*. Sots-art is a term used to refer to unauthorized socialist art—an ironic imitation of pop art—and was a movement originated by the older generation of artists (such as Vitaly Komar, Alexander Melamid, Eric Bulatov, and Il'ia Kabakov) who were critical of the Soviet system (Yurchak 2006, 250). The key figures in the movement began to utilize the tropes of socialist realism but subvert them by substituting established symbols, such as busts of Lenin, with subtle reworkings, such as utilizing the faces of loved ones. In this way, *Sots-art* questioned the ideological basis upon which socialist realism, specifically late Stalinist socialist realism, operated (Figures 2.3 and 2.4).

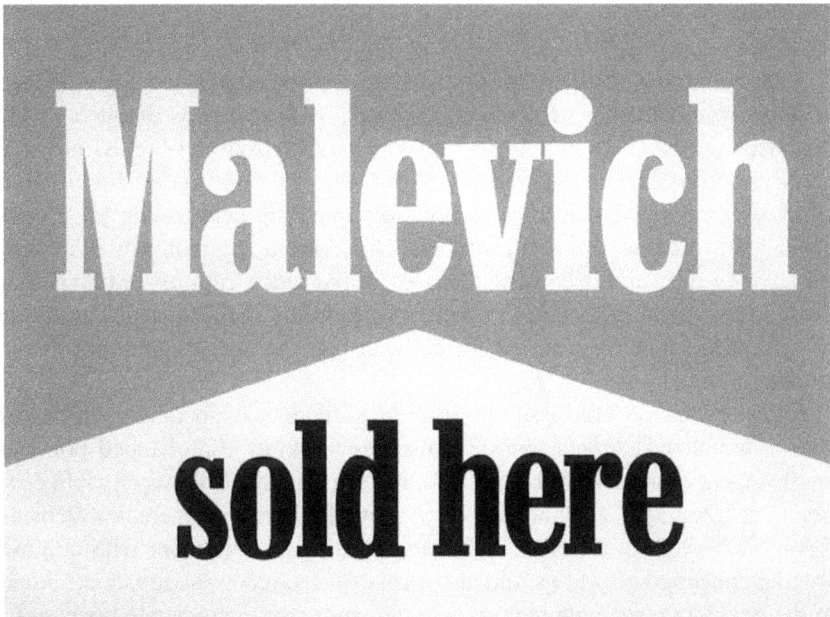

Figure 2.3 Alexander Kosolapov. *Malevich Sold Here* (1989, Acrylic on Canvas, 52″ × 80″). Courtesy of the artist.

Figure 2.4   Alexander Kosolapov. *Campbell's Borsch* **(1989, Oil on Canvas, 74″ × 96″).** Courtesy of the artist.

Such parodying of official tropes was also embraced in Cuba, and this idea of Sots-art in Cuba has begun to be explored by Juan Carlos Betancourt. He discusses the practice of a number of key figures from the "failed utopias/ rebel children" generation (the generation that came of age in the 1980s), and how they responded to Soviet iconography and perestroika. He argues (2012, 69) that they are a "generation who share a common praxis in how they appropriate and deconstruct Soviet propagandist culture—a praxis that proves the critical connection of their poetics to the socialist realist aesthetic whose corpse had been buried formally in Havana at the beginning of the 1980s."

By the 1980s in Cuba, assumptions behind the idea of socialist realism had been internalized. Artists found themselves working in a changed political environment characterized by a continuing sense of siege, focus on rapid economic development, and anti-Soviet currents. In this atmosphere new debates among artists about different styles and political commitment with culture, and the concerted effort to avoid any form of foreign domination, contributed to the development of approaches and demands that demonstrated occasionally conflicting elements of the different iterations of socialist realism. In the 1980s, as in the rest of the time period examined, with the exception of the early 1960s, socialist realism was not mentioned explicitly, but remained a looming force in the background. Equally, throughout the entire time period examined in this book, socialist realism in Cuba remained a polemical subject, not only because of the assumptions and stereotypes surrounding the paradigm, but also because of the Revolution's central tenet of national sovereignty, coupled with the pursuit, and development, of a type of socialism that sought to depart from the ossified variant in Europe, and the focus on Latin America as an alternate pole to the historic domination of Europe or North America. Subsequently, socialist realism has become a point of parody and critique in both the former Soviet Union and Cuba. It remains a point of reference in much of Cuban cultural production today, as does the parodying of the dogmatic doctrine it became and the global political era this represents:

> How I need you Karina, he thought when he opened the fridge and eyed the dramatic loneliness of two possibly prehistoric eggs and a piece of bread that could easily be a survivor from the siege of Stalingrad. He dropped the two eggs in heterodox fat tasting of mutually hostile fry-ups, toasted the two slices of bread on a flame that managed to melt their heart of steel on the end of his fork. A hundred percent socialist realism. (Padura Fuentes 2009, 148)

SOCIALIST, REALIST, AND INTERNATIONAL(IST)

This chapter has explored the development of socialist realism and the ways in which it reflected the nation-building project of the USSR. It has also highlighted the approach's inherent internationalism and the ways in which it initially brought together disparate artistic approaches. It has demonstrated the centrality of culture in Soviet society, its instrumentality in the shaping of economic development, and the ways in which it has been understood in various contexts throughout the history of the USSR.

Cultural development in the USSR is sometimes viewed as a series of discrete historical periods, each isolated from the other, in the political, social, and economic evolution of the nation. 1917 can be viewed as a point of rupture, a dislocation from Imperial Russia's history, culture, and politics and the creation of a new political landscape. However, these functionally "discrete" periods are closely interrelated and share many of the same concerns such as the preoccupation with being cultured and the educative role of culture, in addition to being equally susceptible to landmark political events. However, the Revolution and the subsequent victory in the Civil War changed the priorities of Russian society. Culture came to occupy a central role, and popular, accessible forms of culture increasingly gained centrality, the nadir of which was the late Stalinist period with its reductive approach toward culture for which the term "socialist realism" has become shorthand in Cuba.

The early years of the USSR were characterized by competing approaches to culture, put into practice by different institutions, an enthusiastic outpouring of creativity and a determinedly inclusive atmosphere. This was the first manifestation of one of the features of Soviet culture, and cultural policy: debate. Debate and reconfiguration was at the heart of Soviet culture and therefore at the heart of socialist realism, which was the clearest product of Soviet culture. Intimately linked to economic production, the iterations of socialist realism reflect the shifting governmental, and societal, goals of the USSR. The cultural sphere was a space of contestation for different ideas about the Revolution, concerning the best approaches and priorities. This debate, which occurred at all levels and among all artistic forms, became increasingly codified as the focus within the Revolution turned ever more inwards, before once more opening up to external models, but it remained a constant factor. Because of this, culture and cultural policy in the USSR cannot be analyzed in terms of a simple top-down approach but rather a continuous process of debate and reconfiguration, even during the most restrictive periods of Soviet history.

As this chapter has demonstrated, socialist realism was an approach that provided a conceptual infrastructure upon which to build and implement policies and an idea that sought to link culture to the wider political, social, and economic developments of the time in the journey toward socialism. At a practical level in 1934 it ended a prolonged period of in-fighting between literary groups and was the result of an ongoing process of debate at all levels of society regarding the reconciliation of the USSR's cultural history and its new historical direction. It was both an approach that sought to propel the country toward socialism—future-gazing within a theoretical framework— and a democratic style that ensured "culture" could be understood by all sectors of society, cultural institutions (and their functionaries), irrespective of their level of education.

Finally it is worth reiterating that the concept of socialist realism had a strong international element to it. As a cultural product, and a process, the method had the potential to be exported to other countries to help cement or inspire political change. Such qualities made socialist realism a potentially invaluable tool in establishing the USSR at the forefront of socialist culture, to accompany its self-proclaimed position at the vanguard of socialist theory. The method had successfully encouraged the assimilation of other cultures, with their re-elaboration into a distinctly Soviet, politically committed, cultural product. As a distinctly "Soviet" entity, socialist realism was a flashpoint for criticism from other socialist countries which departed from Soviet theories. Socialist realism therefore had a number of appealing characteristics: as a cultural approach with intimate links to rapid economic development that had (seemingly) successfully transformed the country from a feudal, peasant society that lagged behind the larger European nations into an urban, industrialized proletariat society in a matter of decades and also as an internationalist art form that could help defeat a colonial legacy.

NOTES

1. Of these heated polemics, the key debates have been collected together by cultural critic, Graziella Pogolotti in *Polémicas culturales de los 60*.

2. Kaier and Naiman (2006) offer a detailed discussion of the rise of realism in theater and the privileging of a variant of the Stanislavskii system.

3. The International Stalin Prize or (*Mezhdunarodnaia Stalinskaia Premiia za ukreplenie mira mezhdu narodami*) was renamed as the "International Lenin Prize" in 1955 following Khrushchev's secret speech and the ensuing de-Stalinization campaign. Previous winners were encouraged to trade in their medals for new ones without Stalin's image. In Soviet memoirs Brecht's award is referred to as the "Lenin Prize," whereas in Western accounts it is known as the "Stalin Prize" (Gardiner 2014, 203).

4. The "Bulldozer Exhibition," as the "First Fall Open-Air Show of Painting" came to be known was one of the first exhibitions of unofficial Soviet art. The exhibition was organised by Alexander Glazer, Oskar Rabin, along with other Lianozovo artists (the name for the school of artists that maintained its coherence throughout and after the Thaw, their work was figurative and often not far removed from "official" styles, but with a critical gaze), and joined by Komar and Melamid (Solomon 1991, 75, 89–90). The exhibition was held on the outskirts of Moscow, in Beliaevo, and was destroyed almost immediately by the authorities with bulldozers and fire hoses. The event attracted international attention and the Soviet authorities were embarrassed into announcing that there was permission for another show at Izmaylovo Park (Solomon 1991, 90).

Chapter 3

Cuban Cultural Policy, 1959 to 1975

Diversity and Rising Nationalism

Between 1959 and 1965, the Cuban Revolution had a heterodox ideology, which resulted in an inclusive and dynamic atmosphere with constantly forming institutions that sought to cater to the developing needs of the Revolution.

There were three primary trends that contributed to this environment. On the one hand, the Revolution was an ideological mix, which included emancipatory, revolutionary, nationalist ideals (Félix Varela, José de la Luz, Carlos Manuel de Céspedes, Ignacio Agramonte, Antonio Maceo, José Martí), and socialist and nationalist ideals (Antonio Guiteras), as well as the continuation of the nineteenth century independence movement and the 1933 Revolution. However, on the other hand, particularly among trade unions and sectors of the intelligentsia, there was a pro-Soviet, socialist, Marxist-Leninist current that was strongly influenced by the October Revolution. However, yet another ideological strain was anti-communist, anti-imperialist, and nationalist. Each of these currents entailed different approaches to the building of a national culture and specific foci of interest. However, confronted with the task of the cultural reconstruction of the nation, it became imperative that these diverse ideological currents be reconciled into a unified patriotic movement, with a coherent cultural identity and agenda.

The power and centrality of culture, and the establishment of a clear national identity, had been key ideological components in the liberation movements against Spain and the concepts of *cubanía* (Cubanness) that had subsequently emerged. The goals of the rebellion that enthroned the Revolution had these codes of *cubanía* at its heart. The Cuban concept of national identity drew on several codes which, briefly, included agrarianism, a belief that the countryside held "an almost sanctified connection with the past heroism and the future glory of the 'real' Cuba"; collectivism, moralism, activism, internationalism, and later youth (Kapcia 2000, 85–92, 201–02). Thus began a decade (1959–1969) of searching, characterized by rich and creative debates, an unprecedented political dynamism and polychromatic nuances (Díaz Sosa 2006, 79). However, affected by Cold War tensions, particularly in the period 1960–1969, the Revolution moved inexorably closer to the USSR. Moreover, the pragmatic early adoption of some of the pre-1959 communist party structures, and the predominance of pro-Soviet individuals in positions of power, suggested the privileging of Marxist-Leninist politics and the move toward a cultural approach that did not necessarily recognize Cuba's specificity.

The rapid radicalization of the population, due to landmark political events and the founding of the Cuban Communist Party (Partido Comunista de Cuba, PCC) in 1965, to some extent united these increasingly disparate ideological currents. The PCC was dominated by members of the guerrilla group, the Movimiento 26 de Julio (M-26-7), and championed a distinctly Cuban brand of communism that did not renounce its international aspirations, its focus on national liberation or its ideological debt to figures involved in Cuba's historical struggles for independence. Neither, however, did the founding of the PCC mean that the revolutionary government renounced its ideological affinity with the USSR (particularly with the early years of the October Revolution and the actions and approaches of the Bolsheviks). As fear of attack from external factors/forces increased among the population, the open debates became progressively internalized, as the government's imperative moved toward defense of the emerging nation. The search for the expression of an inherently Cuban ideology and identity had not ended by the 1970s, but rather had been relocated within the developing institutional structures. The focus moved from organization at a higher institutional level to a more individual level, and greater focus was placed on national identity. The erratic proliferation of cultural institutions, the uneven development of cultural forms (literature, theater, dance, plastic arts, music) before the rebellion, and the subsequent differences in their administration in the Revolution, meant that there were not necessarily clearly defined boundaries between institutions, leading to multiple interpretations and applications of cultural policy, grouped around distinct cultural hubs.

The apparent discursive hiatus that the institutionalization of the debates of the 1960s created, and the increased focus on the individual in a period that demanded heightened mobilization and defense, led to the promotion of more dogmatic codes of behavior and the privileging of cultural production that clearly embodied the codes of *cubanía*. With the First Congress of the PCC and the ideological clarity this brought, enshrining the ideas of Martí, Marx, and Lenin into the new constitution, cultural policy began to anticipate the needs of the Revolution, rather than respond to them. The subsequent relationship with the USSR, and the remaining worries surrounding this relationship, were to a large degree quarantined by being irrevocably subsumed to the codes of *cubanía*, but within a Marxist-Leninist, internationalist framework.

ORGANIZATIONAL POLES AND ORIENTATION

Four artistic forms were well established before the Revolution, with international recognition and corresponding dedicated, high-quality institutions: ballet (Ballet de Cuba), music (National Conservatory, Municipal Conservatory Amadeo Roldan, Group of Musical Renovation), the plastic arts (San Alejandro Academy), and literature (the University of Havana and influential literary magazines *Ciclón* and *Orígenes*). There was also a strong tradition of self-imposed exile, particularly of literary figures, in protest at the scant cultural opportunities available under the Batista dictatorship. Theater, however, was underdeveloped and had no associated educational institution. It was restricted to small, short-lived *salitas*, run by individuals on a vocational basis outside the hours of their regular jobs, and a nascent theater group, Teatro Estudio, which had been founded in 1958 in response to the perceived cultural inadequacies of the Batista era. The group had begun working toward cultivating a Cuban theater and had produced a manifesto detailing its commitment to this effect (Linares et al. 1989, 311). Cinema was also underrepresented officially but played a significant role within Nuestro Tiempo and the film club at the University of Havana.

The cultural world responded rapidly to the Revolution, and the immediate post-rebellion period was characterized by a remarkable diversity in the forms and styles of cultural expression, and a proliferation of small cultural groups. Cultural heavyweights, such as writer Alejo Carpenter, returned to partake in the nation's cultural rebuilding and groups were rapidly formed around specific cultural magazines that followed disparate trajectories. Two particularly important nuclei were *Lunes de Revolución*—focused on spreading knowledge about the European and North American vanguard, and without a specific political philosophy (Anon 1959), roughly centered around Carlos Franqui and Guillermo Cabrera Infante—and *Hoy Domingo*—focused on socialist type of cultural expression expounded by Carlos Rafael Rodríguez, Juan Marinello, Manuel Navarro Luna, and Nicolás Guillén (López Segrera 1985, 12). Two key cultural institutions were formed very quickly, and a broad and inclusive cultural policy, or rather a lack of explicit directives, was adopted, celebrating all forms of cultural output and expression. The first of these institutions was the Instituto Cubano de Arte e Industria Cinematograficos (ICAIC), directed by Alfredo Guevara, a student friend of

Fidel and member of the PSP who had supported the rebellion from Havana. ICAIC was one of the Revolution's flagship institutions, committed to fostering high-quality, politically aware cinema. It was founded on March 20, 1959 as a non-military alternative to the Rebel Army's film unit. Many members of ICAIC had been members of Nuestro Tiempo and a number had trained at the Centro Sperimentale di Cinematografia in Rome. Casa de las Américas (Casa), founded on 28 April by Haydeé Santamaria, a former M-26-7 rebel and Moncada veteran, was the second institution of the Revolution with the aim of promoting pan-Latin American cultural dialogue.

The First National Meeting of Poets and Artist in Camagüey (between 27 and October 30, 1960) echoed the desire for greater cultural interaction with Latin America and also reflected the anti-imperialist sentiments articulated in the First Declaration of Havana. The meeting was held with the idea of unifying and co-ordinating the creative and intellectual efforts of the artistic community with that of the Revolutionary Government. The manifesto, *Towards a National Culture Serving the Revolution* was produced as a result. It emphasized the unity that existed between the intellectual and creative worlds before moving on to highlight the negative influence of colonialism and imperialism on the development of a Cuban culture, and the fact that the Revolution had now given the people the power to participate consciously in the development of a national, revolutionary culture (Gordon-Nesbitt 2012, 217). Education was also prioritized and focused on incorporating previously marginalized sectors of society and equipping them with the necessary skills to be active participants in the new society. Initially, education programs centered on political instruction, through the Schools of Revolutionary Instruction (EIR), and basic literacy (the 1961 Literacy Campaign) but, once these were established, soon included culture.

ESTABLISHING AN ORGANIZATIONAL TRADITION

The creation of the National Council of Culture (CNC) and then the National Union of Cuban Writers and Artists (UNEAC) established official organs that catered for the specific needs of the Revolution's artists and intellectuals. In theory the two institutes had different roles that clearly delineated their respective fields of influence and organizational capacity. However, the uneven development of different cultural expression in pre-Revolutionary Cuba, and their perceived varying strengths as educational tools, somewhat blurred the boundaries between these two institutions.

The first of these two key bodies to be founded was the CNC, in January 1961, responsible for cultural education, mobilization, and organization, replacing the Ministry of Education's (MINED) Cultural Directorate. Like the Cultural Directorate, the CNC was subordinated to MINED, and, with the exception of the years 1964–1966, it reported directly to the Council of Ministers in order to give it greater autonomy from the State (Gordon-Nesbitt 2012, 153). Edith García Buchaca (PSP), Mirta Aguirre (PSP), and Vicentina Antuña (Ortodoxos), were all founding members of the CNC and occupied positions of considerable power.

The CNC began by unifying and centralizing the organization of cultural matters and produced the first annual plan by the end of 1962, for implementation in 1963. Culture was divided into four main sections: theater and dance, plastic arts, music, and literature (Manzor-Coats and Martiatu Terry 1995, 60). 1961 also set the essentially pragmatic tone for the cultural policy of the 1960s and beyond. The 1961 debates, held at the Biblioteca Nacional, in the wake of the *PM* affair,[1] culminated in Fidel's *Palabras a los intelectuales* (Words to the Intellectuals), which assumed the support of artists and intellectuals for the Revolution's aims, unless explicitly stated otherwise. *Palabras* was also a clear demonstration of the pragmatic Cuban solution of not coming to a clear resolution regarding the freedoms for, and responsibilities of, the artist in a revolutionary, socialist, society. By saying "within the Revolution everything, against the Revolution no right" (Castro 1961a) Fidel, as Weiss has observed, "set the terms for both an expansive cultural mandate and concern about how and by whom the borders of 'inside' and 'against' would be determined" (2011b, xii-xiii). However, the speech also had more concrete suggestions. In *Palabras*, Fidel identified the need to improve organization within culture and highlighted the CNC as the organ responsible for recognizing and fulfilling the needs of artists and intellectuals—through dialogue with them—and organizing cultural activities and dissemination throughout the island (Castro 1961a). The speech also mentioned the second general cultural institution, UNEAC, which would publish two dedicated cultural magazines, *Unión* and the *Gaceta de Cuba*, in which public debate among Cuba's intellectuals would be encouraged. UNEAC was a non-partisan, umbrella organization that brought together all revolutionary cultural groups within a designated cultural space. In highlighting the success of cultural groupings and unions in other socialist countries, García Buchaca suggested that UNEAC was conceived as an umbrella institution because of the relative lack of a cultural organizational tradition within Cuba (1961, 82–89).

UNEAC was to be the arbiter of cultural quality, it was divided by artistic form, and each component was autonomous. UNEAC members were grouped according to different artistic modes of expression: literature, plastic arts (sculptors, painters, ceramicists, architects, and photographers), music, theater, cinema, ballet, and dance. A section for cinema, radio, and television was added later (Gordon-Nesbitt 2015, 74). UNEAC was responsible for the work plans for literature, plastic arts, music, and ballet, the CNC for theater and dance, and ICAIC for cinema. The CNC still organized cultural activities across all artistic forms (Anon 1970b). Structurally, UNEAC was comprised of an Executive Committee, and branches according to artistic form such as literature, music, and plastic arts that coordinated the activities of their respective forms, a publications committee, and an auxiliary editorial board for *Unión* and *Gaceta*. Entry was dependent on a body of high-quality work that demonstrated an element of continuity. Applications would be considered by an admissions committee, with the possibility of appeal to the higher levels of the UNEAC (García Buchaca 1961, 86–87).

However, the predominance of PSP activists, and the orthodox Marxist-Leninist view of the role of culture under socialism that this seemingly implied within the CNC, as well as the structural similarity between UNEAC and the Soviet Writers' Union, were not universally welcomed. These fears of Stalinism were to some extent acknowledged, if not addressed, publicly in the First National Congress of the Writers and Artists of Cuba, held August 18–22, 1961.

> When defining the character and aims of the Union of Cuban Writers and Artists, their differences are perfectly established [. . .] from the character and functions that other organizations have to play, such as the Trade Union of Artists [. . .] In all socialist countries the existence of these two types of organizations for many years has yielded a very positive experience that we should know how to take advantage of for our artists and, in general, for culture. (García Buchaca 1961, 88–89)

In addition to acknowledging an awareness of similar socialist institutional structures, the Congress also built on the manifesto of the 1960 meeting. It discussed the role of artists and intellectuals as defenders and educators through their diverse creative work, and the nature of art in a socialist society, rather than analyzing the emergent revolutionary opus. Once again, culture was aligned with the struggle against imperialism and the fight for genuine independence, while the importance of the rescue and revalorization of national traditions was emphasized.

The organizational and educational impulse, demonstrated by the Literacy Campaign and the establishment of the EIRs, now moved into the cultural arena, manifesting itself in the *aficionado* and *instructores de arte* movements. The creation of an Escuela Nacional de Instructores de Arte (EIA) had first been called for in May 1961, and such a school dedicated to fostering amateur involvement in culture was ultimately created in 1962, allowing Cubans from socioeconomic and racial groups that had traditionally been marginalized from culture to begin taking an active role in cultural creation. The missions of the arts instructors were threefold: (1) to help develop an interest in the different art forms among people who had not received formal education; (2) to stimulate individuals with creative talent; and (3) to assist in the organization and activities of the performing groups of *aficionados* (Matas 1971, 433). By 1965 1,093 instructors had graduated in the specializations of theater, music, and dance and were hailed as a cultural army ready to bring culture to the most isolated areas of Cuba: "with which they formed a true army of cultural promotors distributed throughout the country, preferably in the zones most isolated from the urban centres" (Anon 1970b). Expression-specific cultural movements were also developed, such as the creation of the Escuela de Brigadistas de Artes Plásticas, which travelled around the country giving slide-shows and talks on the history of plastic arts (García Buchaca 1963a, 20). The *instructores de arte* movement had two important functions: it helped to democratize culture and to deal with the country's cultural under-development. This Cuban specificity was emphasized in the CNC's 1962 report on cultural activities. José Garófalo—the Coordinator for the province of Havana—pointed out that *instructores de arte* had not been necessary in the USSR or Czechoslovakia, because the population already had a sufficiently developed cultural level, unlike in Cuba (Garófalo 1962, 40).

The *aficionado* movement, complementary to the *instructores de arte*, also began in 1962 and became very closely related to the CNC's cultural promotion programs (García Buchaca 1964, 45). A government initiative, it was designed to develop the population's interest, knowledge and participation in the various facets of "art" and was accompanied by an annual *aficionado* festival (Conte 1965). The *aficionado* movement was also focused on the development of revolutionary cultural forms and values, and the education that, it was anticipated, participation in the movement would provide. Vigilance against imperialist penetration of the cultural world was also closely linked to the *aficionado* movement, where the assimilation of the best of universal culture had been highlighted as a priority area, to avoid having it being imposed on Cuba from outside (Reyes and Anon 1972). Finally, by its very nature the community-based *aficionado* movement implied a creative collective.

To some extent the *aficionado* movement parallels the drive to encourage *samodeiatel'nost'* (amateur creation) in the postwar USSR (Tsipursky 2016; White 1990). The concept of *samodeiatel'nost',* that emerged during the Russian civil war and early years of the USSR was defined by the state as amateur artistic creation in the fields of theater, choral music, dance, fine, and decorative arts and classed this type of production as a form of folk art, which was separate from the professional sphere (Anon 1955b). When discussing the phenomenon, Mally translates it as "amateur theater" and argues that it "came to stand for a new Soviet approach that would foster collective interaction and bring about productive social results" (Mally 2000, 23). The paradoxes inherent in theater, but particularly within the *aficionado* and *samodeiatel'nost'*

movements, were also the same in each country: amateur theater was a powerful form of cultural expression in the democratization of culture and by
extension the Revolution; however, given its mass participatory nature, it was
also a potentially destabilizing force if improperly managed.

Headway was also made regarding higher-level creative education,
and plans were drawn up to turn the former country club for the elite, in
Cubanacán, into the Escuela Nacional de Arte (ENA)—inaugurated on the
symbolic date of July 26, 1965 (Loomis 1999, 129). UNEAC's official
organs, the *Gaceta de Cuba* and *Unión*, began publication in April and May
1961 respectively, and the following year the Hermanos Saíz group, which
mobilized youth cultural activities for upcoming artists that were not yet
eligible for UNEAC membership, was founded (Anon 1962a). The CNC had
also begun signing cultural exchange programmers with socialist countries or
countries sympathetic to the Cuban Revolution. They included the promotion
of Cuban culture abroad and, in 1962, twenty-four Cuban painters toured
the "brother" socialist countries of Czechoslovakia, Hungary, Romania, the
USSR, and Poland (Pogolotti 1962), and in the same year the first Casa de
Cultura for a "brother socialist country," Czechoslovakia, opened in Cuba.
The following year a Cuban *Casa de Cultura* was established in Prague
(Antuña 1963, 9). 1962 ended with the First National Cultural Congress.

1963 heralded a more systematic and increasingly centralized organization of culture. The CNC's annual preliminary plans (*anteproyectos*) began,
heavily focused on points eight and nine of the Revolutionary Government's
ten-point plan. The plan, which had been presented to cultural assemblies
throughout the country's provinces, linked cultural activity to the Revolution's greatest needs, emphasized taking culture to the people and focused
on the training of artists and cultural educators and raising the general
population's cultural level (Anon 1963b). The authority of the CNC was
also advanced, and its remit now included the coordination and direction of
all cultural activity at a national and local level and the rescue of national
traditions. A spate of organizations with objectives concordant with these
goals of organization and orientation sprang up over the year. They included
a school for cultural cadres that began teaching in 1963. The purpose of the
school was to create cadres at all levels (national, provincial, municipal, and
rural) and include courses on political orientation, and intensive courses on
general culture which covered history and artistic, literary, and scientific
culture. Students from the working and peasant classes were admitted on the
basis of their aptitude for cultural work. These courses lasted three months
on an alternating basis, so that students were not taken away from production (Anon 1963b, 23). At the same time, the first cohort of *instructores de
arte*, "children of the Revolution, forged by it," began to graduate from their
courses (Pita Rodríquez 1963, 24). In reporting the graduation of 220 of the

theater cohort, Félix Pita Rodríguez emphasized the *instructores'* roles in helping to create a politicized, socialist art that served the Revolution and was capable of responding to the historical moments from which it was born. He also emphasized the core duty of the *instructores de arte* was to help raise the cultural level of the population in the shortest time possible, an essential element of strengthening the Revolution (Pita Rodríguez 1963, 14).

The CNC's authority in the plastic arts was extended with the creation of the Directorate of plastic arts, which subsequently took responsibility for all activities pertaining to this field: exhibition, acquisitions, and conservation. It was also responsible for overseeing artistic education, material provision, artists' travel, artistic and literary competitions and their juries. In this way the CNC's dominion over culture became almost absolute (Gordon-Nesbitt 2015, 195). Cultural organization was specifically addressed in the First National Plenary of Cultural Coordinators, held between July 10 and July 14, 1963. Grass-roots cultural organization also continued with the founding of the first domestic *Casa de Cultura* within Cuba. The *Casa* was founded in Manzanillo in the space occupied by the former Spanish Colonial Society of Manzanillo, as a way of keeping Cuban culture alive. The creation of the *Casa* was supported by a number of individuals, which included Miguel Ángel Botalín (Provincial Cultural Delegate), Manuel Navarro Luna, Celia Sánchez, and Manuel López Oliva. In an interview López Oliva reports being inspired by an article he saw in a cultural publication as a boy about the Bulgarian *dom kul'tury* (López Oliva et al 2015a). The *Casas de Cultura* would ultimately become a national phenomenon in the 1970s, acting as a network of social spaces where all could enjoy and experience cultural activities and training.

With the close of an initial period of intense organization began an era of trenchant polemics regarding different cultures and aesthetics within the Revolution. This period coincided with the CNC becoming autonomous (Gordon-Nesbitt 2015, 196). This period of cultural (and ideological) polemics is commonly thought to involve a CNC-led promotion of socialist realism versus an ICAIC-led endorsement of aesthetic plurality and focus on the reality of the revolutionary binary (Bonachea and Valdés 1972b, 497). This approach is useful in that it acknowledges the uneasy relationship between the pre-revolutionary political parties that were suddenly brought together under the aegis of the Revolution and exacerbated by the necessary co-opting of some of the PSP's structures into the post-rebellion political landscape. However, continuing to view the 1963–1965 period in this manner makes inevitable a reading of the 1971–1975 *quinquenio gris* period as the culmination of the CNC's persistent efforts to fit Cuba blindly into the Soviet socialist mold. Moreover, this perspective fails to include a recognition that the 1963–1965 period was characterized by an open and polemical atmosphere across all spheres of revolutionary life, as a sustained and acute political debate was developing regarding the appropriate models to follow in the Cuban process. Such a view also only marginally recognizes that Marxism was becoming an increasingly mass phenomenon among the population thanks in part to the work of the EIRs but also to the geopolitical events in which Cuba was enmeshed, which inevitably radicalized the population.

These polemics by no means paralyzed cultural activities, however, and by 1964 30,340 cultural events had been organized with an uptake of 11,000,000. 21,000 of these events were held outside of the city of Havana, with an uptake of over 7,000,000 (García Buchaca 1964, 43). Cultural organization continued apace into 1965, as did political organization and orientation. The ideological distance some had identified between the USSR and the Cuban Revolution began to widen still further and the publication of Che Guevara's (henceforth Che) "El socialismo y el hombre en Cuba" marked a shift in ideology and in the role of cultural practitioners. The text became a seminal piece of cultural policy that signaled the beginning of a more inward-looking focus on the development of a national character and a Cuban route to socialism. Che's idea of the *hombre nuevo* was at the core of the radicalizing, mobilizing, and increasingly anti-sectarian current of the late 1960s. This *hombre nuevo* was seen as an actor in the construction of socialism who was an individual, but also a member of the community, which interacted, as a collective, with the revolution's leaders (Guevara 2006, 52–53). Closely linked to the concept of the *hombre nuevo* was the development of a revolutionary consciousness, which entailed cooperation, sacrifice, struggle, political loyalty, and dedication to revolutionary heroes and legends (Frederik 2012, 10–11).

As a result of the need for self-definition, and the perceived attack on the nation, a search began for a clearly defined institutional structure and doctrine in culture and politics. In addition, the interaction with external cultural currents, even if conducted with the aim of adapting these currents, was increasingly viewed askance. Greater attention was placed on unity, the Cuban national character, and the continued integration of the population into culture. The new political unity was reflected in the official publications and *Revolución* merged with the former PSP newspaper, *Noticias de Hoy,* to become *Granma,* the official organ of the PCC. *Granma* was the yacht on which members of the M-26-7 movement sailed to Cuba from Mexico in order to start the rebellion of 1958. By naming the official newspaper of the Party after the boat, the PCC, and Communism in Cuba, was inextricably linked to armed struggle, the legacy of the 1953 Moncada attacks, and the figure of the *guerrillero.*

By the end of 1965, the circulation of numerous creative currents and differing interpretations of Cuban socialism no longer sat comfortably alongside a Revolution that was increasingly moving toward a clear definition of what it stood for (Fay 2011, 418–19). Culture became increasingly linked with politics, education, social production and the Revolution's international fight against underdevelopment.

The continued active cultivation of a culture of political engagement also contributed to the active cultivation of a politicized culture: a determined effort was made to continue educating the population about the importance of culture as a form of social production which could be used to help overcome the conditions of underdevelopment. In 1966 the CNC produced a didactic pamphlet for general dissemination that brought together articles regarding culture in Cuba, previously published in UNEAC's *Gaceta de Cuba*. The introduction to the booklet examined the meaning of "culture," emphasizing the emancipatory potential of culture under socialism, that it was at the heart of any growth as an individual or as a society: "culture is a synonym of growth" (Anon 1966a, 3).

A complementary program to educate workers culturally also began in 1966. It began in the Gerardo Abreu Fontán factory before being taken to other factories whose industries represented a large portion of the nation's production. Key cultural figures from different cultural forms presented to the audience at each event (Pita Rodríquez 1966, 36–37). The aforementioned scheme echoes Aleksei Popov and Nikolai Pogodin's forays into the factories in the Urals with Pogodin's play *Poem of the Axe* in the 1930s.

Finally, while Cuba appeared to be moving ideologically away from the USSR and toward Latin American-wide Revolution, aesthetically it began to move closer to at least one aspect of Soviet culture: architecture, with the proliferation of the Soviet prefabricated housing system, and later its Cuban adaption, from 1963 onward. The buildings, which could be a maximum of five floors (after which a lift had to be installed) were economical to produce and assemble and provided a (short-term) solution to the housing crisis that was threatening Havana.[2] The proliferation of these prefabricated, homogenous, concrete buildings demonstrated the government's continuing commitment to the ideals fought for in the Batista-era rebellion (in this case housing) but also seemed to offer incontrovertible evidence that the country's cityscape and everyday life was progressively being "Sovietized."

DEFENDING THE NEW MAN

The heterodox currents that had characterized the discourse of the first half of the 1960s began to move toward orthodoxy toward the end of the decade. A pronounced sense of isolation began to set in, and unity became increasingly important in the face of continued overt and covert aggression from the USA, including CIA-funded cultural programs like the Congress for Cultural Freedom. Perhaps in response to some of these fears, some of the economic principles that characterized culture under capitalism, which were still in existence in Cuba, were abolished with the rejection of copyright for creative works and the founding of the Institute of the Book (Instituto Cubano del Libro, IdL) in May 1967. Culture continued to play a key role within society, and freedom of creative expression, the political nature of art, and the idea that art should be politically committed in whatever form it took, were all emphasized. Cultural effervescence was once again linked to the M-26-7 and the Revolution, with the visit of the *Salon du Mai*, in celebration of the anniversary of the Moncada attack of 1953. The active participation of the cultural sector in the nation-building project was reiterated in October 1967, when Casa issued a declaration that emphasized the role of the intellectual in the Revolution, and hence the US interest in co-opting intellectuals. In an environment in which the enemy was invisible, Cuba's historical cultural and aesthetic affinity with the US and Europe now began to present potential security problems. In turn, this meant that research into Cuban folklore and traditions and the rescue of these forms of expression were of ever-increasing value, and as such also became a way to protect artists who might otherwise have had problems, such as the emerging music style *Nueva Trova* which would come to be a celebrated revolutionary form or the later musical grouping *Grupo de Experimentación Sonora* which encompassed the Nueva Trova movement. Finally, Che's death in Bolivia, and the CIA's part in it, provided irrefutable proof that the Cuban Revolution was under attack. In some aspects (symbolically and economically), this seemed to herald the end of an epoch and an inevitable return to the Soviet style of constructing a socialist Revolution. However, as Clayfield observes, guerrilla movements continued to emerge and the image of the "heroic guerrilla" endured, serving for many as inspiration to realize the dream of a hemisphere-wide revolution (Clayfield 2013, 74).

A subsequent series of events seemed to provide further proof that the Cuban government was assimilating the USSR's historical modus operandi. In October 1968, Padilla was awarded the UNEAC prize for *Fuera del Juego*, a cycle of poems modeled on outspoken Soviet poets like Evgenii Evtushenko, Nikolai Voznesenskiii and Bella Akhmadulina, who were all tolerated by the system but constantly pushed the boundaries. Padilla had learned of these poets and their work during his time as a correspondent for *Prensa Latina* and admired their sense of moral responsibility (Prieto 2012, 126). In theater, Arrufat was awarded the UNEAC prize for his work *Los siete contra Tebas*. These events provoked a sustained controversy that ended with the publication of both works, but with a disclaimer from UNEAC condemning both pieces. To an interested external viewer it would, perhaps, have been difficult not to see attitudes influenced by the USSR in these events. Over the previous months, Padilla had openly attacked the vice president of the CNC (Lisandro Otero and his novel *Pasión de Uribe*) and defended Guillermo Cabrera Infante, who had broken with the Revolution, entered self-imposed exile, and been expelled from UNEAC. Arrufat had worked with Cabrera Infante on *Lunes* and *Ciclón* and was also openly homosexual at a time when stereotypical hypermacho characteristics were being emphasized. These events, and the failure of Cuba to condemn the Soviet invasion of Czecho-slovakia, set alarm bells ringing in Latin American and European intellectual circles that were ready to see the malign shadow of the Stalin-era USSR pulling the strings behind "restrictive" actions and driving the country inexo-rably toward the historical type of intense cultural regulation implemented by Zhdanov in the USSR twenty years earlier. The annual Writers' Conference in Cienfuegos, held the same month as the UNEAC prizes, responded to these events with the production of a declaration that emphasized the writer's duty to contribute to the Revolution though their work. Toward the end of the year, a series of articles against Padilla and Arrufat began to appear in *Verde Olivo*, the cultural publication of the Fuerzas Armadas Revolucionarias (FAR), signed by the previously unknown pseudonym "Leopoldo Avila." The impact of the commotion surrounding *Fuera del juego* and *Los siete contra Tebas* rumbled on into 1969, leading to a number of discussions and declarations regarding the role of the intellectual in the Revolution, including the Havana Cultural Congress, and Casa marked the 10th anniversary of the Revolution with a round table examining the intellectual in this first decade.

The failure of the 1970 ten million tonne *zafra* (sugar harvest) marked a turning point, which saw a subsequent aligning of institutional structures that governed Cuba's relationship with Cuba. There was also an increasing emphasis on the active participation of the artist in society and their active contribution to the development of the Cuban economy. Fidel issued a strong self-criticism that signaled the beginning of a move away from the economic ideas expounded by Che and a necessary move closer to the USSR, the only ally that was capable of salvaging the floundering economy. The Revolu-tion's inexorable slide into the Soviet camp must have seemed almost com-plete when the government accepted that socialism was a transitory stage on the path to achieving full communism, which—intentionally or otherwise—privileged a certain ideological current. Accordingly, there began a sustained period of institutionalization, previously synonymous with bureaucracy, anathema to the Revolution's ideological currents of the 1960s.

1971 seemed to confirm that Cuba was swiftly becoming a satellite state. A number of events occurred throughout the year that would appear indicative of a progressive "Sovietization" of the country. In chronological order these events included: the construction of Alamar predominantly using prefabricated systems and the Soviet zoning system (Figure 3.1); the implementation of the law against ideological deviationism; the closure of the Department of Philosophy (staunch defenders and promoters of non-Soviet Marxist theories); the meeting of the Directors of Writers' Unions of Socialist Countries in Moscow; the passing of the anti-parasite law; the arrest of Padilla; the exhibition of Modern Soviet Architecture held in the Museum of Fine Arts; a photographic exhibition on the development of "space science" in celebration of the 10th anniversary of Gagarin's space flight in the Cuban Academy of Science. In addition the First National Congress on Education and Culture was held, ushering in a more regulatory and restrictive interpretation of culture and its role. Shortly after this Congress, the poet Padilla issued a suspiciously Stalin-epoch-style self-criticism after being released; Luis Pavón Tamayo, the former editor of the cultural magazine of the FAR, became head of the CNC; and greater regulations were implemented in the cultural field, which included closer examinations of artists' lifestyles. In the political arena, Raúl Roja conducted an extensive tour of the USSR and other socialist countries; Cuban cinema won four prizes at the Moscow Film Festival; Cuba and the USSR signed a protocol for Economic and Scientific collaboration; Soviet ships arrived in Havana, and on two separate occasions Aleksei Kosyguin and Andrei Kirilenko visited Cuba and its seemingly most aesthetically "Soviet" area, Alamar.

Figure 3.1   Housing Unit in Alamar. Photo courtesy of the author.

However, simultaneously a number of other, perhaps less well-reported, events demonstrated a continued commitment to culture, education, Cuba's Latin American identity, and the emerging sense of national identity and *cubanía*. These were a continuation of the ideals expressed in key cultural fora, such as the Tricontinental, the 1968 Congresses, and the Second Declaration of Havana. The Basic Rural Secondary Schools (ESBEC), that were constructed in 1971 were indicative of the ongoing commitment to the education of the population, and of the Revolution's promise to combat the inequalities between the country's urban metropolis and the rural peripheries. Eduardo Galeano's *Las venas abiertas de América Latina,* detailing the destruction of a continent at the hands of imperialist forces operating within capitalism, received an honorary mention in the Casa literary prize; the *Concurso 13 de marzo* (in honor of the student revolutionary group the Directorio Revolucionario 13 de marzo, founded by José Antonio Echeverría) was created; the Cuban Rooms at the Palacio de Bellas Artes opened (on 26 July); the exhibition *Popular Latin American Art,* exhibited in the windows of San Rafael Street between Galiano and Prado, in celebration of the Moncada attack, was held once again linking the (plastic) arts to the Revolution; the new academic year saw the highest intake of students in the history of the Revolution (Fornet 2013, 167), and the *Primer Salón Nacional Juvenil de Artes Plásticas* opened in the Museo Nacional de Bellas Artes. Finally, Alamar, while clearly deeply influenced by Soviet aesthetics, provided a much-needed solution to the housing crisis that had enveloped Havana, demonstrating the Revolution's ability to adapt and assimilate the best of other cultures, and was representative of the movement away from the traditional bourgeois and classical centers of the city (Scarpaci, Segre, and Coyula 2002).

CULTURE OF THE MASSES, FOR THE MASSES: REDEFINING MASS CULTURE

By 1971 the institutionalizing drive of the previous years moved down a level in an effort to address the inequalities between the urban and rural centers. Greater attention was placed on internal organization and unity, leading to the rise of socialist realism as a method of organizing culture. Moreover, the continued sense that the country was under attack, and its increasing isolation from Latin America, meant that the open debates of the 1960s had been internalized, ideas of national identity became expressed in a more bellicose nature, and hypermacho ideas—focusing on romanticized ideas of the *campesino* and the *guerrillero,* and the prizing of heterosexual sexual practices—began to circulate. These ideas mixed with the decolonizing drive, which moved the creative focus from the metropolis to the *campo*, and the continuing commitment to education in order to give as many Cubans as possible ownership of the emergent cultural imaginary as "the greatest resource of an underdeveloped country is the people itself" (Anon 1970b).

Thus began a period which has come to be known as the *quinquenio gris*. The period was characterized by a more regulatory approach toward culture, and narrower parameters within which its practitioners were permitted to operate, which directly impacted on cultural production, above all in theater. The *quinquenio gris*, and its treatment of culture and society, seem to present obvious parallels with the USSR during the Stalin regime, suggesting what might be construed as a demonstrable Sovietization of Cuba. Contemporaneous publications would seem to support this. Over the five-year period, reference to the USSR appeared more frequently in *Granma*; in 1969, there were fifty-seven articles that mentioned the USSR, leaping to 129 in 1970 and then dipping to 103 in 1973, before increasing again to 155 in 1975. However, a re-reading of the period suggests a more complex situation than Soviet imposition or Cuban appropriation of Soviet cultural methods and ideas. Some investigations into this topic have already been conducted by Jorge Fornet (2013)[3] and Hortensia Montero Méndez (2006).

As previously discussed, 1968 marked a liminal point in the conception of culture based on the ideology of the Revolution, and to fully understand the seemingly new direction in which the Revolution had begun to move decisively in 1971 it is necessary to re-examine trends that began to emerge at this moment. The January 1968 Havana Cultural Congress heralded the beginning of a strong focus on anti-colonialism, the Third World, and the more active societal role required of the artist, particularly those immersed in the revolutionary process (Gallardo Saborido 2009, 149). The conscious deconstruction of pre-existing discourses further fused the political and artistic responsibilities of the artist. Artistic production and cultural development necessarily became an essential element of the mobilization to both defend and advance the Revolution (Weppler-Grogan 2010, 144). Valdés Paz also identified it as marking the beginning of a rupture between the Cuban intellectual world and the European Left, who applied European models of socialism to the Cuban reality without recognizing its specific condition of underdevelopment (Valdés Paz 2015). Within culture, the decolonizing process manifested itself in an ideological deconstruction of the dominant critical discourse(s) (Villegas 1989, 505). Cultural figures attempted to reconcile combating the residual effects of colonialism and the borrowing of Western cultural traditions and tropes with the need to create authentically Cuban intellectual spaces to foster organic discourses. Cuba's search for an economically outside the United States' influence also involved distancing itself from the traditional cultural hubs of Paris—where many pre-revolutionary Cuban artists had studied—and later New York, seeking out alternative centers as part of the island's "recalibration towards novel, non-aligned and post-colonial poles" (Fay 2011, 421). This recalibration also caused (or allowed) the revolutionary government to assert its leadership in the international arena and thus to a more active resistance to perceived Soviet "meddling" in Cuban affairs.

This situation in Cuban culture in the late 1960s and early-to-mid 1970s was analogous to what Yurchak terms the emergence of the "Imaginary West" in the late Soviet period. Yurchak (2006, 34–35) defines the Imaginary West, which emerged in the 1950s and came to dominate the lives of young people in the 1970s and 1980s as "a local construct and imaginary that was based on the forms of knowledge and aesthetics associated with the 'West,' but not necessarily referring to any 'real' West." The creation of the Imaginary West, and its inextricable linking to late Soviet culture, stemmed from the discussion in the USSR in the 1940s about cosmopolitanism versus internationalism and the evaluation of cultural production from the correct ideological standpoint (Yurchak 2006, 163). The concept opened up "space of interpretation of what concrete foreign cultural forms might mean in different contexts" (Yurchak 2006, 164). The same applied in Cuba in the attempts to create authentic Cuban culture, the concept of "good" and "bad" foreign influences, forms, and subjects, was a local (often intensely so) construct which was constantly shifting imaginary.[4]

In its bid to create a Cuban, yet international, culture and develop different artistic forms, foreign cultural forms, their meanings and their dangers meant different things in different context. This was further complicated by the enduring sense of siege and the way the CNC tried to counter foreign influence with a renewed focus on clearly "Cuban" elements of culture. Practically, what this meant was that the CNC began to focus more actively on the countryside and the inclusion of peasants in the nation's intellectual life through sustained education and organization—one of its founding principles (CNC c.1973). The cultural gaze of the nation had turned to the countryside and its inhabitants: an area which had great cultural and political significance in the history of the nation and which embodied elements of nostalgia, notions of purity, cultural authenticity and a genuine national heritage (Frederik 2012, 2–5).

ARTISTIC FORMS AND LOCAL NORMS

Within the theater these objectives were evident in the formation of Teatro Escambray, a troupe that was firmly focused on both Cuba's provinces and the role that theater could play in the development of the Revolution and in addressing regional and local concerns (Rudakoff 1996, 78). The group's move to the isolated region of the Escambray came in part out of a strong sense of frustration; its members felt that theater in Havana reflected colonial culture, mostly with plays from the European repertoire, within a traditional style of performance—in short, plays that spoke of foreign concerns and foreign cultures (Tunberg 1970, 48–54). Other theater groups that emerged, or changed their orientation in 1968/1969, also demonstrate the shifting attitude toward culture and increasing focus on the younger generation that had been "formed" within the Revolution and the evolution of the Revolution's ideology. Teatro Estudio broadened its remit (the creation of a national theater) to create a cultural hub with a strong educational and collective bent, Teatro Tercer Mundo had a specific geopolitical focus and a more "militant" approach toward revolutionary commitment and social behavior, and Teatro Joven—which operated as a collective—became recognized as an official troupe. Finally, a series of cultural interchanges were planned from later in 1971, geared toward artistic and technical improvement, principally to help with the technical shortcomings of the *aficionado* movement (Quesada 1972).

The plastic arts reflected the increasing preoccupation with defense, development and national identity in a slightly different manner that focused on the promotion of young artists (as products wholly of the Revolution) and a broadening of the definition and reach of "art." A systematic professionalization of the plastic arts began in 1969, with plans to continue rolling out this organizational scheme over the following years, reflecting the drive for greater organizational unity within cultural policy (Anon 1970b). The mobilizing capacity of the plastic arts was celebrated, as were the art's close links to the country's productive forces. Moreover, in the same way that Teatro Escambray was celebrated as the best exemplar of theater and mass culture in the Revolution, the poster movement (discussed in chapter 6) was particularly celebrated as a national product that was conceived of and produced completely within the Revolution.

The 1971 First National Congress on Education and Culture, as with the 1961 Biblioteca Nacional meetings and 1968 Havana Cultural Congress, responded to these emergent trends. The Congress reflected the desire for a greater cultural unity and for a more forensic examination of past cultural trends and productions, in order to combat potentially damaging tendencies. The resolution from the Congress stated that emphasis should be placed on the development of revolutionary values through historical analysis, the use of Third World solidarity themes, and a new look at contemporary revolutionary conflicts (Lent 1988, 64). The Congress also stressed the drive to eliminate (malign) foreign tendencies within the cultural world in the continuing battle against cultural imperialism in any form, from any source. The sense of isolation and attack had become entrenched, and, to a certain extent, codified in cultural policy. The ramifications of this were subtle but pervasive and clearly led to some uncomfortable interpretations of the parameters within which cultural practitioners should fit. The mobilization of culture in the defense of the nation and therefore the role of the artist as a combatant (but also educator) placed new, *macho*, demands on the cultural practitioner. Masculinity and hyper-masculinity became more desirable characteristics and cultural expression become more bellicose. That the 1971 Congress addressed both education and culture (even though the latter was a last minute addition to the program to help deal with the extraordinary events preceding the congress) is significant. Culture and Education had been linked to one another in 1970 in the CNC's *Cultural Policy of Cuba,* which was reproduced later as a report for UNESCO in 1972: "it is our understanding that while education and culture lie in different areas, they nevertheless are part of a single complex and require to be dealt with simultaneously" (Anon 1970b).

The failure of the ten-million ton sugar harvest, the decisive act to lift Cuba out of poverty and underdevelopment, had demonstrated unequivocally that the technical education of the Cuban population was failing, and therefore prolonging the nation's state of dependency. As a result, a concerted effort to remedy this pervasive skill deficit began in all spheres of Cuban society. In this respect culture occupied a particularly powerful, and privileged, position as it bridged both worlds. Culture was in itself an educative tool, but it was also a form of social production that, when mobilized correctly, contributed to the development of the nation and national economy both directly and indirectly (Otero 1971). The valuing of culture in the continued defense and development of the nation and the economy also hints at the continued "Latin American" strain of socialism and a very practical application of the words of the Revolution's enduring ideological forefather, José Martí: "being culturally educated is the only way to be free" (Martí 1963 289).

In this light, the presence of the USSR in the Revolution during the *quinquenio gris,* and beyond, can be read as taking on another function. This is not to completely negate any ideological affinity between the Cuban Revolution and the USSR, but rather to highlight that the *quinquenio gris* was more complex than the idea of the USSR's cultural and structural imposition on the Cuban Revolution. It was also the year that Teatro Político Bertolt Brecht was founded: a political theater group that in some respects, due to its very pronounced political commitment and the predominance of productions from Socialist countries in its repertoire, functioned as a designated Soviet/Eastern European space. Concurrently, *Revolución y Cultura,* which dedicated a significant amount of space to the plastic arts in its publications, and constantly engaged in dialogue with the official cultural policy, began to be published regularly.

It is precisely during this more regulatory period that the plastic arts began to play a more active role in mass culture and the continental struggle for independence. Less affected than theater by the normative demands placed on them by interpretations of cultural policy, perhaps because of their well-established status or the less clear narrative of visual culture, they responded to the foci of the 1971 and 1968 congresses and established themselves at the heart of Latin America's continued fight against imperialism. Under the auspices of Casa, the First Meeting of Latin American Plastic Arts was held in 1972. The meeting proposed a central role for art in the fight for justice against imperialism. A program of activities was devised that helped situate the struggle on a local and continental level, encourage the development of a system of signs and symbols for the revolutionary struggle and engage the population (Gordon-Nesbitt 2012, 348–52). The Second Meeting of Latin American Plastic Arts, held in October 1973, expressed solidarity with Chile, and assessed how the objectives of the 1972 meeting had been achieved and the effectiveness of art in fighting imperialism, in addition to formulating specific action plans.

The mobilization of the plastic arts in this way coincided with the beginning of a sustained period in which Cuban students studied culture and art at Higher Education level, and which saw the creation of the National Union of Workers in Arts and Entertainment (SINTAE) and of a school for the improvement of cadres, with courses lasting 90 days or two years (Anon 1974e, 4). The teaching and dissemination of art began to be systematically reorganized and a report was published outlining the new directives for the teaching of art in Cuba, with the aim of forming ISA, providing art education at higher level. The report emphasized that the system would be restructured following the recommendations of Soviet advisors, that Marxism-Leninism would become a mandatory topic on the curriculum, and that the MINED would be responsible for teaching at the basic level, and would approve the study plans for general teaching, while the CNC would be in charge of teaching methodology, technical skills and artistic specialties (Anon 1974b). Plans were also made to incorporate artistic education more fully into the curriculum at the ESBECs, with two hours a week dedicated to culture and art classes with seminars focusing on culture's ideological force and its influence on societal behavior (Martínez 1974). 1974's work plan from the CNC underlined the Council's continuing focus on revolutionary culture, on equalizing cultural disparities and on the mobilization of culture in the defense of the nation. This was to be achieved through the critical assimilation of world culture, the study of cultural values of countries fighting for their independence, the study and assimilation of the experiences of the socialist countries, the study of the character and origin of Cuban culture, the tactical mobilization and promotion of cultural forms according to their social impact, the elevation of the ideological content of cultural magazines such as *Revolución y Cultura*, and the continued promotion of young artists (Anon 1974e).

The First Congress of the PCC cemented the intimate relationship between education and cultural production and development of a culture that genuinely interested and resonated with the masses. That the masses should be sufficiently educated to understand vanguard artistic movements that responded to and engaged in dialogue with the political concerns of the time (in a way that had not been possible when Cuban artists responded to the October Revolution, due to the population's low educational level), was a concern (PCC 1976c, 467–502). In the PCC's programmatic resolutions, it committed itself to the continued roll-out of cultural installations and their material bases and the continued professional organization of artists and writers, in order to critically assimilate the best of universal culture and articulate it in a culture of and for the people that was reflective of the aspirations of the Revolution. In order to achieve an educated citizenship that was both capable of understanding vanguard art movements and producing an art that reflected the new societal values, the PCC committed itself to holding days of culture and fostering co-productions with socialist, Caribbean and Latin American countries, in addition to incorporating art education into citizens' basic instruction (PCC 1976b, 111–13). Books and translations that would deepen the Cuban population's knowledge about the other socialist countries were also identified as an educative cultural tool (PCC 1976c, 473).

THE GREAT APPROPRIATION

The period 1965–1971 can in some ways be viewed as analogous to China's "Great Leap Forward," due to the frenetic nature of institutional formation and economic organization, geared toward lifting Cuba out of underdevelopment and the rapid achievement of communism. By the same token, the late 1970s and very early 1980s can be viewed as Cuba's Great (Cultural) Appropriation. During this period, there was a deeper fusion of economy and culture, the latter of which was ambitiously developed in all its forms, including amateur. There was also an intensified drive to assimilate the best of universal culture, deepen understanding of Latin American culture and articulate Cuban national culture within a socialist international framework. This period was characterized by the systematic effort to remedy the technical shortcomings that inhibited the coherent expression of national characteristics and perpetuated Cuba's state of dependency. Ideologically, Cuba and the USSR still differed, but there was more common ground, specifically the idea that socialism was a path through which to achieve communism. Pragmatically speaking, this served both parties well: the USSR remained the leading light of Communism and was able to play the role of "big brother," guiding Cuba through the transition and helping the island's technical development by educating Cubans in all subjects in the USSR (which would also demonstrate the prowess of the Soviet educational system), while Cuba was able to take advantage of the technical knowledge that it lacked. This indeed implied looking to the USSR and the Socialist Bloc for useful cultural aspects, organizational or technical. Consequently, there was a proliferation of cultural scholarships for Cuban students who excelled to study in the USSR and Socialist Bloc: Bulgaria for opera, the USSR, Ukraine and Poland for painting, monumental art, and sculpture. For students wishing to specialize in theater, destinations included the GDR, USSR, Hungary, Poland, Bulgaria, and Czechoslovakia to specialize in theater direction, dramaturgy, puppet theater direction, scenography, costumes, lighting and in the GDR a specific specialization in organization and planning of theater and in the specialization of Brecht's theater. Upon their return, these scholars were expected to teach at the planned Higher Arts Institution (ISA) (Quesada 1972, 29).

The CNC's Directive No.1 for the development of work in 1975 laid out the path for culture for the following year. The Directive was comprehensive but among its plans and directives emphasized the need to strengthen and develop Cuba's cultural relations with socialist countries and particularly the USSR (in accordance with the norms and directive of the meeting of the Ministers of Culture of Socialist Countries the year before). The Directive also emphasized the need to make the most of the advice from Soviet specialists and stressed that Marxism-Leninism was to be taught so that it would ultimately be viewed as the foundational base upon which creativity was built, rather than "just" another subject in the curriculum (Anon 1975c). Finally a darker chapter in cultural politics seemed to be coming to a close as the CNC's strictures against homosexuality, which had so particularly affected theater, were abrogated in 1975 and those marginalized by the edicts of the *quinquenio gris* had their wages paid retrospectively (Kapcia 2005, 156).

The First Congress of the PCC resulted in the elaboration of a more detailed cultural strategy (as opposed to simply reflecting attitudes, as in 1961, 1968 and 1971). The Thesis and subsequent Resolution outlined culture's educative and emancipatory role in the new Cuba and that the aim of the PCC was to establish a climate favorable to the creation of art and literature that would ultimately be of benefit to the world. The experience of the USSR in cultivating a culture that was aimed at combating man's exploitation of man and the establishing of a state that encouraged the national expression of its constituent peoples was hailed as a particularly valuable example from which to learn (PCC 1976c, 473). A more marked cultural participation from youth (who had been suitably educated through the system of artistic education) was identified as an area of focus. The youthful participation was linked to the nation's continued fight against imperialism and cemented the political and militant nature of artistic creation in Revolutionary Cuba:

> The enemy tries, with copious resources, to take advantage of the cultural and artistic needs and aspirations of the youth to influence them via pseudo-cultural elements and deforming customs. Our aim is to educate their thinking and the feelings of our youth about culture and human values with Marxist-Leninist criteria so that they might use it as a weapon, from the very depths of their person, against the antihuman ideology and the corruption of reaction and imperialism. (PCC 1976c, 495–96)

The structural weaknesses that had perhaps affected UNEAC's capacity to respond to events in the 1960s were also addressed in the 1975 Congress of the PCC, as cultural, political and technical education of educational figures was assigned to the CNC and MinEd (and then to MinCult), and UNEAC, which had to guarantee that it operated on the basis of collective direction and democratically elected positions, was charged with supporting, promoting, and defending Cuban artists (PCC 1976c, 499).

The work of UNEAC, which was tasked with organizing cultural exchanges, co-productions and educative translations, was also recognized as of equal importance to the CNC: "the tasks related to the promotion of culture and the maximum enjoyment of a cultured existence for the whole population, are tasks that are as inalienable as the tasks of improving the material conditions of life and education" (PCC 1976c, 501). In addition to recognizing culture's formative value in society, the document acknowledged the need to improve material conditions for cultural expression. This declaration marked the beginning of sweeping reforms of cultural policy, which are often interpreted as "pragmatic responses from a revolutionary regime confronted with unfavorable social and political circumstances" (Eligio 2009, 180).

The evolving, more inclusive, atmosphere seemed to be confirmed by the inauguration of two key new institutions: ISA, providing University-level art education, and MinCult, replacing the CNC. Significantly, the former Minister of Education and M-26-7 urban coordinator, Armando Hart, was Minister of Culture. MinCult was concerned with the development of the material and technical bases of art, the problems that were related to material resources, funding and technological development, artistic education (organized along the lines of the national education system), and all cultural aspects of cultural dissemination (Báez and Hart Davalos 1986, 11). ISA was housed in the ENA, symbolic of the new institution's encouragement of individual thought and expression and the recognition of non-Soviet aesthetics. The new Constitution that had been drawn up the year before was also ratified, institutionalizing the Revolution (Azicri 2000, 112). The Constitution ended a period of prolonged debate between different proponents of socialist models—radical-Guevarist-*fidelista*-nationalist versus orthodox-Soviet-PSP (Kapcia 2014, 133). The broadly inclusive sentiment of *Palabras* was resurrected (replacing the exclusive interpretation of the speech that had appeared to predominate between 1968 and 1975) and the freedom of artistic expression was guaranteed (PCC 1976a). The State's continuing commitment to the democratization of culture was codified as the Constitution reaffirmed the State's role in cultural education, encouragement and cultivation of the masses (PCC 1976a, 31). MinCult's commitment to supporting the development and dissemination of culture and the greater focus on cultural cooperation and interchange with the USSR were confirmed with a series of protocols signed with the USSR in June 1976. The protocols concentrated on Ministry-level cultural cooperation, and cooperation in the performing arts between 1976 and 1977, and a plan on cultural and scientific cooperation for 1976 to 1980 (Ginsburgs 1987, 159, 425).

With internationalism now having been enshrined in the Constitution, and the critical assimilation of external cultures now being a priority, the revolutionary government's cultural focus turned outwards once more. A renewed emphasis was placed on the idea of the nation, and on national culture within a wider socialist culture. To some extent, this translated into a celebration of the individual within society—which fitted with the CNC's 1970s (re)definition of mass culture as the "sum of strong individualities developed fully as a result of the process of personal liberation, fostered by the revolutionary event which occurred in our country" (Anon 1970b). Some rights were gradually restored to artists, such as authors' rights and royalties, which were reinstated in 1977 for the first time since their abolition in 1967.

1976 represents, then, not a turn away from the USSR and the end of a period of supposedly pernicious Soviet-style influence, but rather a clarification of the basis of the cultural relationship between the two countries and the structural apparatus that directed culture. The PCC's *Thesis and Resolution* on artistic and literary culture, the ratification of the 1976 Constitution, and the inauguration of MinCult organized the Revolution's cultural spaces and, in articulating the role of the intellectual and the anticipated forthcoming cultural tasks, left less-ambiguous spaces in which alternative interpretations of the role of culture and its practitioners could be promoted, or indeed denigrated.

Such uncertainty regarding the Cuban relationship with the USSR demonstrates the complexities and conflicts of deterritorialization and reterritorialization and the "unequal appropriation of knowledge and art" (García Canclini 1995, 240). The deterritorialization of culture and knowledge cannot be reduced to particular movements or cultural codes and policies, but rather "their meaning is constructed in connection with social and economic practices, in struggles for local power, and in the competition to benefit from alliances with external powers" (García Canclini 1995, 241). Thus Soviet culture (in its broadest sense), for the Cuban revolutionary government and cultural apparatus, was therefore a product of imperialism and hegemonic intentions, but also the "realism of common people's culture" (Yurchak 2006, 164), reflective of the prizing of "popular culture." These conflicting perceptions continued to co-exist throughout the 1970s and 1980s, informing and reflecting emergent cultural policy.

NOTES

1. The short film *PM* was ultimately banned from public distribution, and the surrounding furore contributed to the dissolution of the Lunes group, the series of debates that culminated in Fidel Castro's "Palabras a los Intelectuales." *PM* was produced by Saba Cabrera Infante and Orlando Jiménez Leal for Lunes's weekly peak-time television program LUNES de TV. The film was aired and received a favourable review from Néstor Almendros, a fellow member of Lunes, (Smith-Mesa 2011: 84). The film seemed to glorify Batista's Cuba and jarred more than it should in the euphoric days of the immediate Revolution, and in the face of increasingly hostility between the USA and Cuba, the response to the film was more severe than it otherwise might have been (Chanan 1985: 101). It was felt that *PM* was politically and aesthetically irresponsible because it followed its chosen stylistic model too closely and uncritically (Chanan 1985: 103). Smith-Mesa considers the *"PM* affair" reflected the fact that every effort was being made to gain Soviet support, including in the field of culture (Smith-Mesa 2011: 91–92; 281–82).

2. Pedro Ignacio Alonso and Hugo Palmarola have explored the presence and adaptation of the KPD/Gran Panel Soviético in Cuba and Chile in detail (2009, 2014a, 2014b).

3. Fornet's principal focus is on the pivotal year of 1971, and the years surrounding it. His analysis focuses principally on the first half of the decade. He sees 1971 (and the years immediately preceding it) as essentially a debate about power, self-determination, and national sovereignty.

4. Regarding imaginaries of the "other" side of the Cold War, Ivan de la Nuez has written extensively about ideas of the East in the West. In particular, the rise of an "Eastern" aesthetic in the West since 1989 and an ongoing fascination with culture in countries that fell within the socialist camp, and often the specifically Soviet camp (de la Nuez, 2013). Loss has explored the way that Cuba, to a great, extent had historically identified with the West both socially and culturally. In exploring this she has highlighted how this pre-revolutionary affinity would prove problematic later on (Loss 2013, 81).

Chapter 4

Cuban Cultural Policy, 1976 to 1986

Inscribing Cuba in the International

Toward the end of the 1960s, the Revolution's direction and priorities were beginning to shift, from outward-looking perspectives to more internally focused ideas. Guerrilla movements within Latin America were failing, the death of Che in Bolivia in 1967 had profoundly affected the perceptions regarding the viability of Guevara's idea of a moral economy based on and influenced by ideas of social justice. Cuba's economy was floundering, and concerns about defense were increasing (Lévesque 1978, 147). In January 1968, Cuba hosted the Havana Cultural Congress, which, as discussed in chapter 3, heralded the beginning of a strong focus on anti-colonialism, the Third World, and the more active societal role required of the artist. The UNEAC's congress held at the end of the same year signaled a greater emphasis on active contribution of the intellectual to the revolution, the active political role of art, and a focus on national identity (Casal 1971, 460). The net result was that artistic production and cultural development necessarily became an indispensable component of the mobilization to both defend, and advance, the Revolution (Weppler-Grogan 2010, 144). These cultural priorities meant that there were competing demands on cultural practitioners who sought to combat the residual effects of colonialism in culture, but also borrowed from Western cultural traditions. Reconciling these demands with the need to create authentically Cuban intellectual spaces to foster organic discourses was particularly difficult because of their seemingly contradictory nature. Partly as a result of closer economic collaboration with the USSR, and the shift in policy that this seemed to imply, there was a change in cultural administration by the 1970s. A new, different set of debates and struggles emerged, to be played out over the next decade as the emphasis shifted toward the "conservation and development of art of immediately popular origin" in the bid for a national culture (MinCult 1986, 5). This change occurred mainly within the institutions of the CNC and the UNEAC, and more orthodox ideas and a more prescriptive approach to culture began to gain ascendancy, for a time (Weppler-Grogan 2010, 146–54).

From the mid-1970s onward, the focus began to shift outwards, yet paradoxically, also remained steadfastly focused inward. Concurrently, Cuba also began to inscribe itself more fully into socialist internationalism through the rescue of national folklore and tradition. The net result was an increased focus on economic development and a drive for total equality and equal opportunity in the cultural world. This was manifested in areas such as the re-structuring and refining of cultural organization in a bid for unity, educational excellence, mass participation and efficiency in order to give as many Cubans as possible ownership of the Revolution.

However, at first glance, the late 1970s and 1980s seem to offer little in the way of landmark cultural policy. In part, this is due to the fact that debates, at least for the remainder of the 1970s, remained largely internalized as a result of the 1971–1976 *quinquenio gris*. A closer analysis reveals the existence of multiple strains of thought: orthodox Marxism, Latin American Marxism, and revolutionary socialism. Some found common ground around certain ideas, such as the emergence of a genuinely Cuban culture. Others had opposing stances to certain ideas, such as the nature of the relationship between culture and productivity (superstructure versus a more holistic approach), or what unity might look like within culture. Yet more were not always clearly identifiable and tended to merge with the changing dominant strains of thought, but occasionally surfaced—best evidenced by attitudes toward Martí and Cuban traditions. The organization of the cultural world, and the clear demarcation of the roles and boundaries of each institution, appeared to have been set: MinCult was concerned with guidance, technique and methodology, while the municipal and provincial authorities of the *Poder Popular* administered the cultural centers and facilities. National defense was clearly still the priority for cultural and political leaders, and, within culture, this defensive impulse manifested itself in the drive for a united front within the cultural world, quality and clarity in artistic production, and a clearly defined role for artists and intellectuals. This defensive requirement also demanded that the population—and specifically artists and intellectuals—have an adequate ideological and political education, which would allow artists and audiences to assimilate the best of universal culture without the antagonistic politics and history that elements of this culture was potentially imbued with. Attitudes such as these led to the beginning of the embedding of socialist realism in both the aesthetic and organizational senses in the late 1970s. Perhaps the most important impact that the siege mentality, which developed because of a prolonged sense of attack and increasing isolation, had on culture during the 1970s and 1980s was in the fervent focus on the development of clearly identifiable revolutionary Cuban forms and styles of national expression.

Concurrently, the Revolution entered what was arguably its most utopian/egalitarian phase, leading to greater focus on the nation's youth and the prioritization of widespread dissemination of, and access to, culture. The heightened level of attention placed on the Revolution's younger generations was also an expression of the emerging concept of *cubanía rebelde* which particularly prized youth. Hope for the *nuevo hombre* of socialism thus moved toward the *aficionado* movement, which also fitted with the cultural apparatus's focus on the rescue and investigation of national and regional traditions, as well as the search for national culture in popular and mass culture. Additionally, culture came to be viewed as an economic stimulant and key developmental tool, resulting in a sustained focus on the greater integration of different cultural forms and of culture into the economy. Cultural plans and congresses were articulated within the same timeframe as the socioeconomic *quinquenio* plans, which also fitted with the cycle of PCC Congresses (1976–1980 and 1981–1986), which in turn called for clear organizational structures and accountability.

Finally, throughout this period, there was a change in the official approach toward the USSR, from using it as a model to3 learn from (visible in the proliferation of scholarships to the USSR to improve the technical knowledge of students in a Higher Education setting), to positioning Cuba as its equal (i.e., the wording in the 1976 Constitution) and then restricting the relationship to the public performances of alliance (for examples, co-productions to celebrate significant Soviet anniversaries). However, these myriad, coterminous currents each seemed to privilege different interpretations of socialism and different ideas of the role of culture and the artist within the Revolution and other national liberation movements. While institutional clarity was achieved, informal and formal discursive spaces in the cultural world remained, and policy was applied erratically. The decentralized system meant that "basic decisions in cultural matters rest [ed] with the community" (Sarusky and Mosquera 1979, 23). Kapcia (2008, 107) argues that "Cuba's revolutionary ideology was a complex, contested and evolving body of values and beliefs rather than a predetermined set of doctrines." In keeping with this, I argue that *Palabras*, the 1976 PCC's *Thesis and Resolution* on literary and artistic culture, as well as other key moments of policy articulation, were able to be used to praise or criticize a work, or justify a particular institution's or section's approach.

CUBAN CULTURE IN "OUR" AMERICA

The 1976 *Thesis and Resolution* on artistic and literary culture to some extent prioritized education and research within Cuba's creative sphere. This impulse was also inextricably linked with the drive to improve the organizational clarity and coherence of the cultural world. This was seen as a way of ensuring high-quality cultural production and as a necessary step toward the greater integration of artistic production into the country's economic structure and drive: indicative of the growing perception of culture as an economic stimulant and developmental resource.

Constructive criticism, that is, the viewer critiquing a piece of work to make it better and thus contribute to the Revolution, formed the backbone of this renewed prioritization of education. In the PCC's Thesis and Resolution on Artistic and Literary Culture, criticism was presented as a cohesive activity that would ensure a high quality Cuban form of art. Moreover, a Cuban art that had safely assimilated the best of world culture, regardless of its socioeconomic or ideological origins, and re-articulated it into a Cuban setting. Cultural criticism was also therefore an indispensable tool in the defense of the nation and the nurturing of a national culture (PCC 1976c). The *Thesis and Resolution's* section regarding criticism closed with a reminder of the heightened state of change that the Cuban population found itself in and with a call to the youth of the nation to embrace their role as critics. After 1976, concerted efforts were made to improve the political and ideological education of the Cuban population in order to equip them with the necessary skills to be productive critics.

Despite the renewed focus on criticism, the institutionalizing drive of the early 1970s had not disappeared by the latter half of the decade and, after the founding of MinCult, a number of institutions continued to be created after fulfilling a number of the goals set out in the 1975 Congress of the PCC. For example, the 1975 Congress' call for a greater focus on studying Cuba's national traditions led to the founding of the Center of Martian Studies (Centro de Estudios Martianos) on 19 July 1977. The center had the aim of demonstrating the links between the revolutionary democratic goals of Martí and the socialist ideology of Marx, Engels and Lenin (Hart Davalos 1977, 57). In some ways, the center was demonstrative of the deeply entrenched relationship between culture and the political tasks of the nation. However, it was also indicative of the potential inscription of the "Cuban" into the internationalist narrative of socialist Revolution, articulated by Martí: "graft the world into our republics, but the trunk must be of our republics" (1963, 18). And also somewhat reminiscent of the 1928 nationalities policy of the Soviet Union. The nationalities policy was closely linked to the USSR's foreign policy and internationalist goals. It aimed to position the USSR as a future model for a global political order which respected the rights of all nations (Suny 1998, 285). The development of national cultures was encouraged, although Soviet Russian culture occupied the primary position in the family hierarchy of cultures. The other Soviet republics were encouraged to celebrate their national cultures and histories, but also had to emphasize ties with Russia and the progress afforded by their annexation to the Russian Empire (Suny 1998, 288). Manifestations of nationalism were punished harshly, but patriotism was promoted; the definition of these two manifestations was fluid and contingent on the politics of the day.

Returning to Cuba and the Center of Martian Studies, the increasing tendency to view the country as a composite part of Latin America and the Caribbean—what Martí termed "Nuestra América"—also allowed both these views regarding the construction of socialism via nationalism and internationalism to co-exist. In 1977, a variety of changes were made to existing institutions that placed an emphasis on promoting Cuban culture, while balancing this with the ever-closer relationship to the Soviets. Some institutes were amalgamated and new organizations were created to fulfill ongoing cultural-political needs. Two such institutes which facilitated further informed cultural exchange were the Higher Pedagogical Institute for Foreign Languages (ISPLEPL) and a filial to the Pushkin State Institute for Russian Language. Meanwhile, the centralized publishing house, the IdL, was dismantled into separate specialized publishing houses in what Kumaraswami and Kapcia argue was an attempt to rectify the errors of the *quinquenio gris* and simultaneously formed part of the ongoing commitment to institutionalization (2012, 122).

As part of the drive to further democratize culture and the belief in culture's emancipatory potential, two key cultural movements were also revived: the *instructores de arte* and the *movimiento de aficionados,* which laid the foundations for the creation of the *Casas de Cultura* in each municipality. After the Second Congress of the UNEAC, these two movements, but particularly the *aficionado*, became increasingly important in the nation's cultural policy. The *aficionado* movement was progressively valued as a vehicle that enabled the people to directly participate in the creative process, for its educational capacities and as a form of cultural creation that also fed back into the people's creative process, thereby helping to raise the quality of the work produced and awareness among the people. The revival of these movements laid the foundations for the creation of a nationwide network of *Casas de Cultura.* The *Casas de Cultura,* which were distributed across each municipality, were designed to enhance "the notion of cultural democratization and mass participation in a collective good" (Kapcia 2008, 106). The *Casas de Cultura* organized and ran the *aficionado* movement, and were responsible for all cultural activities at a community level. They aimed at raising the educational level of the population, disseminating culture and providing recreational opportunities; they did not, however, train professional artists

(Sarusky and Mosquera 1979, 25–26). It would appear that, as Judith Weiss has suggested (1985, 124), and as Manuel López Oliva asserted in an interview (López Oliva 2015a), the network was founded directly from the Soviet model of *Doma kul'tury* (palaces of culture). The systems share a name, the same purpose of mass political and cultural education and enlightenment as well as the national structure of organization (White 1990).

However, the creation of the *Casas de Culturas* was, as Kapcia argues, not just an implementation of a foreign model but also the "formalisation of a more organic process" and coincided with an increase in addressing the training of professional art teachers at a national and continental level (Kapcia 2005). Changes were also made to the higher education system for the arts and ISA began to develop a postgraduate course training teachers in Marxist-Leninist aesthetics (Rodríguez Alemán 1977, 100).

Toward the end of the year, and against the backdrop of the build-up to the celebrations of the 60th anniversary of the October Revolution, the Second Congress of the UNEAC was held. The Congress, which also included a resolution on the 60th anniversary of the October Revolution (UNEAC 1978c), was opened by the President of UNEAC, Nicolás Guillén. Guillén emphasized the unity of the cultural world, the role of the artist and intellectual in the continuing fight for national liberation and the permanent need to defend the nation against those who would seek to interrupt this emancipatory process. In doing so he presented the Revolution as the continuation of the liberation movements begun in the nineteenth century, thereby emphasizing the "Cuban," and to some extent negating the "Soviet," in the Revolution:

> As we the Cuban writers and artists now meet under the great shadow of the Father of the Nation, we are clearly aware of the responsibility we assume, of the duty we undertake, ready as we are to strengthen the liberating process of Cuba and its national synthesis every day: from Céspedes to Martí, from Martí to Fidel Castro. (Guillén 1978, 36)

Guillén acknowledged the diversity of expression and opinion among the creative world, but simultaneously emphasized the unity of the Revolution by likening the arguments and disputes among artists and intellectuals to those within a family. He also clarified the need to assimilate the best of culture—from different, and possibly even antagonistic, political outlooks—in the synthesis of a Cuban, socialist culture. He did this by grounding his argument in Lenin's accommodating approach toward bourgeois art during the October Revolution and his opposition to the desire to destroy all links with previous culture in a bid to create truly proletarian art. Guillén reiterated the role of the artist and intellectual, firmly locating them within the Revolution's internationalist aspirations/outlook: to produce art that was linked to the Revolution's fight and that might serve as a guide or inspiration to further struggles for national liberation. Throughout all this he stressed that the enduring high quality of cultural production remained a key concern. Finally, he finished by rejecting all forms of cultural chauvinism and reiterating the value of bourgeois culture when it contributed to the growth and development of a Cuban culture. However, he also emphasized the need to nurture and defend, by all means possible, the nascent national culture, which was rooted in two opposing, but equally valid, cultures: that of the African slave and that of the colonial Spanish. By doing so, Guillén acknowledged the seemingly contradictory cultural currents, but subsumed them under the umbrella concepts of "Cubanness" and "socialism." This approach of Guillén's paralleled the Soviet discussion of socialist realism as concurrently national and socialist.

A second reading of Guillén's opening speech also offers some insight into some important ideas and currents that fitted into the emerging national narrative that had begun to be articulated by the new constitution. In his speech, Guillén provided a concrete example of the (inter)cultural chauvinism that he had declared had no space in the Revolution. The merging of these two sides of Cuban identity into a unified Cuban national identity remained true to Ortiz's concept of the Cuban *ajiaco*, the emblem of the Cuban concept of "transculturation." Transculturation, and specifically the idea of the *ajiaco*, emphasized the blending of cultures, rather than the domination of one at the subjugation of the other (Ortiz 1963, 100).

The speech also indirectly extolled the value of the role of the critic in socialist cultural production, through nuanced and informed criticism the best of these cultures could be neutralized and assimilated into Cuban culture. This reassertion of the benefit of recognizing the value of "bourgeois" art was a practical application of some of the goals put forward in the 1975 Congress of the PCC. In his closing speech, Hart built on Guillén's argument, referring back to the Dentro/Contra paradigm in Fidel's *Palabras a los intelectuales*. He argued that previous difficulties experienced over the past decade and a half had arisen through a misinterpretation of *Palabras a los intelectuales:*

> The deficiencies, difficulties, and the achievements that have existed during the period between UNEAC's First and Second Congresses, are in part related to the greater or lesser understanding that each one has had the deepest essence of Fidel's words, when in a succinct thought he proclaimed 'Within the Revolution everything, against the Revolution nothing,' or when he said 'art is a weapon of the Revolution.' (Hart Davalos 1978a, 63)

For Hart, the best way to defend the emerging national culture and ensure high-quality was through the recognition, study, and assimilation of the

Latin American and Caribbean roots of Cuban culture into socialist cultural expression (Hart Davalos 1978a, 63). In this vein, Hart also issued a call to bring debate back into the public sphere, in contrast to the internalization of debates in the early 1970s. Debate, the Minister of Culture argued, was a way of defending Cuba from malign forces. At the same time, he located the forthcoming Cuban experience in the shadow of the achievements of the USSR in educating the country (Hart Davalos 1987b, 167).

Thus criticism was also identified as an essential tool for the cultural development of the country, and as a way of avoiding unnecessary individualism that would separate the individual from the collective and reality. Hart called for the coherent application of the cultural policy set out in 1976. He extolled the organizational achievements of MinCult and the moves it had made to combat the lack of organizational tradition within the creative world. He also emphasized that the preparations for the Congress, conducted over the previous ten months, had revealed that there was a common substrate of ideas and unity of opinions that linked the different artistic forms together (Hart Davalos 1978b, 170–86).

With his position established, Hart explored the different ways in which cultural policy could be applied, and highlighted that organization, and an approach that was not specific to individual artistic forms, but rather holistic, were the keys to the effective implementation of said policy: "only with an comprehensive vision of the phenomenon of culture and analyzing the relationships between the different arts, could these play their role in the revolutionary transformation of society" (Hart Davalos 1978b, 175).[1] A dedicated body—the Popular Council of Culture—was created to coordinate interaction between the state apparatus and the working masses in culture. Ultimately, the closing speech was deeply pragmatic, elaborating on the ways in which cultural policy could be applied, warning of the potentially damaging approaches and tendencies within culture, and, above all, highlighting the ways in which a cultural production of a higher quality could and should be achieved. In his closing words: "Martí said: 'justice first, art after.' Justice has triumphed! Forward Art!" (1978a, 76) articulated the overriding preoccupation of the 1970s and 1980s: with socialism established and systemic inequalities addressed, how should the nation create a high quality, authentically "Cuban" art?

CULTURE IS NOT A LUXURY

The PCC and UNEAC's call for greater cultural interaction and exchange with the USSR had already begun to manifest itself at an institutional level. A protocol of cooperation between the Soviet and Cuban Ministries of Culture and a plan of cooperation between the Union of Painters of the USSR and the UNEAC, for the period 1978–1980, were signed in February and April 1977 respectively (Ginsburgs 1987, 426).

Later in the year, the importance of culture to the spiritual and economic development of Cuba was forcefully rearticulated by Hart at the IX Meeting of the Ministers of Culture of the Socialist Countries, held in Moscow in July 1978. In a speech concerning the meeting's first point of action—the role and place of culture and art in the fulfilling of the socio-economic development plans—Hart explained the Cuban government's approach to culture. It was necessary, he explained, to take a two-pronged approach toward art and culture when considering its role in socioeconomic development: first, its role in solving the problems of occupying workers' free time and second, the influence of art on material production (Hart Davalos 1978c, 9).

Regarding the first approach, Hart signaled that art and culture were valuable practices because they facilitated a greater understanding of reality and aimed to provide spiritual satisfaction to the people. Because of this, art and culture were particularly useful ways of learning about and understanding the human condition. Hart posited that if workers spent their free time in increasingly cultured ways, this would have an economic impact as it would create a demand for culture and cultural products that needed to be satisfied. This would potentially create a cycle of positive feedback: if workers spent more of their free time in cultured activities, this could create a strong craft movement, which, in addition to its artistic and entertainment value, would have dual economic value (product and process). Hart considered that this hypothetically liberating development was dependent on a greater cohesion between different sectors of Cuban society and a fundamental change in the way that art and artists were viewed by society (Hart Davalos 1978c, 14–15).

Hart argued for the greater integration of culture into the Cuban economy. An essential component of this was the assimilation of the best technological and scientific advances in the international community, and their re-elaboration into a Cuban cultural context that also recognized the value of traditional methods of cultural production. This necessarily entailed a closer relationship between art/culture and industry/economy, which was in turn based on an informed understanding of the value of culture and heightened cultural appreciation. Design was hailed as a particularly good example of the close interaction of culture and industry given that its core aim was to produce something to settle the spiritual and material needs of the population. Hart singled out the plastic arts as an area that was poised for greater investigation into the interaction of art and industry, and the subsequent production of products for everyday consumption. This laid the way for projects which forged links between economy and culture, which emerged from the late 1970s onwards. Technical mastery and the greater unity between different cultural genres were deemed essential for the more integrated relationship between art and socio-economic development. Aesthetic requirements and scientific progress were considered the driving forces behind the demand for the greater integration of different aspects of culture. The discovery of this point of convergence of culture, technical mastery, and scientific development was regarded as providing the greatest range of possibilities for artistic expression. Hart also reminded the conference of the interrelation between material production and intellectual production. The speech closed with Hart arguing for the use of new methods of mass production to help produce a cultured, educated, discerning population that could partake in the cultural life of the nation and produce high-quality art.

Cultural production that was integrated into the Cuban economy was also hailed as means by which Cuba could break out of its cycle of dependency on sugar and earn valuable hard currency. This demanded a change in the way cultural investment was therefore viewed:

> For its development, the country requires an important source of investments that it is essential to prioritize to the maximum. This requires that any important investment in culture should be analyzed not only from the angle of its artistic or literary meaning, but also from the point of view of its economic interest and even its potential for exports. We cannot afford to have culture as a luxury. Our cultural development should also serve, as far as possible, as a source of internal revenue, and as a way to acquire foreign currency. In addition to the strictly cultural principle, which cannot be underestimated, criteria of affordability must also be taken into account. And these two aspects are perfectly reconcilable. (Hart Davalos 1978c, 23)

Therefore, Cuba's cultural history had to be reassessed with a financially oriented eye. Hart highlighted the fact that the cultural diversity that was characteristic of Cuba was in global demand, and that this necessitated a greater recognition of some of the constituent elements of Cuban culture, such as the popularity of the Spanish language and the international recognition and diversity of the Cuban plastic arts (Hart Davalos 1978c, 25). Cuban music—most likely popular music—was singled out as a form of artistic expression that had many universal characteristics that made it potentially attractive to large sections of the world. Because of this, there were many opportunities for exchanges, and moreover as an artistic form that had creative input coming directly from the people. Hart's call for the re-evaluation of the relationship between art and material production was the continuation of the ideals of the 1953 rebellion and implied the prizing of culture and cultural expression. In addition, Hart's suggestion that art and culture be linked more clearly with industry was not a complete change of direction of cultural policy—indeed it can be seen as an extension of *Palabras a los intelectuales*, which was in part an affirmation of the new and important role artists and intellectuals would occupy in a time of great socio-economic change (Kumaraswami 2009). However, while *Palabras* had touched on the idea of an international cultural economy, Hart was now articulating the idea more fully, clearly linking artists and intellectuals to the international and national economy.

Steps had already been taken to bring cultural production into the economic sphere and an official institution dedicated to this task was quickly established. The Cuban Fund of Cultural Assets (Fondo Cubano de Bienes Culturales, FCBC), which still exists today, has the aim of promoting and commercializing works of art from artists working in the plastic and applied arts, which are comprised of decorative arts, and the wide-ranging manifestations of artisanal work and design (MinCult 2016). The FCBC as a national organization was created in 1978 (Alonso González 2017, 139) with a provincial branch inaugurated the year before (Mesa 1977).[2] Cultural activities and cooperation were planned along the same timescale as the economic *quinquenios*, as the particular skills of the artist were increasingly integrated into the country's economic development.

The linking of culture with socioeconomic production in a bid to construct the socialist modernity more fully had clear historical antecedents outside of the Revolution. The linking of the two areas has echoes of the positive interaction of art and culture with economy and industry that can be found in the Bauhaus movement, Constructivism (the object-as-comrade), the New Deal (in programs that stressed the interrelatedness of culture with all areas of life such as the Treasury Relief Art Project, the Federal Theater/Art/Music/Writers Projects), and, lastly, Dobrenko's interpretation of socialist realism as the real producer of socialism through the consumption of socialist realist cultural production.

Perhaps because of this—the setting in which the Minister of Culture made his 1978 speech, and the lack of definition in how this greater integration of culture and economy was to take place—Hart's ideas were also able to be interpreted and applied in a reductive manner that viewed culture as rather than base (Marx 2010). By 1979, it had become clear that the government considered that the educational challenges the country had faced in the early years of the Revolution had been overcome. In consequence, the focus had shifted toward raising the quality of cultural production within Cuba, both as a means of further educating the people, but also as a way of articulating the emergent national identity. This attitude, and that cultural development, was synonymous with social development and economic progress, is evidenced in Sarusky and Mosquera's UNESCO 1979 report on the cultural policy of Cuba. The report detailed the development of the country's cultural infrastructure, the aims, implementation of, and reasoning behind the country's cultural policy. In doing so, the report reiterated the close relationship between education and culture and alluded to the shift in investment in culture after educational goals had been met (Sarusky and Mosquera 1979). ISA was flagged as a key formative institute and emblematic of the Cuban government's approach toward art and culture:

> The Instituto Superior de Arte will provide training to licentiate and doctoral level in: music (composition, musicology, orchestral conducting, choral conducting, string instruments, wind instruments, percussion instruments, the guitar and singing); the scenic arts (acting, drama, theater); and the plastic arts (engraving, painting, sculpture). Consideration is being given to the possible inclusion of town planning, interior design, furniture design, toy design and stage design in the plastic-art section. The institute serves as the center for instruction in the various specialized fields, the objective being to train all-round artists and teachers who take a global view of art, who understand, and are receptive to each form of artistic expression. The university-level artists graduating from the institute will have a guaranteed place in society and will be able to devote themselves to creative activities without any concerns or difficulties. In addition to providing specialized artistic instruction, aesthetic education forms part of the general education system, since it is considered to be inseparable from the all-round formation of the human personality. (Sarusky and Mosquera 1979, 39–40)

Culture continued to be actively linked to the fight against the colonial legacy and imperialist aggressions, and cohesion in the cultural world and cultural production once more became closely related to the better defense of the nation. Culture became the subject of passionate mobilization drives that focused on organization, inclusion and unity—a by-product of which was a demand for greater structure, coherence, and accountability.

Against the backdrop of increased economic dependency on the USSR, the Cuban government's organizational drive and focus on the creation and consolidation of dedicated cultural institutes continued. Greater links between the different artistic forms were encouraged. The unity of the cultural world having been established, at least to some extent, with the founding of MinCult, the focus on raising the cultural (production) level, resulted in a progressively close working relationship between official cultural institutions and the PCC to achieve the goals set out in the 1976 *Thesis and Resolution* on artistic culture. Institutional organizational coherence (internal and external) was subsequently prioritized. Within this organizational drive there was a focus on political and ideological education as a means to guarantee quality and widespread cultural participation, and in this aspect, the *aficionado* movement played a particularly active role.

In July 1979, in keeping with the PCC's commitment to investigate national and regional folklore, and build cultural links with the Caribbean and Latin America in particular, Cuba hosted the third festival of Caribbean culture,

Carifesta. The theme was "A Rainbow of Peoples under One Caribbean Sun" (Carifesta 2016). The festival, which runs to this day, celebrates the folklore traditions of the Caribbean and is held as a way of deepening understanding of the region's collective cultures. It is also a way of bringing the community together and combating the isolation of its constituent countries (Carifesta 2016). Events were held in Havana but also in Matanzas and Santiago de Cuba as part of the celebrations. Folklore had also come to occupy an important position in Cuba's international cultural dealings with the USSR, helping to control the degree of interaction between the two countries. Folklore, and culture that overtly drew on national traditions, were effective ways of mediating any influence due to the protection afforded by its historic nature. For example, the 1979 *Dni kubinskoi kul'tury* (Days of Cuban Culture) celebrations, which took place across the USSR, showcased the Ballet Nacional de Cuba, members of the *Nueva Trova* movement, folklore ensembles, choirs and *Teatro Estudio* (Anon, Hart Dávalos, and Vélez 1979, 139–140).

Public culture, or at least one aspect of it, in Cuba was given its own institution when the Advisory Board for the Development of Monumental Sculpture (Consejo Asesor para el Desarrollo de la Escultura Monumentaria, CODEMA) was created in 1980 (Alonso González 2017, 139). CODEMA was responsible for the analysis and approval of monumental sculpture, and the restoration and construction of monuments. The continued institutionalizing focus was also evident in Cuba's international cultural policy, and cultural relations with the USSR were further consolidated when a protocol on the Intergovernmental Soviet-Cuban commission on cultural cooperation was signed on April 7, 1980. A further agreement between the USSR and Cuba on cooperation in the field of culture, education and science was also signed at the same time (Ginsburgs 1987, 426; TASS 1980). Agreements such as those signed with the USSR were of the type recommended in MinCult's 1980 report "objectives, techniques, and methods for cultural promotion" (MinCult 1980). Such reorganization of the way in which the two countries interacted also reflected the overwhelming focus on bureaucratic efficiency of the Brezhnev administration. This focus was centered around two theories of *nauchno-tekhnichestaia revolutsiia* (scientific-technical revolution) and *nauchnoe upravlenie obshchestva* (scientific management of society), minor ideological innovations characteristic of the increasingly immobile Soviet political system (Brudny 2000, 59).

The continuing focus on anti-imperialism, anti-colonialism, and defense was thrown into sharp relief by the landmark Mariel boatlift. Early in 1980, hundreds of Cubans, disenchanted with the Cuban system and the economic situation in the country, sought asylum in the Peruvian embassy. On 21 April, it was announced that discontented Cubans would be allowed to leave Cuba if they were collected by boat from the Western port of Mariel. By September, 124,779 Cubans had left the island with the USA's assistance. This perhaps contributed to the continuing focus at the Second Congress of the PCC (December 18–20) on defense of the nation. The Second Congress was also significantly geared toward socioeconomic development. It brought together economic nationalism, cultural promotion, and education in the defense of the nation. The Congress' main report celebrated the cultural achievements of the Revolution, the consolidation of cultural agencies and the subsequent work done by MinCult and UNEAC, and the emergence of a "coherent cultural policy" (PCC 2011a, 15). Between 1975 and 1980, eight new vocational art education schools were in the process of construction, with over 5,000 students enrolled in the sixteen basic and twenty-one intermediate art schools and ISA. The *aficionado* movement had also increased significantly, and by then Congress had reached 250,000 members in 33,000 groups (up from 200,000 members in 18,000 groups in 1975) (PCC 1980, 25). The movement was singled out for yet further development as part of the continuing drive to further relate culture to material production (PCC 1980, 26). Finally, culture was formally linked to national defense, with the establishment of a new recruiting policy "for drafting more and more young men with an ever higher cultural level, men who are more generally capable in every sense, for active military service" (PCC 1980, 46). In addition to rearticulating the PCC's commitment to the *aficionado* movement, the report extolled the progress made in the application of cultural policy and the resultant cohesiveness in production. The plastic arts, perhaps due to their ability to be widely disseminated rapidly, were an area of a special interest:

> Progress has been made in defining the main guidelines for artistic and literary production. Measures will be taken to change the traditional concept of plastic arts and assign them a broader social role, relating artistic work to production. (PCC 1980, 26)

The *Resolutions* on literary and artistic culture echoed the main report's focus on youth, the need to build greater links between art and industry, the importance of political education within culture, and the militant nature of the artists in the Revolution. It called for a greater focus on the quality of production in the scenic arts, the increase in the influence of Cuban music on youth, and the greater linking of the people and the creators in the field of plastic arts. Within the plastic arts monumental and mural sculpture were highlighted as a particular area for focus over the next *quinquenio* (PCC 2011b). The renewed focus on the merging of cultural and material production fitted with the upcoming *quinquenio*'s (1981–1985) emphasis on economic protectionism, in part to be achieved through increasing exports and replacing imports with national products (PCC 1980, 35). The Second Congress also discussed the Strategy for Socioeconomic Development through to the year 2000, the planning of which had begun in 1978. Once more, material cultural production was linked to the strengthening of the Cuban economy: "in the industrial sectors that produce consumer goods, specially [*sic*] in the food and light industries, development must be based on meeting consumer demands and increasing export products, promoting local arts and crafts" (PCC 1980, 42). The economic and organizational focus on culture extended into the way artists were paid, with the trial of a new payment system and regulations within theater in the collectives in Havana between November 1981 and April 1982 (Sala 1985, 32).

Toward the middle of the 1980s, the anti-colonial drive that had begun in the latter half of 1968 had effectively become institutionalized and there was a gradual move away from the appropriation of Soviet technical skills toward the application of these skills in the elaboration of a Cuban culture that built on studies of Cuba's national heritage. Uncorroborated interviews suggest that this move away from the USSR as a model was reflected in ISA in both the plastic arts and theater sections. Specifically, it was visible in the difficulty some postgraduate students returning from the USSR experienced in being accepted to do their social service and the decision not to renew the contracts of the Soviet theater educators. The preceding events of 1981, such as the *Volumen Uno* exhibition and the First Meeting of Latin American and Caribbean Dramatists, were indicative of this shift in focus and of the drive to develop Cuban cultural expression more fully. The subsequent process of renewal after the 1971–1975 period had ignited a new wave of cultural creativity and this renewed enthusiasm created something of an artistic boom in the 1980s. New genres developed, and areas such as the plastic arts, which were quicker to respond than other mediums, "thrived in a fertile and open space, clearly connected to contemporary art trends in Latin America, Europe and the United States" (Tonel 2009, 180). Concurrent with the continuing anti-imperialist sentiment a "guardedly more relaxed pluralism" developed (Manuel 1990, 311), building on the calmer 1976 constitution that echoed Castro's *Palabras* speech: "artistic creation is always free as long as its content is not contrary to the Revolution. The forms of expression in art are free" (Documentos 1977, 138).

The Third Congress of UNEAC in 1982 confirmed the more tolerant attitude toward cultural practitioners and reiterated the constitutional provision that artistic creativity was free as long as its content did not run contrary to the Revolution. The Congress emphasized that the essence of Cuban cultural policy was to promote a broad popular movement around culture, so that it could facilitate both precision and high aesthetic standards with the "broadest creative freedom for the masses, artists, and writers that spring from them" (Lent 1988, 60). In these more democratic conditions, culture flourished and "the self-confidence and self-reflexion on the part of the writers [and other cultural forms] in the 1980s was reflected in the quantity and diversity of the cultural debates and publications organised to celebrate the landmark of twenty five years of Revolution" (Kumaraswami 2007, 76).

In 1983, one of the first clear applications of the call to link culture and material production was put into practice. TELARTE (discussed in chapter 6) was an experiment in mass distribution with artists contributing designs for textile painting (Camnitzer 2003, 114–15, 351). A similar project, "arte en la fábrica," which was based on an idea by the artist Flavio Garciandía also began: artists went to factories and planned work using available materials normally used for industrial production (Camnitzer 2003, 116). Projects such as this echo the early revolutionary projects, such as Tveresat, the ROSTA windows, and Theatrical October, in theater and cultural education conducted in the 1960s, and the onus on collectivity exemplified by the Teatro Escambray. The integration of art and industry/productivity, and the individual into the collective also possibly draws inspiration from Russian Constructivism. The Constructivists saw art as a political tool that was intimately linked to the rest of society, artists were considered artist-engineers that formed part of a collective (Kaier 2005). They attempted to achieve this by entering the realm of industrial production more fully and promoting art's utility and combatting the commodification of objects found in capitalism. Part of this involved attempting to imbue the everyday object with a political consciousness, producing useful objects that sought to forge a conscious, socialist relationship "between human subjects and the mass-produced objects of modernity" (Kaier 2005, 5).

The differing and competing currents of thought, and their attitudes toward the USSR and socialism, coalesced around the Monument to Lenin in Parque Lenin at the beginning of 1984. In what Alonso González considers to be evidence of Cuba's use of heritage in the negotiation of international relations with the USSR, there was significant debate surrounding the construction and inauguration of the monument designed by Soviet architect Lev Kerbel and Cuban counterpart Antonio Quintana. González (2017, 146–47) argues that from 1980 the USSR and Cuba had been in discussions about the monumental, socialist realist monument, with Soviet bureaucrats and artists and architects offering materials and workers (Alonso González 2017, 139). The Soviet side, including vice-presidents and ministers of culture, had argued for inaugurating the monument in November 1982, in commemoration of the 65th anniversary of the October Revolution. In contrast, the Cuban side pushed for July 26 in commemoration of the Moncada attack, and the use of local materials to avoid interpretations of the monument as evidence of Cuban subordination to the Soviet superpower (Alonso González 2017, 146–147). The monument, built using Cuban marble, was eventually inaugurated on January 8, commemorating the 25th anniversary of the Revolution, definitively presenting the monument as a Cuban accomplishment and sending a clear message about perceived Cuban subservience to the USSR (Rodríguez 1984). 1984 was also a landmark year for architects, who, after having been reorganized into the Higher Technical Centre for Construction in 1963, were now grouped into the Union of Cuban Architects and Construction Engineers (UNAICC). UNAICC had been created in 1983, but was not officially founded until a year later. Later, a Sociedad de Arquitectos was created within the UNAICC and when architecture was eventually included in UNEAC, and it was done so under the title of *Diseño Ambiental* (environmental design), in a departure from what Loomis has argued was the 1970s Soviet-styled valuing of architecture for its constructive capabilities and negating its artistic capacities (Loomis 1999, 147).

During this time of competing ideas and approaches to culture under socialism, cultural debate came to the fore once again and new voices entered the dialogue. In 1984, a cultural magazine, *Temas,* was founded, dedicated to cultural investigation across the cultural forms and economy.[3] A large portion of its content was drawn from studies conducted by various research centers. A good number of the articles addressed the economy of the cultural sphere, reflecting the wider, coherent, concerted effort that was being made to consolidate the links between art and the economy. This effort to integrate the two spheres was undoubtedly heightened by the upcoming prospect of the renewal and renegotiation of the trade agreements with COMECON and the USSR in 1986 for the following *quinquenio*. In some ways, this focus prioritized the organizational drive that had begun to emerge in the Second Congress of the UNEAC and Hart's 1978 Ministers of Culture meeting, but, at the same time, it also added renewed vigor to the search for, and articulation of, distinct Cuban cultural expressions. Practically, this resulted in different applications of policy toward the same goals. Some programs and directives focused on improving the quality of workers' free time, such as plans for galleries, exhibitions, museum exhibits, improvements made to the national cultural network. Others focused on integrating artists more practically into economic production (TELARTE, arte en la fábrica, Alberto Lescay's winning entry for the Antonio Maceo sculpture in Santiago de Cuba, cultural exchanges and tours abroad). Yet more programs and directives focused on improving the quality of cultural production and the reach of cultural integration as a primary step to the first two approaches. This last approach included criticism, education, the search for new expressive means through greater dialogue between artistic forms and expression, and, of course, organizational improvement:

> It is not enough to want to work in interdisciplinary teams if the administrative, economic, and methodological conditions that make it possible are not created, although formally, specialists in various branches of art are integrated with these teams. (Navarro 1985, 114)

These different strains of thought and approaches toward culture that were united by a common goal arguably led to what can be viewed as a "peaceful coexistence" between different aesthetics, or a dynamic and pluralistic organizational socialist realism. The discussions surrounding "revolutionary art form(s)," the "dentro/contra" argument, the focus on public debate, public contact, and constructive criticism, or other aspects of the key policy documents discussed in this chapter, functioned as a useful umbrella term that allowed cultural practitioners to pursue their own aesthetics safely within the Revolution. This approach was similar to the way that, in the 1930s, socialist realism functioned as a convenient (empty) term that would help to unify the factionalized cultural community and provide a democratic style that would ensure that culture was understood by all sectors of society, regardless of their class origin or educational level (Robin 1992, 11). Moreover, the 1980s in Cuba were particularly focused on facilitating the crossover of "elite" and mass culture (educating the population and democratizing culture further), and in using art and culture more generally to produce (exportable) socialism ready for popular ideological and material consumption.

However, there was also potential for the beginnings of the application of socialist realism as an aesthetic approach as clear archetypes of the Revolution definitively emerged. These archetypes were a continuation of the ideas of the early independence wars and the Moncada assault, the emphasis on the Latin American and Caribbean elements of Cuban culture, the veneration of key cultural figures and the emphasis on the artist as *guerrillero*.

In 1986, a month before the Third Congress of the PCC, MinCult produced a report clarifying its structure, role, and goals (MinCult 1986). MinCult reaffirmed its commitment to the promotion and protection of high-quality art and culture and explained that this occurred on two distinct but inextricably linked planes, the artistic-cultural and the social-cultural. It also synthesized ideas about the importance of national patrimony, cultural diffusion, debate, education, and reiterated the internationalist aims of the development of a Cuban culture (MinCult 1986, 3–4). The report articulated the Ministry's commitment to a sustained and systematic dialogue between artists, intellectuals as collectives and individuals (MinCult 1986, 11). In a deeply egalitarian move, the report significantly broadened the term *aficionado* to include both those who generate artistic activity and those who enjoy the art, thereby giving cultural ownership to the majority of the Cuban population. The *aficionado* movement was celebrated as the embodiment of direct public creation, and its inherent reflexive educational capabilities (MinCult 1986, 4). In many ways, the report set the tone for the cultural policy for the forthcoming *quinquenio*, particularly as there was no resolution on artistic and literary culture in the Third Congress in December.

The second half of the period that this research encompasses demonstrates a changing approach toward the USSR. At the end of the 1960s and the beginning of the 1970s, the gaze of the cultural authorities had turned inwards in a defensive bid. However, from the mid-1970s onwards, the focus began to shift outwards, yet perhaps paradoxically, also remained steadfastly focused inward as defense remained a priority. The revolutionary government began to inscribe Cuba more fully into socialist internationalism through the rescue of national and regional folklore and tradition. Concurrently, an increased focus on the development of the Cuban economy and a utopian phase that saw a drive for total equality and equal opportunity began to be felt in the cultural world. This was manifested in areas such as the re-structuring and refining of cultural organization in a bid for unity, educational excellence, mass participation and efficiency, the emphasizing of *aficionado* and *instructores de arte* activities, in order to give as many Cubans as possible ownership of the Revolution, the privileging of criticism as a means of ensuring quality, the weight given to technical mastery and high quality output; the linking of culture and economy, and the focus on interdisciplinarity. However, the defensive element of the dominant ideology privileged different aspects of cultural organization and different, occasionally conflicting, approaches. Strong anti-imperialist and anti-colonialist sentiments still persisted, which affected the way that cultural forms and works were viewed and discussed. Moreover, the emphasis on clarity, unity, and the continuing call for culture to reflect the Revolution's reality gave rise to different perceptions of art within the Revolution, resulting in the presence of organizational socialist realism and the beginnings of the aesthetics of a distinctly Cuban socialist realism. Puñalez-Alpízar considers this period to have been the period when socialist realism naturalized (2012, 355). These coexisting currents of thought and application of cultural policy meant that in Cuba the USSR was viewed as a legitimate source of education and inspiration. But, at the same time, it was also regarded as a potentially imperial force focused on subordinating Cuba within the hierarchy of the international socialist movement. This led to the pragmatic—and sanctioned—adoption of elements of the Soviet culture and policy, the rejection of others, and the development of a performative element regarding the public relationship between the two countries (see Figure 4.1). The public performance of the alliance between the two countries ultimately allowed each to reaffirm their legitimacy, but also ensured a degree of separation that permitted the Cuban leadership to pursue their own path of socialism. This is to some degree evidenced by the significant increase in the frequency with which interaction with the USSR occurred at an official level (state visits, exchanges, collaborations, exhibitions) from the early 1970s through to the mid-1980s, contrasted with the gradual move away from Soviet culture toward Latin American and Caribbean culture.

Figure 4.1   Monument to Lenin, Lenin Hill, Regla. The bronze face of Lenin was added in 1984 by Thelvia Marin. However, a commemoration to Lenin had been in existence on the hill since 1924. Photo courtesy of the author.

NOTES

1. Hart expressed a similar sentiment when discussing the relationship between art and economy, in which he argues the individualism of an artistic form reduces its overall value, and that this approach could be applied to the art-society relationship (Hart Davalos 1978c, 19).

2. From 1987 onward, the FCBC has organized the Feria Internacional de Arte-sanía (FIART) an annual artisanal fair often held in PABEXPO that brings together artisans from all over Latin America and the rest of the world with the chance to exhibit and sell their products.

3. Another, better known, magazine also called *Temas* was created in the early 1990s and is still running today.

Chapter 5

Theater

Staging the Revolution

Theater occupied a conflicted position within the Cuban Revolution in the period under investigation. Its immediate and participatory nature was both an advantage and a disadvantage: theater helped viewers re-contextualize meanings and aims within the goals of the Revolution, but, because of its inherent instability, theater was also considered a potentially subversive form (Kapcia 2005, 141). Because of its underdeveloped status—the relative lack of Cuban playwrights and established theater groups—and the fact that because of all this it was a "ground zero" for revolutionary culture,[1] theater had the potential to become a flagship revolutionary art form. However, because of the predominance of foreign models and foreign styles, its bourgeois roots, the initial prevalence of pre-revolutionary intellectuals, its popularity, and the stereotypes surrounding its practitioners, theater increasingly became an arena where different interpretations of the role of culture and implementation of cultural policy were contested.

Theater was an indispensable component in the creation and diffusion of a culture that genuinely reflected the needs and the interests of a large sector of the population. Moreover, as an effective vehicle which facilitated the propagation of new values and cultural perspectives in the rest of Latin America (Cole 2002, 42), it lent itself easily to the international aspirations of the revolutionary government. This inherent internationalist character further augmented the importance that theater held for all currents of political thought within the Revolution. Theater became a site of experimentation for emerging articulations of a national narrative that was sensitive to the needs and demands of the Revolution and its people. This was particularly true of approaches to past cultures and the idea of the new socialist citizen.

However, unlike the plastic arts, Cuban theater was not able to capitalize on its international prestige and push the boundaries of cultural policy. Inextricably linked with the economy and ideas of "Cubanness" and ideas about the *hombre nuevo*, a distinction, and value judgment, was increasingly made between professional and *aficionado* theater, and their perceived role models, as the Cuban authorities turned their backs on accepted cultural centers. Theater's history in Cuba also began to work against itself. To begin with, the presence of these pre-revolutionary professionals helped the rapid dissemination and development of theater as a revolutionary art form, but it also set the stage for later reactions against perceived cultural imperialism and colonialist mind-sets. Therefore, theater was always closely monitored by cultural institutions and figures, and never granted the autonomy that other institutions such as ICAIC or Casa were. Precisely because of this, theater provides an interesting insight into how culture interacted with politics and how different cultural impetuses were reconciled with cultural policy and production.

PRE-REBELLION THEATER

By the 1940s, increasing economic stability in Latin America and rising development levels created a sense of optimism that formed the basis of new cultural expression, from which theater (and eventually film) sprang (Matas 1971, 427–428). The Spanish Civil War (1936–1939) and WW2 also contributed to the development of Cuban theater, as a number of Spanish intellectuals and artists emigrated to Cuba (such as director and writer Cipriano Rivas Cherif, actress Margarita Xirgu, writer Rubia Barcia, actor Francisco Martínez Allende, and architect Rafael Marquina). Rivas Cherif and Xirgu founded the Municipal Academy of Dramatic Arts in 1941, which became an experimental theater in 1953 (Matas 1971, 429). In 1944 Teatro Popular (TP) was created, directed by Paco Alonso. Closely linked to the PSP, TP encouraged the writing of more socially committed drama and held performances in factories, theaters, and public plazas. It also staged the first works by Soviet authors in Cuba: Leonid Leonov and Konstantin Simonov. TP's existence was, however, short lived and it closed down in 1945 as part of the wave repressing communism and associated entities (Anon 1996, 219).

During this period, which has come to be known as the era of the *salitas*, theater flourished, and a taste for something "more ambitious and durable" than previous theatrical experimentation developed (Matas 1971, 430). The net result was that between 1954 and 1958, a range of small, but permanent, theaters proliferated (Matas 1971, 430). The artistic ferment of the 1950s was also reflected in the provinces, particularly in Camagüey and Oriente (Matas 1971, 431).[2] Throughout the 1950s, the theater section of the cultural society Nuestro Tiempo supported these achievements and was also engaged in a program of research aimed at broadening theater (Matas 1971, 431). The theater section was under the guidance of actor and director Vicente Revuelta, who was also one of the founding members of the seminal theater group Teatro Estudio, now a theatrical institution.

The limitations that characterized pre-revolutionary theater ultimately turned out to be an advantage. The advent of radio, able to reach isolated audiences in their homes, dealt a blow to the popularity of theater in institutional spaces. Economic concerns also hindered the growth of independent theaters: venues were small and admission prices, given the disposable income of the average spectator, could not exceed a dollar (Matas 1971, 431). As a result, theaters could not pay adequate salaries to their actors or technicians, so many sought employment in radio or television, only participating in theatrical productions in their spare time (Matas 1971, 431–32). However, these restrictions helped create a space and dynamic that allowed for more experimental and political theater to develop in theater halls. Theater groups had little support from producers, the government, and even the theater-going public (Tunberg 1970, 43). Theatrical repertoires had, since at least the 1930s, a strong focus on European drama and eschewed Cuban playwrights (Woodyard 1983, 57). The privileging of European theater had occurred because European productions were profitable and the majority of the Cuban artists who took on the task of developing theater in the 1950s were either members of the first dramatic schools in Cuba, or had trained abroad.

These factors notwithstanding, theater within the Cuban Republic planted a number of new ideas in the cultural consciousness of the island, which would become more strongly articulated during the Revolution (Kapcia 2005, 102). One of these dormant ideas was the beginning of an articulation of a national narrative through the appropriation of a colonial era theater style: *Teatro Bufo* (theater of the buffoon). *Bufo* developed in the middle of the nineteenth century, at the peak of the slave trade and when the island had its highest percentage of black inhabitants. As part of the performance of *Bufo*, white actors blackened their faces and painted their lips white. *Bufo* was similar to minstrels in the USA, but also differentiated itself, as its scripts had more developed storylines and the content reflected and reacted to Cuban history and contemporary social issues (Frederik 2012, 43). The three stock characters, *el negrito*, *la mulata*, and *el gallego*, ultimately came to be seen as the three distinct social and ethnic groups of the new Cuban nation, and therefore, an early articulation of a sense of national identity (Frederik 2012, 43). Because of this, and the fact that audiences were taking the opportunity to celebrate their nationalism during performances, *Bufo* was banned during the internal conflict known as the Ten Years' War in Cuba (1868–1878). Once

Cuba separated from Spain in 1898, and became the property of the United States (from which it did not become independent until 1906), *Bufo* theater incorporated the US citizen as the new enemy and in performances the three national Cuban types were seen to act more collaboratively (Frederik 2012, 46). In this way *Bufo* clearly laid the basis for a demonstratively Cuban theater during the late nineteenth century (Kapcia 2005, 56). Moreover, although the pre-revolutionary archetypes in *Bufo* were forcibly erased after 1959, they actually persisted in the twenty-first century perceptions of the Cuban character, which looked back to images of pre-revolution society (Frederik 2012, 43).

By 1958, theater had gone from being deeply traditional to "Havana's most innovative and avant-garde artistic form," exemplified by experimental theater locales such as the Talía, Hubert de Blanck, Atelier, Sótano, Arlequín, Idal, and Arcoiris (Kapcia 2005, 101–102). A key group of the cultural vanguard was Teatro Estudio. This group, formed in February 1958 by eight actors, sought to produce more clearly "revolutionary" work. One of the founding members was Vicente Revuelta, who, after returning from Europe in 1954, brought a more systematic approach to acting, inspired by the Stanislavskii system (Kolin 1995, 91–92). The theater group had strong links to *Nuestro Tiempo*, and prior to the Revolution received clandestine lessons in dialectical Marxism from Mirta Aguirre (Santana 1983, 15). Teatro Estudio can be traced back as the principal source of Cuban revolutionary theater and, for the first decade of the Revolution, it remained the central theatrical institution in the country (Martin 1990, 42–46).

(AMATEUR) THEATER: A KEY TOOL OF
SOCIAL AND POLITICAL CHANGE

As the Revolution rapidly fused art and politics, theater responded particularly quickly to the new society (González Rodríguez and Winks 1996, 104). 216 productions were staged in Havana alone during 1959, and 264 in 1960, in marked contrast to 172 in 1958 (González 2003). Unlike in cinema, which saw the emigration of nearly all pre-revolutionary figures involved in the industry, the majority of playwrights and directors active prior to the Revolution remained in Cuba (Matas 1971, 433). Until its closure on November 6, 1961, *Lunes de Revolución*, the cultural supplement of the newspaper *Revolución*, was a "loyal and persistent friend" to theater (Leal 1962), which focused on theater both nationally and internationally, providing the main forum for discussion about this form of expression. *Lunes* also briefly boasted its own theater group, Teatro Experimental de Lunes, which showed *La Leçon* (*The Lesson*) and *Les Chaises* (The Chairs), both by Romanian-French playwright

Eugène Ionesco and directed by Rubén Vigón in Sala Arlequín on January 12, 1959 and again on February 2 (González 2003, 335–339).

In January 1961, theater was subordinated to the former-PSP-dominated CNC. The CNC's role in theater was myriad. It coordinated cultural events throughout the country, approved or rejected proposed projects from artists and writers, gathered information about foreign culture and disseminated it, controlled bookings on a national and regional basis, and allocated the budget (Tunberg 1970, 44). The choice of which plays and productions to stage fell to the theater group, and the group's director would then present these choices to the CNC's theater section for approval. If approval was not forthcoming, the director could ask for feedback and then appeal the decision. However, concert readings by professional groups and amateur productions did not need approval from the CNC (Tunberg 1970, 43). In his analysis of the development of Cuban theater, Tunberg asserts that by 1970, the date his work was published, no proposal had been rejected or censored (1970, 43).

Once a script was approved, a group's director could then go to the *almacén* (the national costume and scenery workshop) and borrow existing costumes and scenery. If new costumes or scenery were required, the group was billed for it. Production costs did not include rent, as each official theater group had its own theater and the government absorbed the utility costs (Tunberg 1970, 44). Dramatic artists were granted secure financial backing in the form of a salary and professional status, thereby allowing them to dedicate themselves entirely to their creative endeavors. A professional was considered to be any individual who either drew a salary from the CNC, or who had a job that was closely related to their artistic field. To become a professional it was necessary either to have a contract from the CNC for a particular project or to be a member of a theater group which had a general contract with the CNC. These (renewable) contracts were generally granted annually, but were not particularly binding. Individuals could switch groups, change projects, or leave theater altogether (Palls 1975, 68).[3]

It is worth noting that there has been little further research conducted regarding the system of organization and valorization of theater, plays, and theater practitioners. In part, this stems from the historiographic legacy created by the *quinquenio gris* that still contributes to a general unwillingness among theater specialists in particular to discuss the specificities of the period today. This is particularly the case with regard to researching the system with which the CNC approved and graded plays, actors, and troupes, which is generally known as the *sistema de valorización*. This is because the *sistema de valorización* was, and still is, perceived to be intimately linked to what was called, in the furor of 2007 when Pavón appeared on the program *Impronta* on Cubavisión, the *parametrización* of actors which was so destructive to theater during the *quinquenio gris* and immediately after.

Theater's immediacy made it a particularly powerful tool for incorporating working men and women into cultural activities. This was arguably capitalized upon by the EIA which had a dedicated theater section. Part of the duties of the *instructores de arte* was to help with performing groups of *aficionados'* organization and activities (Matas 1971, 433). These *aficionado* groups were organized in labor centers all over the island with the aim of attracting and educating large audiences, so that professional theater groups would have a popular foundation (Matas 1971, 433). Amateurs also had a number of options available to them if they wished to try to become professional playwrights. They could submit a work to the theater section of the CNC or directly to a theater for criticism. Alternatively, they could send a work to Casa for one of its literary prizes, or to UNEAC for publication or consideration for the David Prize for unknown, unpublished, and unproduced writers. They could also arrange an amateur production and hope that it would be picked up by a professional group (Woodyard 1983, 58). Regional amateur theater competitions, open to all theater groups, were held annually in renovated theaters throughout the provinces (Tunberg 1970, 45).

Different styles of theater proliferated in Havana; in 1962 the Teatro Lírico and the Teatro Musical de la Habana were founded. The Teatro Lírico focused on operas, operettas, and *zarzuelas*—Spanish lyrical theater that includes spoken and sung text—and the Teatro Musical focused on foreign or national contemporary musical plays. Both theaters had their own orchestras and were allocated particularly high budgets on account of the demands of the form (Matas 1971, 433–434). The CNC created another theater group, the short-lived Conjunto Dramático Nacional (CDN) in 1962, which ran until 1966 (González 1985, 64).

Although still predominantly Havana-centric, revolutionary theater began to take hold in Cuba's provinces, with the development of groups which incorporated local cultural and historical traditions, such as Cabildo Teatral de Santiago which was created in 1961 in the eastern province of Oriente (Manzor-Coats and Martiatu Terry 1995, 45; Tunberg 1970, 52). By 1963 professional groups were established in the provinces in an effort to decentralize theater (Martin 1994, 155). Despite the new organizational structure and coordination of efforts, theater activities had begun to decrease significantly in 1962. This was in part because a large section of the traditional theater audience, the middle class, had left or was in the process of leaving the country, and also because Havana audiences still preferred "light" amusement such as musical comedy and vernacular variety shows (Matas 1971, 434–35). Possibly in response to the decline of audiences at cultural events, the CNC began to seek to further coordinate cultural activities and, between December 14 and 16, 1962, it held the First National Cultural Congress. The focus of this congress was on mobilization and the promotion of cultural exchange between different mass organizations (Gallardo Saborido 2009, 89). Each province outlined its program of work in the cultural field, with the aim of encouraging direct participation in cultural activities (Gordon-Nesbitt 2012, 290–91). However, theatrical production stalled after theater was amalgamated into the CNC and was then further affected by the move toward insular introspection, and indigenous cultural codes (rather than a focus on the formation of new cultural narratives) slowly began to take hold, in the face of increasing international hostility and isolation (Fay 2011, 413–14).

After the first Escalante affair of March 1962, which ended the "inevitable phase of sectarianism," theater gained its own official journal (Benedetti 1971, 8). *Conjunto* was a Casa publication, and therefore, unaffiliated to any one group, with an office in Havana, where the significant majority of theater was still focused. The publication, whose name paid homage to the collective nature of theater, began production in mid-1964. It appeared relatively regularly and involved a wide range of Cuban and Latin American researchers and dramatists (Tunberg 1970, 44–45). The journal's form remained relatively constant but the editorial board experimented with different approaches. David Fernández was the editor for the first three editions, then critic Rine Leal was in charge until the tenth edition. From 1972 the journal was under the control of Galich, a Guatemalan *dramaturgo* and researcher. The first issue, July–August 1964, included an interview with the Czechoslovakian director Otomar Kreycha, head of the National Theater of Prague, and Josef Svoboda, his scenographer (Layera 1983, 35). Kreycha had been invited by the CNC as part of the celebrations of Shakespeare's fourth centenary. He had originally planned to direct Vsevolod Vishnevskii's Optimistic Tragedy but then changed to *Romeo and Juliet* (Fernández 1964, 9–10). *Romeo and Juliet* was popular in Central and Eastern Europe during the Cold War and had become politicized (Loehlin 2002, 65). Kreycha and Svoboda had staged the play in 1963 with a particularly innovative set design and clear political undercurrents as Czechoslovakia was "struggling to find an alternative to both Western capitalism and Soviet totalitarianism" (Loehlin 2002, 65).

By 1965, attendance in Cuban s had surpassed one million annually, an increase of 1,000 percent from 1958 (Martin 1994, 154). Around the same time, the first wave of students from the Revolution's educational institutions had begun to graduate and form their own theater groups, such as Teatro Joven, which sought to relate theater to the revolution. It was a collective of four actors, six actresses, and five technicians, with playwright Raul Macías serving as literary advisor and "big brother." The group operated as a collective, majority decisions were the rule, and members usually shared the directorial chores from production to production. The group became professional in November 1969, when their two-year obligatory social work, in lieu of military service, which had consisted of rural theatrical tours, was completed. Theater attendance was to become affected by the deteriorating relationship between Cuba and the USSR as the direction of the Revolution began to shift toward intense (grass-roots) radicalization from 1962 onward (Kapcia 2005, 121). By the end of 1965, a cultural Revolution that encouraged and supported numerous creative currents and differing ideologies was "anomalous in a country for which the conclusion of the rite of passage had become a national imperative" (Fay 2011, 418–419). The new political infrastructure "and the doctrinal impetus that drove it, moved towards absolute definition" both in the field of politics and culture (Fay 2011, 419). The articulation of unity, a coherent national identity, and the mobilization of resources became privileged characteristics. Moreover, artists' interaction with external cultural currents, even if conducted with the aim of adapting these currents, "was now tainted with the stain of potential treachery" (Fay 2011, 417). Theater, which had not produced a clearly Cuban revolutionary art form, was particularly susceptible. As the cultural world became increasingly polarized, some high-profile figures emigrated: Guillermo Cabrera Infante in 1965 and Carlos Franqui in 1968 (Fay 2011, 418–19). Moreover, pre-revolutionary prejudices, despite the profound social, cultural, and political transformations within Cuba "lingered malignantly on" (Fay 2011, 416).

Homosexuality became an obvious point of confrontation and issues regarding the lifestyle, perceived or real, of certain individuals became increasingly evident, with the Military Units to Aid Production (Unidades Militares de Ayuda a la Producción, UMAP) beginning to be used for purposes other than "disciplining" wayward youth in 1965 (Gallardo Saborido 2009, 106). This concern with sexual orientation was to become particularly pernicious within theater, which also had to contend with actions based on the stereotypes that surrounded not only the artistic form but also the characteristics and sexual preferences of practitioners. These prejudices, and the suspicion of cultural professionals with pre-revolutionary ties, would become more pronounced toward the end of the 1960s and in the early 1970s. I consider that these prejudices and stereotypes led to a hypermacho and chauvinist expression of national identity which led to further regulation of theater.

1968—ARTISTS BECOME MEN
AND WOMEN OF ACTION

By the time of the Havana Cultural Congress, theater had become increasingly stratified and, between 1968 and 1970, individuals in theatrical groups began to divide into new subgroups (Benedetti 1971, 21). Artists felt increasingly stifled by the government's prescribed, specialized, theater groups and felt a growing disjunction between living the Revolution as citizens and as artists (Martin 1990, 42). As a result of these preoccupations, there was a fundamental redefinition of theater regarding the changing direction of the revolutionary process. This "mediation of 1968," sought to resolve some of the tensions within Teatro Estudio between different interpretations of formal innovations and the search for revolutionary culture (and differing geographical focuses) (Pianca 1989, 519). As a result, two different theater groups were formed in the conscious search for a greater cohesion between theory and practice (Pianca 1989, 519). These two groups were the Havana-focused Los Doce, which focused on closed experimentation in the capital, and Teatro Escambray, which looked to the countryside and greater interaction with the historically marginalized and impoverished peasants. Los Doce, headed by Vicente Revuelta, was an experimental group which sought to challenge the limits of what was accepted as theater (Martin 1990, 42). The group experimented with Jerzy Grotowski's ideas of "Poor Theater" and did not give public performances for a year. Grotowski was highly influential in experimental theater. His concept of "Poor Theater" emphasized an actor's connection with the audience, and the audience's participation in a production (Wiles 1980, 142). Los Doce embodied one of two important goals of the cultural authorities—collectivity. However, in keeping its experimentations in theater confined within the group, albeit with the aim of improving future performances for the public, the group in some ways fell short of ideas regarding widening participation in culture.

Teatro Escambray was firmly focused on Cuba's provinces and the role that theater could play in the development of the Revolution. Teatro Escambray moved to the Escambray Mountains with a mandate to "develop and perform theater based on regional issues and driven by local concerns" (Rudakoff 1996, 78). This was an isolated, impoverished region with a history of violence (Rudakoff 1996, 79). The choice of location was significant in another way: the Escambray Mountains were a particularly strong symbol of the Revolution. There had been two National Fronts that fought in the 1959 rebellion, the ex-Directorio Revolucionario Estudiantil group of 1958 split over whether to join Che's group and attack Santa Clara (one group, under Faure Chomón did) or to remain apart (as did the other section, the Segundo Frente Nacional de Escambray, under Eloy Gutiérrez Menoyo). Gutiérrez Menoyo's men became the anti-Revolution guerrillas of 1960–1966 and remained in the mountains and fought against the Revolution's forces until 1965. Teatro Escambray used sociological techniques to research social problems of development in the countryside and then converted the findings into theatrical performances for those who had been the subject of research. The first topic, chosen by the Escambray people, was husband-wife relations and local society (Rudakoff 1996, 81–82). Members of Teatro Escambray talked with local residents at their homes and in the cane fields, where performances were then held, which, because of the relevance of and familiarity with subject matter, sometimes drew the viewers in, resulting in interruptions and interventions from the viewers (Rudakoff 1996, 77–78).

Teatro Escambray's first investigation was conducted between November 5, 1968 and December 6, 1968. It was planned in conjunction with the regional Party and, to maximize any potential effect, the group was divided into three committees which traversed the region's municipalities of Trinidad, Topes de Collantes, Condado, Caracusey, Cumanayagua, La Sierrita, Manicaragua, Mataguá, Jimbacoa, Güinía de Miranda, Fomento, and Báez (Corrieri et al. 1978, 35). On its tours, the group stayed in each location for one week and would then perform two different plays—one at the beginning of the week and one at the end. Teatro Escambray used farce as a basic form and this style shifted the focus in Cuban popular theater from "dialectic and formalised structure to aesthetic concerns and highly theatrical, imagistic performance" (Martin 1990, 42). Every three months, the group would make a circuit and return to the first village to begin the tour again and to see what social and cultural progress had been made (Tunberg 1970, 55). Members of Teatro Escambray eventually formed groups elsewhere, such as Flora Lauten and Teatro La YaYa based in the Santa Clara Mountains, and Albio Paz who founded Teatro Acero, based in a steel factory in Havana (Martin 1994, 130).

Practically, Teatro Escambray's relocation to the regions also solved a problem of over-crowding. By 1970 Havana boasted nineteen official theater groups, comprising of thirteen theater companies and six dance troupes (Anon 1970a, 18), in comparison to the six that had existed in 1958 (1970a, 44).[4] Between them these groups had staged 1,042 works: 788 premieres and 254 revivals (Anon 1970a, 24–25). By 1970 the problem of a surplus of theater professionals had become twofold: there were not enough theaters in Cuba to keep all professionals in regular work and there were no immediate plans to create more professionals until the CNC could demonstrate the need for them. Moreover, budget troubles also meant that the CNC had frozen all new contracts (Martin 1990, 46). Contracts represented the majority of the CNC's theater budget: in 1969, of the 16 million pesos assigned to the CNC, 15 million of them were spent on salaries (Martin 1990, 42–46). This created a real problem for unestablished theater professionals seeking to break into the market. Teatro Escambray's high-profile relocation to an impoverished rural setting paved the way for other groups to follow suit, thereby helping to combat the saturation of the Havana theater world, and further cementing the close relationship between culture and politics as the group actively sought to become an "agent in the Cuban revolution" (Tunberg 1970, 48). The group's move reflected the revolutionary government's aims for the further democratization of culture through the widening of participation and the importance placed on the idea of the collective.

What was left of Teatro Estudio after the split also changed; in October 1968 Raquel Revuelta, a leading film actress and a founding member of the group, became its director (Tunberg 1970, 44). She considered Teatro Estudio's fundamental purpose to be the creation of a national theater and attempted to transform the group's theater into a cultural center which included music, dance, painting, and poetry. A number of new programs were established, including a cycle of classical theater, plastic art exhibitions, poetry readings, concerts of contemporary music, and production of new plays (Tunberg 1970, 47). An emphasis was placed on Teatro Estudio's collectivity; every theater artist or craftsman was expected to make an individual contribution to the whole of the production (Tunberg 1970, 48).

Toward the end of the 1960s, theater groups with more explicitly ideologically militant or Third World focuses also began to proliferate, such as Teatro Tercer Mundo (T3M), which combined a clear focus on the axis of underdevelopment—Asia, Africa, and Latin America—and a more orthodox approach toward revolutionary commitment and social behavior. Many of T3M's actors had toured Mexico in the summer of 1968 with TD and some of those involved had decided that, in order for Cuban theater to properly relate to the Revolution, an element of the range of theater being practiced in Cuba should be overtly political. The CNC supported this idea and T3M was formed in February 1969 (Tunberg 1970, 49–52). For unclear reasons, it was the only professional theater group in Cuba that did not need to have its script approved by the CNC for proposed productions, but it did require budgetary approval. The group had two guiding principles, that theater must be taken to the people—which saw free productions, staged outside to audiences averaging about 1,500 in size—and that the drama they stage must be revolutionary (in form and in content) and should relate to T3M's commitment to world-wide socialist Revolution. The group operated strict social, personal, and professional criteria for potential members, and applicants had to prove their commitment to the Revolution, with evidence such as a consistent record of voluntary labor. Nor did the group accept drug users, those considered sexually promiscuous, or homosexuals (Tunberg 1970, 49–52). According to Tunberg's research on theater during this period, the group had made a conscious decision, taking into account the Marxist argument that an artist cannot be viewed separately from their work, or society, not to accept homosexual actors in a bid to broaden the reach of their theater:

> Tercer Mundo feels that homosexuality is a manifestation of how economic and cultural imperialism has affected Cuba and that to call one a homosexual in any country would be to call him alienated; thus, to eliminate alienation between Cuban culture and the people one must insist on a 'normal' lifestyle on the part of its actors. (Tunberg 1970, 53)

T3M's stance was intimately linked to the "incessant fight against the [perceived] residues of the colonial heritage" (Vitier 1971, 7) which underpinned educational and cultural production from the late 1960s onward. The exclusionary strictures of T3M are evidence of two currents that had begun to emerge in the cultural arena. In one sense, the group's entrance requirements reflected the increasingly hypermacho atmosphere that was developing due to the increasing presence of ex-guerrillas, and associated publications, in the cultural and political apparatus (such as Pavón and *Verde Olivo*). However, the focus on combatting erroneously perceived alienation caused by homosexuality was paradoxically also demonstrative of the desire to further democratize culture and to involve new audiences, as seen in other groups such as Teatro Escambray. This seemingly inconsistent stance is an example of the multiple currents of thought regarding culture's role in the Revolution. These currents continued to exist well past 1965, and at times coexisted and others contradicted each other. Furthermore, the change in key figures within cultural administration could also explain the privileging of certain ideas and creative demands that led to the beginning of the circulation of a certain type of narrative socialist realism in Cuba, which demanded didacticism and clarity.

These nascent hypermacho, nationalist, and regulatory tendencies were further exacerbated by the increasing suspicion with which intellectuals active prior to the Revolution were viewed, as the revolutionary government increasingly felt under attack from external forces. The expulsion of Cabrera Infante from the UNEAC in August 1968, and the simultaneous departure of Carlos Franqui, added to the increasing suspicion with which pre-revolutionary intellectuals were being viewed, particularly if they did not have explicitly revolutionary stances or were linked to these ideologically difficult figures. These more regulatory and exclusionary sentiments had already been growing in strength on a more grass-roots level, due to the increased pace of post-1965 radicalization, but would become more aggressively articulated in the early 1970s when "the promises of the Cuban Revolution met the realities of governing [and] the government pushed to put forth one unifying definition of what it meant to be revolutionary" (Ford 2010, 367). In doing so they emphasized the importance of the *aficionado* movement, cultural democratization and mass participation, in place of the cultural "elite."

QUINQUENIO GRIS (1971–1975/6)

The regulatory tendencies that had begun to develop from 1968 onwards were intensified by the 1971 National Congress of Education and Culture in the drive to eliminate foreign tendencies and signs of cultural imperialism in the creative world (Casal 1971, 463). The Congress, and its closing declaration formalized, to some extent, the hypermacho focus of the following years:

> The cultural mediums cannot serve as a framework for the proliferation of false intellectuals who seek to turn snobbery, extravagance, homosexuality and other social aberrations into expressions of revolutionary art, removed from the masses and the spirit of our Revolution. (Documentos 1977, 52)

With the promotion of new cultural figures, such as Armando Quesada and Jorge Serguera, along with some, such as Pavón, from the military, the constituent roles of culture began to be (unofficially) separated out through the privileging of different currents and approaches. I suggest that, within theater, its intrinsic educational value became its most prized element. The prizing of this educative potential fostered didactic approaches toward the art form which increased as the revolutionary government strove toward cultural democratization. However, this was by no means a monolithic approach and alternative attitudes to culture in socialism persisted.

In the early 1970s a system of international scholarships that would further help the development of Cuban theater began to be implemented. These scholarships formed part of the educational drive that was linked to the process of reassessment and focus on raising the quality of production after the failure of the 1970 *zafra*. It was planned that the awards would be offered between 1973 and 1980. In 1972 there were twenty-one approved individuals for the scholarships, and it was hoped that this number would rise to thirty the following years.

More generally, the cultural authorities placed the emphasis on assimilating universal cultural elements, and synthesizing a national culture that confronted Cuba's colonized past (Documentos 1977, 51–56). Artists and intellectuals had their religious beliefs, sexual orientation, relations with acquaintances and colleagues abroad, and other aspects of their personal lives, scrutinized (Weppler-Grogan 2010, 147).[5] Theater, which was still valued for its educational and agitational capacity, had initially enjoyed a high degree of freedom.

However, it began to face a greater degree of censorship and limitation (Ford 2010, 367). The playwright and poet Antón Arrufat came under intense attack for his most recent collection of poetry, *Escrito en las puertas*, accused of having a "poetic expression defeated by its own lack of consistency and poetic veracity" (Avíla 1969, 13). He was marginalized for the following fourteen years, when none of his existing or new work was published, and, although his work was gradually accepted again, his theatrical work was not (Gallardo Saborido 2009, 186). Other artists found that they could not find a public forum for their work, some were unable to take trips abroad, and others, like Arrufat, received jobs in which they were unable to constantly pursue their creative interests (Weppler-Grogan 2010, 147). For the same reasons that theater ensembles had been seen as didactic vehicles as an important feature of the socialist Revolution, theater was now considered particularly dangerous (Layera 1983, 42):

> We were all guilty, in fact, but some were more guilty than others, as could be seen in the case of homosexuals. [. . .] As incredible as it may seem to us today [. . .] it is not preposterous to think that this was the foundation, let's call it theoretical, that served in 71–72 to establish the 'parameters' applied in the high-risk labour sectors, as they were the magisterium and, above all, the theater. It had been concluded that the mere influence of the teacher or actor on the student or the adolescent viewer could be risky. (Fornet 2009, 16)

As part of this greater regulation of theater and the effort to further educate the Cuban population in cultural matters, the official theatrical organ, *Conjunto,* which had remained unpublished between 1968 and 1971, was resurrected. It began circulation again in 1972, under the permanent editorship of Galich, with a more militant line that was clearly committed to the Third World and to art as a service to social causes (Martin 1990, 44).

This educative focus changed the priorities within theater. Historically, the idea of a "sophisticated" theater audience traditionally referred to an audience familiar with the codes and techniques within the Western classical tradition (Villegas 1989, 507). Therefore, the cultivation of new theoretical models for discourse and the understanding of works in their own historical context meant that there was a concerted move toward amateur movements and theatrical works which incorporated "the people," either through giving voice to their concerns or encouraging their participation. *Aficionado* theater proved to be a source of redemption, or escape, for some individuals who had fallen foul of the *quinquenio gris* in other artistic areas. One such example is Antonia Eiriz, a visual artist and member of *Los Once,* who came under scrutiny from the CNC, possibly through her prior association with the cultural supplement *Lunes.* Eiriz faced much public criticism for her controversial work *Una tribuna para la paz democrática* (1968), particularly from some of the more dogmatic cultural figures, some of whom advocated stereotypical socialist realism (what I term high Stalinist socialist realism) (Anreus 2004, 13). In particular Anreus identifies printmaker Carmelo González as an advocate of socialist realism. By the end of the year, Eiriz had stopped painting, in protest, and in 1969 she resigned from teaching art in Cubanacán (Anreus 2004, 13). She eventually began to teach children and adults from the Committees for the Defence of the Revolution (Comités de Defensa de la Revolución, CDRs), in her native municipality, Juanelo, to make figures from papier-mâché. These efforts gradually developed into a movement of amateur art practitioners that gained national recognition, and the papier-mâché puppets were used in plays, whose theatrical sets, as well as writing, were created by members of the CDRs (Weppler-Grogan 2010, 152).

The more didactic approach toward culture was also reflected in the types of work that won Casa's theater prize between 1970 and 1975.[6] Winning works dealt with explicitly revolutionary themes, focused on Latin America's history or culture, or adapted European culture to the Cuban setting and reconfigured it for a Latin American context. In 1970 no prize was awarded while in 1971, Raúl Macías (the "big brother" figure to Teatro Joven) won the award for *Girón: historia verdadera de la Brigada 2506*, which dealt with the events surrounding Playa Girón, presented a strong critique of the United States, and looked outwards at the achievements of the Revolution (Ford 2010, 364–67). Macías had spent time abroad, including studying in Moscow in the early 1960s (he later served as a translator of Soviet Russian-language works) and in Libya and Angola, (Ford 2010, 364). In 1972, the Uruguayan playwright Antonio Larreta won, with *Juan Palmieri*. The piece shows, from the perspective of his mother, the political awakening of her son, a young student who is deeply affected by the death of Che in 1967. It guides the audience through the political events between 1967 and 1969, beginning with the death of Líber Arce, the first student shot during a protest in Montevideo on August 14, 1967. Reminiscent of the perceived tenets of late Stalinist socialist realism, the play was commended for its simplicity, maturity, accuracy of the political commitment made, and the historical setting, and its successful appropriation of structures from bourgeois theater (Casañas and Fornet 1999, 80). In 1973, Víctor Torres, part of the amateur theater movement in Chile, won with *Una casa en Lota Alto*, a dramatic representation of ideological and generational conflicts within a coal-mining family. The piece also highlighted the artificiality of theater, with the actors explaining that they were representing factual events, drawing on data compiled by social scientists, in order to motivate the audience into action (Layera 1978, 40). The play's use of dramatic forms imported from Europe and the United States was singled out (Layera 1978, 39), and the piece was hailed by the jury as the work which most clearly reflected the "open form of experimental theater of [the Latin American] continent, which includes the pueblo not only as a consumer but also as a dynamic protagonist in this aesthetic phenomenon" (Casañas and Fornet 1999, 86). In 1974 there were no winners, by consensus, and in 1975 there were three: Jorge Goldenberg, *Revelo 1923* (Argentina); Guillermo Maldonado Pérez, *Por Estos Santos Latifundios* (Colombia); Alejando Sieveking, *Pequeños Animales Abatidos* (Chile), all of which were singled out for their clear ideological stance, historical focus, audacious use of theatrical conventions and balanced structures (Casañas and Fornet 1999,

97). Toward the mid-to-late 1970s, an increasing emphasis was placed on "collectivity" and the interaction between government and people. These two trends, in theory, served to further demonstrate the emancipatory power of the Revolution. In this sense the focus on, and subsequent privileging of, collective-style production and dialogue between the government and people, was similar to theater production during the early Russian Revolution (1917–1924), and the concept of *samodeiatel'nost'* (previously discussed) (Mally 2000, 17–46). When discussing the Russian revolutionary case, Mally identifies this approach as what Victor Turner termed social drama, when groups try to occupy a new space in the (changed) social system (Mally 2000, 19). Through acting, these participants found a way to enter the public sphere—"and thus to lay claim to a new community in which they could have a voice" (Mally 2000, 18). While Mally is specifically discussing the rise of amateur theater in this instance, I would argue that the description also applies to professionals adopting the new art forms of the new society.

The 1976 Casa theater prize demonstrates this argument, in addition to evidencing the internationalist aspirations of the Cuban revolutionary government. The prize was awarded to the Colombian Grupo de Teatro La Candelaria for their piece *Guadelupe años sin cuenta*, which was hailed for taking a collective approach toward the creative process, as "collective creation, [is] the genuine form of our Latin American theater" (Casañas and Fornet 1999, 103). The collective nature of the Cuban Revolution was also demonstrated through a series of strategically important co-productions between 1972 and 1978. These co-productions began with the GDR and Bulgaria; however, the majority were with the USSR.

The increased focus on co-productions flagged up by the 1976 PCC manifested in two further theatrical co-productions with the USSR in 1977. The year 1977 was a symbolic year, being the 60th anniversary of the October Revolution, and the co-productions formed part of wider celebrations taking place. The 1977 co-productions were *The Chimes of the Kremlin* by Nikolai Pogodin in 1940 and Iuri Liubimov's adaptation of *Ten Days That Shook the World* adapted from John Reed's 1919 book of the same name.[7] *The Chimes of the Kremlin* is the second play in a trilogy dealing with the life of Lenin and the Bolshevik Revolution; in the play, Lenin and an old Jewish watchmaker repair the Kremlin chimes so that they can play the *Internationale*. The play was the second time that the directors Evgenii Radomyslenski (then rector of the Shkola-studia MKhAT, the theater school attached to the MKhAT) and Miriam Lezcano had worked together with Teatro Político Bertolt Brecht. Their first venture, staged in 1975, was Boris Vasilev's *The Dawns Here Are Quiet*—a tale about a heroic Soviet attack on German paratroopers by five female soldiers and their male senior sergeant, set in Karelia in 1942. In 1977 the same duo directed Nikolai Pogodin's *The Chimes of the Kremlin* again performed by Teatro Político Bertolt Brecht (Anon 1978c). The staging of *The Chimes of the Kremlin* was then repeated by the troupe in 1978 in the Mella Theater for the celebration of Lenin's 108th birthday (Anon 1978b).

Politically these co-productions served a number of purposes: they helped to fill the gap created by the hangover of fear from the *quinquenio gris*, they were a public symbol of friendship between the two countries, and promised not to upset the status-quo, as they were all on "safe" topics—Lenin and, separately, the fight against fascism. Both plays deal with the October Revolution and ideas about international socialist revolution. By staging them in 1977, and linking them to the celebrations of the October Revolution, the Cuban cultural apparatus was able to focus on celebrating the work of the Bolsheviks and Lenin, to emphasize the focus on internationalism, and to underline the emancipatory and inclusive nature of socialism. This meant that Cuban-Soviet solidarity could be celebrated, while more difficult topics that did not perhaps sit so well with the emerging Cuban ideology (such as Stalinism, peaceful coexistence, détente) did not necessarily have to be addressed in a public forum—in Cuba or in the USSR. But they also helped to contribute to the continuing development of a politically committed, genuine Cuban art. This was clearly articulated by Radomyslenskii, in an interview for the general magazine *Bohemia*; Radomyslenskii emphasized that his aim was to create an authentically Cuban spectacle that took the best of the Soviet piece but adapted it to Cuba's circumstances, languages, and daily life (González Freire 1977, 28).

I would therefore argue that these co-productions are demonstrative of the wider desire to create a national culture, with a universal appeal, but also the belief that socialist culture should be "proletarian in its content, national in its form" (Abashin 2011; Stalin 1952). This approach sat neatly with Cuban priorities and was also compatible with different Soviet ideas of Socialist Realism—both traditional and avant-garde.

Radomyslenskii was interviewed by the Russian-language press, along with Aleksandr Okun' who was a Soviet Artist who appears to have also gone to Cuba to spend some time with Teatro Escambray.[8] Radomyslenskii spent over four months in Cuba (Anon, Radomyslenskii, and Okun' 1977, 134). He and Okun' were aided during their stay by Miriam Lescano, who had already studied theater direction in the USSR by the time of the artists' visit (Anon, Radomyslenskii, and Okun 1977, 135). In discussing the work of Teatro Escambray Okun' drew parallels with the ROSTA's living newspapers—in response to the scarcity of paper—and the early revolutionary theatrical experiments that were linked to this: "Artists create original theater posters: sharp, laconic, direct (like in the time of our 'ROSTA WINDOWS,' against enemies of the Revolution)" (Anon, Radomyslenskii, and Okun' 1977, 137).

The flagship of these Soviet productions in Cuba was undoubtedly *Ten Days That Shook the World* staged by Iuri Liubimov at Teatro Estudio. Ten Days was a loose adaptation of the book of the same name by American journalist John Reed, about the October Revolution and his first-hand experience of the event. Liubimov was a deeply influential director in the USSR, responsible for a demonstrable shift in the style of Soviet theatrical production, and *Ten Days That Shook the World*, first staged in 1965, was one of his landmark productions. He shunned "dogmatic" approaches and uniformity of expression, embraced Brecht's ideas of alienation, and disliked the excessive use of props. At the time of his Cuban production, he was facing criticism in the USSR for his style, as were other directors, such as Anatoli Efros (Beumers 1999, 370–380). For unknown reasons, unlike in the other Cuban-Soviet co-productions, Liubimov did not have a Cuban co-director.

Ten Days had been the Taganka Theater's second production and was a loose adaption, incorporating a range of theatrical forms and songs based on works by Brecht, Aleksandr Blok, Fedor Tiutchev, David Samoilov, Nadezhda Maltseva, and Vladimir Vysotskii (Beumers 1997, 25). Additional material had been added such as references to the suffering of those imprisoned during the uprisings, the fall of the Romanovs and thus the tsarist system, speeches from Lenin, the presence of the character of John Reed in the production, and a discussion of the reception of this book in the United States (Beumers 1997, 26). Only two incidents were taken from the book, and the play was divided into two parts (Beumers 1997, 26). In her detailed examination and analysis of the play, Beumers notes that the play's use of theatrical devices was spread evenly between the two opposing forces, so no one device became stereotyped to a particular type of expression (Beumers 1997, 27). The Taganka's stage adaption also included an element of "total art" as it began outside the theater—revolutionary songs were broadcast, Red Guards checked the tickets and then placed them on bayonets. Women wearing red kerchiefs sold the tickets, spectators had red bows pinned on them and banners were pinned around the foyer. Musicians forayed into the auditorium before the performance and eventually led the audience into the auditorium. Finally, the audience was asked to vote for or against the production upon leaving (Beumers 1997, 31). In this way the audience was an integral part of the event. However, it is unclear if the production was reproduced exactly in Cuba. In 1978, the Colombian troupe La Candalaria won the Casa theater prize, with *Ten Days That Shook the World.* The jury which awarded the prize unanimously commented that the work stood out for its thematic importance in the current context of Latin America. Because theatrical values predominate in it, offering excellent possibilities to develop it as a show. For the resulting work rigorous, serious and of a professionalism having understood how to adequately handle the dramatic language (Casañas and Fornet 1999, 117).

In conversation with the Soviet state newspaper *Izvestiia* regarding the celebrations of Soviet culture, Hart confirmed that the sixtieth anniversary co-productions were linked to the PCC's 1976 *Thesis and Resolution* on artistic culture, underscoring their educative potential:

> Both plays were exceptionally warmly received by the audience. We had the opportunity to exchange experiences with the Soviet artists who had come to attend the Days of Culture, and to see for ourselves that forms of cooperation could be much wider than before. We became more deeply acquainted with the cultural policy of the USSR and, based on the decisions of the First Congress of our Party, will do everything to facilitate the Cuban people's wider acquaintance with the remarkable achievements of Soviet art. (Vernikov 1977)

These co-productions therefore fulfilled a number of purposes. They fulfilled an educative and informative role, they demonstrated the power of collective work and they helped the development of Cuban theater. Finally, they adhered to the cultural agreement signed in 1969 that stipulated that cultural work undertaken between the two countries would take place around the 100th anniversary of Lenin's birth, the anniversary of the Cuban Revolution and the Great October Revolution (Anon 1969b).

1976: REDEFINING THE SOVIET-CUBAN RELATIONSHIP AND INSTITUTIONALIZING POST-*QUINQUENIO GRIS*

Fundamental to the idea of collectivity was the effort to institutionalize, and in doing so streamline, the cultural apparatus. The institutionalizing drive of the 1970s drew heavily on the ideas expressed by Che in "El socialismo y el hombre en Cuba":

> All this implies, for its total success, the need for a series of mechanisms, the revolutionary institutions. [. . .] This institutionality of the revolution has not yet been achieved. We seek something new that allows the perfect identification between the government and the community as a whole, adjusted to the particular conditions of the construction of socialism and fleeing to the maximum of the commonplaces of bourgeois democracy, transplanted to the society in formation (Guevara 2006, 58).

In 1976, this drive reached the cultural world with the formation of the Min-Cult, headed by Hart, together with an administrative reform of key cultural institutions (such as ICAIC, Casa and UNEAC), and a reorganization of regional divisions. New theaters opened and a large cohort of professional playwrights was created—including pre-1959 survivors, such as Carlos Felipe and Rolando Ferrer, and newer artists such as Matías Montes Huidobro, José Triana, Manuel Reguera Samuell, José Brene, Arrufat, José Ignacio Gutiérrez, Nicolás Dorr and Héctor Quintera. Despite these new provisions, experimentation in theater remained limited, in part due to the self-censorship associated with the memory of the regulation of previous years (although, during the *quinquenio gris* theatrical experimentation had never disappeared entirely, as groups such as *Los Doce* trialed Jerzy Grotowski's ideas) (Kapcia 2005, 161–62). MinCult sought to encourage artistic experimentation and innovation within theater, as continued creativity was at the core of both the articulation of a revolutionary national identity and "the very essence of socialism" (Martínez Heredia 1991, 21).

In an effort to ensure that training met the demands of professionalized actors and to better coordinate the number of aspiring actors with the spaces available for them in pre-existing groups, a university-level arts school, ISA, which opened in 1976, became part of Mincult's program (Figure 5.1).

Graduation from the ISA guaranteed a career as a professional, once the artist was qualified as such, job security was assured, and promotion

Figure 5.1   Theater School of ISA, Designed by Roberto Gottardi. Photo courtesy of the author.

made possible. By the mid-1980s, there were over fifty groups fully funded by MinCult (Pianca 1989, 521). Martin reports that audience numbers in 1985 had increased by a factor of ten since 1958, from 120,000 a year to 1,239,333 in a country of almost ten and a half million and that the majority of theater goers were between sixteen and thirty years of age (Martin 1994, 162). The number of productions (staged in formal and informal venues) had also increased from 7,121 in 1975 to 9,617 in 1985 (Martin 1994, 162). Moreover, 70 percent of the plays performed were written by Cubans (Martin 1994, 162). It was during this period that a number of Cuban theater students began to pursue funded postgraduate study in the USSR. As with those postgraduate students from the plastic arts, upon returning to Cuba some found themselves unable to complete their social service at ISA due to their perceived "Sovietness," and fears that they would impose the doctrine of high Stalinist socialist realism. In interviews uncorroborated sources suggest that this was particularly true for those who had studied at the State Institute of Theater Arts, (GITIS) in Moscow and exacerbated by erroneous interim reports from Cuban cultural figures visiting the USSR (Anon 2015). Clearly, by the early-mid 1980s ISA was undergoing an anti-Soviet phase. Graziella Pogolotti, the Dean of the theater section at that time, had chosen not to renew the contracts of the Soviet teachers at ISA who had been there since 1980. When discussing the Soviet teachers in interviews it was felt by some that they did not understand the Cuban students, nor the emotional element of theater (Pogolotti 2015). The removal of these Soviet figures was also part of the solution to the ongoing preoccupation that foreign teachers were teaching Cubans to appreciate and propagate foreign theater rather than concentrate on the development of a genuine national theater (Cano 2015).

However, there was still a divide between theater inside and outside Havana and the problem of providing space for new professionals to enter the theatrical market. To this end a new "umbrella" style, like the original concept of socialist realism, was also created: *Teatro Nuevo*. Within this term Teatro Escambray could be incorporated along with other newly-created groups, particularly those that sought to integrate rural or traditionally peripheral audiences. *Teatro Nuevo* "became an active model of utopia for the socialist system itself—a productive and indisputably positive movement to bring theater and art to the most marginalised rural populations in the country" (Martin 1990, 44). This aspect of theater was considered particularly important, as the education of these rural populations was thought to "be the key to uniting the island's population into one cooperative *pueblo*, or national community" (Frederik 2012, 42–49). While this may have had some initial success by the early 1980s, as Martin observes, the groups, which were formed with actors based in Havana, had ceased to exist (Martin 1994, 163).

A further major motive of the decision to further institutionalize culture was greater economic efficiency as the authorities sought to address Cuba's ailing economy and break away from a cycle of dependence. As discussed in chapter 4, cultural production had become tied with economic development, and specifically using Cuba's culture internationally as a means of earning hard currency. The government's commitment to raising Cuba's international cultural capital was reflected in the government's organization of large-scale public events at home, tours abroad, and new foreign co-productions. One such production was with GDR director, Ulf Keyn. Throughout 1979, Keyn toured around the island with Teatro Político Bertolt Brecht performing Alexander Guelman's *El Premio* (EcuRed 2016), *El Premio* was particularly popular in Cuba and frequently appeared in the repertoires of Cuban theater groups; moreover, by this time Keyn was a regular figure in Cuban theater. In 1972 Ulf Keyn had taught the theoretical bases of Brecht's theater—the first time this had been done in Cuba (Quesada 1972, 26). He had also staged *Galileo Galilei* and *La Madre* in 1974 and 1975 respectively at the Teatro Hubert de Blanck (CTDA 2017). Just a month after the inaugural December 1979 Festival del Nuevo Cine, the Festival de Teatro de la Habana was held. The event functioned as a bridge-building exercise, attempting to break down the barrier between the *Teatro Nuevo* movement and other theater groups, and provincial and international theater groups were well represented at the festival (del Pino 2013). The Festival also dealt with the problem of attending cultural festivals in countries unsympathetic to the Revolution, which might aim to mediate Cuba's cultural hegemony in Latin America. Such events included the Second Festival of Popular Latin American Theater (New York 14–23 August 1980) or the First Festival of the Theater in Latin America, organized by Theater of Latin America (TOLA) in June–July 1979 in Washington D.C. and Waterford, Connecticut (Gallardo Saborido 2009, 153). The first Cuban festival had 352 creative collectives apply of which twenty were chosen to participate in the festival, in total thirty-nine pieces were performed (Anon 1981b, 116).

However, despite the conciliatory idea behind the Havana Theater Festival, the First Festival of Teatro Nuevo was held in the same month, clearly competing with the Havana festival. The *Teatro Nuevo* event was held outside the capital, in Villa Clara, between December 9 and 17, 1979, cementing *Teatro Nuevo*'s status as a style that belonged to the countryside and asserting its independence from Havana's theatrical scene. The second Havana Theater Festival was held in January 1982 and attracted over 43,000 spectators showcasing fifty-nine works from twenty-nine different theater collectives (Anon 1982a). The festival saw playwrights, theater collectives, and plastic artists reconsidering the relationship between theatrical language and content (Woodyard 1983, 57). The festivals were then held biannually until 1987, when the combination of developments in Europe and the deterioration of Cuba's economy made the festival an impossibility (del Pino 2013).

As in the plastic arts in the 1980s, and invariably in part due to the economically driven reassessment of Cuban culture, there was a turn toward analyzing the culture produced in the Revolution. By the 1980s, Cuba's economy was still struggling and subsequent experimentations with market mechanisms were felt within theater, which was now viewed as a potentially exportable commodity. Toward the middle of the decade, a system for increasing the productivity of theater groups was created, which pegged salaries to the number of performances an actor gave each month (Manzor-Coats and Martiatu Terry 1995, 46). Prior to this, a survey had been conducted on the productivity of the main theater groups in Havana. The survey concluded that the existing quotas which had "apparently" been copied from the USSR were unattainably high and suggested alternatives (Sánchez León 1985, 46).

The focus in theater moved toward consolidating the quality of existing theatrical groups and opening up opportunities to individuals without university training. A new funding system, *proyectos*, was intended to address the criticism that innovation was stifled when young energy was channeled exclusively into existing groups without the prospect of building on new ideas encountered during training at the ISA. These *proyectos* would also allow for the formation of projects by actors without university preparation. They would not curtail funding for existing groups but rather aimed to make these groups more receptive to the use of their resources (Layera 1983, 42). This decentralizing approach did not eliminate the need for planning altogether, but shifted the emphasis from building theatrical institutions to making the resources for creating theater available (Martin 1990, 45). The national budget of eleven million pesos from 1980 to 1985 supported twenty-five permanent theater houses, eight open-air theaters, twenty-four cultural centers, two schools of art and a school of ballet (Martin 1990, 56). Martin notes that, despite the limitations placed on theater and cultural mobilization in the late 1980s due to economic restrictions, more Cubans attended theatrical events than in the early 1980s when these economic problems were not so pronounced (Martin 1994). This suggests the crisis in theater in the 1980s was more related to perceived opportunities and creative possibilities than purely economic concerns.

Possibly in response to the crisis in theater, *Tablas*, a quarterly theater magazine, was founded in 1982. The publication, which discussed the problems and possibilities of contemporary Cuban theater, was edited by the Centre for Research and Development of the Scenic Arts, and led by critic and writer Rosa Ileana Boudet and edited by Juan Carlos Martínez. Within the cultural arena attempts were also made to identify emerging trends and

new directions. Between July 19 and 22, 1981, Casa hosted the Meeting of
Theatre Workers in Latin America and the Caribbean (Salado 1981; Anon
1981a). In February 1983 the First Nuevo Teatro International Workshop
was held (Elvira Peláez 1983). The following month, *Tablas* held a round-
table analyzing Cuban theater during the Revolution, and in 1984—Via
Telex—a new critical section was created. Other academic works, such as
Ileana Azor's Origin and Presence of Theater in Nuestra America (1988)
highlighted theater's responsivity to politics. Particular styles, such as *Bufo*,
were also reassessed and their particularly valued characteristics (close links
to the *pueblo* and their capacity to assimilate) were highlighted. *Bufo* was
hailed as a clear example of the assimilation of a foreign culture and its subsequent re-elaboration into something distinctly national. It was also part of a
wider Latin American movement of assimilation of European culture. *Bufo*,
and specifically its acting style, was also highlighted for the way in which the
actors "developed a capacity for improvisation and for establishing a dialogue
with the public which is the root of their popularity" (Vázquez Pérez 1984,
5). Sociological studies were also conducted trying to establish the ten best
puestas en escena (Sala Santos and Sánchez Leon 1986) and analyze the
productivity of theater.

The Revolution's internationalist nature was explored both within and without Cuba. In 1982, Teatro Escambray, the theater group which had come to
embody revolutionary Cuban theater, toured the United States (Acosta 1982).
Within Cuba, the country's links with other socialist countries, particularly
the RDA, were explored, with a co-production between the RDA and Cuba
in 1983, *Humboldt y Bolívar* by Claus Hammel which was directed by Hanns
Perten and Mario Balmaseda of the Volks theater Rostock and Teatro Político
Bertolt Brecht, respectively. Two more co-productions were also done with
the USSR (Teatro Obrazstov and the Lenin Komsomol theater group) in
addition to Cuban participation in international socialist theater events in
Czechoslovakia and Hungry (MinCult 1983, 48). Hammel, president of the
Dramatic Arts Section of the GDR's Writers' Union, reported that he had
had the idea of writing a piece that would link the GDR and Latin America
back in 1964, when he first came to Cuba, but had not written the piece until
1976, when he undertook a new tour around the Latin American continent,
which included stops in Venezuela, Mexico, and Cuba (Espinosa Domínguez
1983, 37). In *Humboldt y Bolívar*, Hammel explored the relationship between
Simón Bolívar, the leading figure in the Latin American independence movement, and Alexander Von Humboldt, the Prussian geographer, explorer, and
naturalist. Humboldt is often credited as the "second discoverer" of Cuba due
to the detailed anthropological texts he produced about Cuba (Figures 5.2
and 5.3). However, in *Humboldt y Bolívar* Humboldt is presented not as a
conquistador, but instead as a "friend" (Espinosa Domínguez 1983, 38). The

Figure 5.2 Statue to Alexander Von Humboldt in the University of Havana. Photo courtesy of the author.

play highlighted the contrast between Humboldt, a humanist scientist who does not consider himself a man of action, and Bolívar, patriotic, transformative politician who is a man of action (Espinosa Domínguez 1983, 38). The

Figure 5.3 Statue to Alexander Von Humboldt, Describing Him as the Second Discoverer of Cuba, Outside Humboldt University in Berlin. Photo courtesy of the author.

play did this by focusing on the reported meetings of Humboldt and Bolívar in the early nineteenth century (Hammel 1983, 43). The work also explored themes of solidarity and internationalism (Espinosa Domínguez 1983, 38).

The entirety of the script was reproduced in *Conjunto*, and the play ends with the liberators of Latin America joining Bolívar on stage as Humboldt leaves (Hammel 1983, 43–104). Thus, Latin America is united once more in its fight for liberation and homage is paid to the enduring and central nature of the *pueblo*:

Bolívar: ¡Humboldt!—!Humboldt!—¡Humboldt! *(From the burning rain of ashes that springs from the volcano emerge the liberators of Latin America. Bolívar is joined by Miranda, San Martín, O'Higgins, Artigas, Hidalgo, Morelos, Martí, Pancho Villa, Zapata, Sandino, Che Guevara, Allende, peasants, workers and soldiers of the people. White, Black and Indian. Also Bonpland, Montúfar, and Rodríguez. Also the Student and the Unknown Woman.)*

Unknown Woman: By a lake
Rugged
Perilous path
Of crossroads and despair
Under many flags
With rags hanging
Dressed in uniforms
Armed with sticks
Pitchforks and submachine guns
Barefoot
In espadrilles and boots
It is moving
Despite the setbacks
Uncontainable
Hopeful
Immortal
The *pueblo*
(Hammel 1983, 104).

Theater and Nation Building

As this chapter has explored, the trajectory and treatment of theater in revolutionary Cuba reveals the centrality of the idea of a coherent national identity for the Revolution, and the power attributed to culture, particularly participatory culture, in the synthesis and articulation of said identity. One of Cuba's most durable national pastimes has proved to be the "textual reflection on the contours of collective identity" (Fay 2012, 13–14). Theater's discursive nature made it ideally suited to helping to articulate, refine, and combine concepts of national narrative and identity. As a result, theater was one of the first cultural forms to visibly respond to the Revolution, was greatly encouraged, and was quickly subsumed into the emerging cultural apparatus. However, theater's mobilizing and participatory potential also meant that, as differences between cultural practitioners became increasingly pronounced, it was viewed with mounting suspicion, particularly as a clearly revolutionary form in such a responsive artistic form failed to arise. As ideas of hypermacho behavior and nationalism became more pronounced this further contributed to greater regulation and the privileging of certain types of theater.

The approach toward theater taken by the CNC and then MinCult also reveals the depth of the initial rift between (wo)men of action (*guerrilleros*) and (wo)men of words ("traditional" intellectuals) and the eventual economic impetus that ultimately led to the reconciliation of the two sides. As Cuba's cultural practitioners attempted to reconcile a colonial past with the development of an indigenous, revolutionary culture, questions of collectivity, and participation were raised. A fissure formed between groups with different attitudes toward foreign cultures. On one side of the rift were the "professionals" who had links to culture prior to the Revolution which, given Cuba's increasing isolation, suggested potentially skewed political alliances. On the other side were the individuals who had begun their creative work in the *aficionado* movement or within the Revolution's cultural framework and therefore had an unquestionable commitment to the Revolution, even if they used imported cultural forms. This opposition between the perceived sectarian tendencies of early professionals of theater and the more collective approaches of amateurs was also deeply rooted in the articulation of a national narrative, and therefore, affected by the ever-present concept of "history."

Fay has argued that history, its explanation of Cuba's past humiliations and failings, and its insights into the essence of Cuban identity and Cuba's future, "became the ontogenetic key" to the synthesis of a coherent revolutionary national identity (Fay 2012, 11). I would argue that within theater, the conflicts engendered by the codes of *cubanía* were most prevalent in the division between professionals and amateurs, or what García Canclini terms as the "art versus crafts" dichotomy.

The oppositions between the cultured and the popular and between the modern and the traditional are condensed in the distinction established by modern aesthetics between art and crafts [. . .] Art corresponds to the interests and tastes of the bourgeoisie and cultivated sectors of the petit bourgeoisie; it is developed in cities, speaks of them, and when it represents landscapes from the countryside it does so with an urban perspective [. . .] Crafts, on the other hand, are seen as products of Indians and peasants in accord with their rusticity, the myths that inhabit their decoration, and the popular sectors that traditionally make and use them. (García Canclini 1995, 173)

However, as the codes of internationalism gained increasing currency within Cuba, and the synthesis of its national identity, "art's" assumed affinities and grounding in the global, capitalist, Eurocentric market came to be seen as a means of pursuing a national cultural "self-sufficiency." Artistic forms that had previously implied an allegiance to this economic structure, could, as with Antonio Larreta's *Juan Palmierei*, be expropriated and reconfigured to a more appropriate cultural, artisan, and historical setting in the fight against cultural dependency, be that on the global capitalist market, or the reigning socialist superpower. This economic impetus helped to reconcile the professional and amateur theatrical movements and channel them into the continued development of the Revolution, and the fight for Cuba's autonomy.

Regarding the "Soviet" presence in Cuban revolutionary theater, from 1965 onward the overlap of different cultural approaches from different periods of Soviet development and the cultural practices of Cuba began to become apparent. As discussed in chapter 2, debate was inherent to the emergent doctrine of socialist realism and the years leading up to the 1934 meeting, where the name began to be used as an umbrella phrase. These polemics were among different cultural groups regarding the best path for the creation of a revolutionary culture and what to do with pre-revolutionary culture. Generally these polemics were grouped around literary journals associated with different movements such as *Krasnaia nov'* (Red virgin soil), *LEF* and *Na postu* (The post), which all sought to be the organizing center of Russian literature (Maguire 1968, 155–57).

For example, on one hand there was the implementation of practices that would appear to run closer to one strand of thinking on the debates regarding the fostering and implementation of a culture that was both socialist and realist of the first two decades of the Russian Revolution. The USSR at the tail end of the Thaw was characterized by a series of shifting open spaces and was seeing a revival of the practices and preoccupations of the early Soviet avant-garde as part of a conscious effort by cultural practitioners to broaden the term "socialist realist" into something that was multi-faceted and encompassed a range of styles (and genres), as long as its core principles were revolutionary (Gardiner 2014; Jones 2006; Beumers 1999; Clark 2000). The social and cultural mobilization campaigns of Khrushchev's administration were modeled on those of the 1930s and were implemented as part of a drive to recapture the energy and faith of the younger generations (Stites 1992, 144). Some of these campaigns used the Cuban Revolution as a source of inspiration both implicitly and explicitly (Gorsuch 2015, 505–06). Concurrently, key figures in Cuba's cultural arena were seeking to establish a cultural system that was broadly inclusive and encouraging of many different currents and approaches.

However, as Cuban-Soviet relations began to deteriorate, the direction of the Revolution began to shift toward intense radicalization (Kapcia 2005, 121). Subsequently, practices that seemed to have parallels with the cultural policy of the USSR more contemporaneous to revolutionary Cuba began to emerge. In the same month that the PCC was founded, there was a more overt linking of theater to ideas of communism with a training course inspired by Bertolt Brecht's methods and theory (Grutter 1965, 16). New theater groups sought to relate culture to the reality of the revolution and to make culture more inclusive. The Conjunto de Arte Teatral "La Rueda," focused on the need to make productions from periods that potentially had little resonance with contemporary Cuban life more applicable (Hurtado 1966, 76). Meanwhile, Taller Dramático searched for an appropriate form of national expression in a number of ways, through the updating of foreign works; though paying particular attention to Cuban authors; and through commitment to experimentation that was ever closer to the needs of the people and the revolutionary objectives (González Freire 1966b, 33). As the Cuban Revolution moved toward clearer definition, a more regulatory current began to emerge. This was in part linked to the unexpected death of Che and persistent economic problems which gave rise to the desire to gain some form of economic independence and the ascendency of more orthodox ideas. These practices include privileging of certain topics and styles through the introduction of prizes, which provided concrete guidance to Cuban playwrights, who might be eager to seek out "safe ground" amid increasing hostility.[9] The continued dominance of Brechtian models and the emphasis on work with an explicit revolutionary bent could also be interpreted as reminiscent of the priorities of Soviet theater in the 1950s (Gardiner 2015).

These tendencies, however, can also be read as a reflection of the shifting preoccupations of the Cuban government, and I would argue that they resonate with the preoccupations of the Soviet avant-garde, in particular the ideas shared by *Proletkul't* and *LEF* that art should organize the psyche of the masses, that the artist was an individual within a collective and that art should be directly relevant to daily life (Maguire 1968, 153–85). For example Brecht, while aesthetically problematic in the USSR, was known for his stance against American imperialism, a fact that was highlighted in the Soviet press surrounding his receipt of the Stalin Prize in 1954 (Gardiner 2014). A focus on clear revolutionary commitment, the importance of participation and collective work, and the role of *aficionados* can also be interpreted as symptomatic of the Cuban government's wider interest in, and affiliation with, Latin America as the Cuban government sought to move away from traditional (colonial) cultural poles. One manifestation of this increased Latin-American focus was in the popularity of *Teatro Nuevo*, embodied in Cuba by Teatro Escambray, a popular form in Latin America and particularly

Colombia, which enabled collective creation and popular participation (Padura Fuentes, Kirk, and Estorino 2002, 122).

By the early 1970s it would seem that, as Damaris Puñales-Alpizar argues (2012), one particular approach to realist, socialist art—that of high socialist realism—had gained ascendency in Cuba as culture became more increasingly regulated and seemed to move closer to the narrow interpretation of socialist realist art. However, I argue that cultural practices had become complicated because the discursive atmosphere which had characterized the 1960s had ended with the privileging of certain production styles. Despite this, the preoccupation with supporting and developing different forms of art that was both socialist and also realist (in the sense that it related to the everyday reality of the average revolutionary Cuban) continued. A particularly bellicose expression of nationalism, which in turn gave rise to hypermacho ideas (as explored earlier) further complicated matters.

The drive to foster an art that was simultaneously socialist and realist, but not "socialist realism" became clearer after the 1975 First Congress of the PCC when it was made abundantly clear that the art of the Cuban Revolution needed to assimilate the best traditions of national culture, appropriate criticism, develop a universal culture and use the most varied and creative forms of expression to fully reflect the world the population lived in (Anon 1975c: 25).

Ultimately, periods of liberalization in the USSR, when, as discussed in chapter 2, some sectors of the cultural world were striving to make socialist realism into something more open and inclusive, converge with open processes of debate in Cuba. Within theater, the adoption of models that would seem to look to the Soviet experience became more pronounced as the political course of the Revolution became clearer from 1965 onwards and moved definitively toward socialism. As Cuba's relationship with the USSR developed and the Cuban government increasingly sought independence the emphasis in culture began to shift, bringing with it different aims and forms of expression. While on the surface it may seem that the 1970s, and in particular 1971 to 1975, brought an approach that was distinctly Soviet, it actually reveals a deeper preoccupation with the development of a national socialist culture that sought to incorporate as many practitioners and styles as possible while maintaining a clear political and social goal. This is more evident in the late 1970s when Cuban and Soviet cultural authorities undertook a number of theatrical co-productions of classic revolutionary plays, seeking to relate them to Cuban reality. Underlying preoccupations of cultural programs and productions suggest that there was a real desire for a national art that was socialist and realist, suggesting that there could have been socialist realism in Cuba, but not in the sense that the term socialist realism—denoting the Stalinist variant—is popularly understood in Cuba or outside of academic circles.

This variant, or variants, allowed Cuba to reassert its independence and vie for leadership of the international socialist movement.

NOTES

1. Ground zero because it had the least "ruins" from Cuba's colonial and neo-colonial history—little had been developed that was clearly Cuban during this period, leaving the form clear for relatively uncontaminated theatrical experimentation within the Revolution.

2. Camagüey had a long tradition of theater: in the early nineteenth century theaters had been founded in Puerto Príncipe, and also in the province of Santiago de Cuba (Matas 1971, 428).

3. For example the playwright, Abelardo Estorino joined Teatro Estudio in 1960 and was contracted by the government as a professional writer in 1961 (Martin 1990, 42).

4. Tunberg (1970, 44) argues that by summer 1969, Havana boasted thirty, largely homogenous, professional theater groups, compared to the six that there had been in 1958.

5. One casualty of the period was the playwright Virgilio Piñera, who fell from grace during the *quinquenio* because of his open homosexuality (Martin 1990, 54).

6. Between the beginning of the Casa de las Américas system of prizes and the break-up of the USSR there were only seven Soviet judges, many of whom were frequent contributors to the Soviet journal *Latinskaia Amerika*. They were; Pavel Grushko (Poetry prize, 1973), Vera Kuteischikova (Artistic-literary essay prize, 1979), Valentina Schiskina (Historical-social essay prize, 1980), Inna Terterian (Story prize, 1978), Venedicto Vinogradov (Essay prize, 1975), Victor Volsky (Essay prize and also extraordinary prize for Bolivar in Our America, both 1977), and finally Valeri Zemskov (Artistic-literary prize, 1987) (Casañas and Fornet 1999). The only Eastern European or Soviet individual to judge a theater competition was María Sten, from Poland for the 1978 award (Casañas and Fornet 1999, 117).

7. Iuri Liubimov and Jan Kopecky had been present at the 1966 Theater Festival which ran from 21 November until 5 December 1966. The Festival coincided with the II Encuento de Teatristas, a theoretical and practical event that brought together 29 delegates from 19 countries over four continents. The countries were Spain, France, UK, UEA, USSR, Italy, Czechoslovakia, RDA, Vietnam, Argentina, Mexico, Chile, Peru, Uruguay, Venezuela, Colombia, Brazil, and Cuba (Beltrán 1967, 166).

8. Aleksandr Okun' exhibited in the Klutchnick Museum and the Kipniger Gallery both in Washington, D.C, and the Skirball Museum in Los Angeles in 1977. Okun' appears to have been heavily involved in the Leningrad underground art scene and emigrated to Israel in 1979 (Okun' 2017).

9. It was not actually until 1967 that an award was actually given for a theatrical work—René Ariza won the prize with his piece *La vuelta a la manzana* (Anon 1967a, 6).

Chapter 6

Adelante el arte

The Plastic Arts in Cuba

The inherent discursive nature of the plastic arts meant that they were able to continually push the bounds of interpretations of cultural policy in a way that theater could not. As a result, the plastic arts, and their new forms that emerged, occupied a special position, acting as a sounding board for the country's cultural policy both inside the Revolution through a process of cultural democratization, and in fighting internal and external colonialism. This was because the form proved particularly adept at generating mobility in Cuban society, both within the confines of the expressly political, but also in the everyday realities (Weiss 2011b, xiv). However, as priorities changed within the Revolution, the roles assigned to the plastic arts began to diverge. This led to the tactical adoption and promotion, or rejection, of certain tendencies by different groups, leading to what could be termed multiple socialist realisms. This was, arguably, further complicated by the self-reflexive nature of the plastic arts, which saw the selective assimilation and re-elaboration of trends that were open to numerous interpretations. A particularly clear example of this can be found in the emergence of the photorealism movement, which seemed to parody both US hyperrealism and the socialist realism of the 1940s simultaneously. Ultimately the discursiveness of the plastic arts led to the development of a distinctively Cuban approach to art, which helped to assert Cuba's independence while maintaining its socialist credentials.

PRE-REVOLUTIONARY PLASTIC ARTS

Prior to the 1959 rebellion, the plastic arts in Cuba already had an established international reputation thanks to artists such as Amelia Peláez, Wilfredo Lam, Mariano (Rodríguez), Mario Carreño, and René Portocarrero. This

143

reputation was built on these artists' expressive reflections, within an international framework, on their country's rich and complex history and the imprints each of its cultures had left in the national imaginary. Thus the plastic arts were always linked with independence struggles and underdevelopment but also remained connected to Western modernism (Camnitzer 2003, 4). This "connectivity" contributed to the artistic form's global promotion as the Revolution's flagship cultural output by the revolutionary cultural authorities. The assimilation of multiple trends ensured a balance of the national and international, which made the plastic arts particularly exportable. The plastic arts in the second half of the twentieth century were thus inherently suited to the internationalist aspirations of the Cuban revolution and this quality was at the heart of the form's development and promotion. Due to the notably diverse historical influx of cultural and ideological influences in the country, artists had a wide heritage upon which to draw.

A distinctly Cuban approach to the plastic arts was consolidated during the period 1930 to 1959, in which insurrectional struggles were also evolving. Two distinct characteristics developed during this period: political/social commitment and a belief in the power of art. These elements had begun with the cultural magazines *Revista de Avance* and *Orígenes* and had been continued by the work of cultural societies such as Nuestro Tiempo. In 1927 the *Revista de Avance* sponsored an exhibition which aimed to "place Cuban art in the context of the new European modernist trends without giving up [its] identity" (Camnitzer 2003, 103). The *Exposición de Arte Nuevo* was accompanied by a manifesto to this effect, seeking to walk the line between nationalism and internationalism (Camnitzer 2003, 103). *Orígenes*, the successor to *Revista de Avance*, also fostered a close relationship between art and literature. *Orígenes* was particularly significant for its artistic covers, a position that *Casa de las Américas* would come to occupy thanks to the work of Umberto Peña. At the time of its publication, *Orígenes's* cover designers were not usually artists; however, the artist Mariano who formed part of the publication's editorial team during the time Lezama Lima played a central role in the magazine was very involved in the publication's visual presentation (de Juan 2007, 139). National and international artists from across the generations contributed to the magazine's covers, and art from the group became notably more Latin Americanist (Camnitzer 2003, 107).

Thus from an early stage the plastic arts were imbued with a strong sense of moral duty and a belief in their transformative abilities. The form's commitment to, and engagement with, politics and the various trends that had left their imprint on the cultural imaginary, contributed to a wide range of aesthetic styles and personal understandings of the "common good." As already seen in chapters 3, 4, and 5 these different stances generally sat neatly within the loose framework of ideas provided by the Revolution in seminal speeches and congresses which demarcated the (outer) boundaries within cultural policy.

By 1959, artistic education had been well established in Cuba for over a century. The Escuela de San Alejandro, which followed the French-Italian school of teaching (focusing on realism and technical mastery), was created in 1817, receiving official recognition the following year (de Juan 1968, 65). The French painter Juan Bautista Vermay, who had decorated the interior of the Templete in Habana Vieja, was the founder (de Juan 1968, 48). In her book *Introducción a Cuba, las artes plasticas,* de Juan stressed that unlike other foreign artists in Cuba, Vermay adapted to the country's mixed atmosphere, but that neither he nor the subsequent directors of the Escuela "knew how to capture the atmosphere of *cubanidad,* naive if you like, that the engravers and popular painters showed" (de Juan 1968, 64). The Escuela offered classes principally in drawing, due to the lack of appropriate materials for other techniques. The first Cuban director, Alejandro Melero, took up the role in 1878 but kept the curriculum focused on the French school, which concentrated on historical paintings and drawings. Melero did introduce access for female students (Camnitzer 2003, 153), thereby helping to break down gendered perceptions of artists. Students of the Escuela included Wilfredo Lam, Amelia Peláez, and René Portocarrero.

In spite of the Escuela's ground-breaking role in the establishment of the plastic arts in Cuba, not all students felt that the tuition allowed them sufficient means of self-expression. Camnitzer comments that the Escuela principally educated through a "negative process," causing students who were uninspired by the methods or focuses of the school to seek alternative, more experimental, spaces, that reflected the creativity, internationalism, and experimentation of the post-war Paris School. One such institution was the Asociación de Pintores y Escultores, founded in 1915 (Camnitzer 2003, 153). Other attempts included following the Mexican Revolution's models, and, on the initiative of the Spanish painter Gabriel García Maroto, creating open-air schools in rural Cuba (Camnitzer 2003, 154).[1] In 1930 the Asociación de Pintores y Escultores was merged with the Club Cubano de Bellas Artes to form the Círculo de Bellas Artes. The Círculo was divided into sections: literature, painting, music, sculpture, and architecture, with later additions of graphic arts (1935), sumptuary art (metalwork), scenic arts (both 1945), and printmaking (1954). The Círculo held regular events with the aim of promoting the development of the plastic arts, and these events included the *Salón Anual de Bellas Artes.* Concurrently, the Escuela Libre de Artes Plásticas, which later became the Estudio Libre, was created by Eduardo Abela in 1936. The Estudio Libre remained operational until

1967, under the new name of the Taller de Artes Plásticas Camilo Cienfuegos (Anon 1980a, 215). The Estudio Libre did not charge for tuition
and was inundated with applications. Moreover, as San Alejandro forbade
its staff from participating in the events of the new institution, Abela used
young artists who worked outside of San Alejandro, such as Portocarrero
and Mariano Rodríguez as a guiding staff (Camnitzer 2003, 155). A more
subtle and lasting result of this early promotion of newer artists was the
demonstration of the power and value of youth through the popularity and
success of the project.

Pogolotti considers that the divisions between the artistic establishment and the newcomers went far deeper than the transformation, under
the influence of the Paris School, of the Cuban artistic idiom. Instead, she
suggests that the transformation of artistic language and political struggle
were elements in the wider project to modernize Cuban society. The intelligentsia was united in the design of Cuban nationhood and, reform of the
plastic arts aside, the vanguard never had any explicit program (Pogolotti
1997, 171–172). This unity, even if superficial, set the plastic arts aside
from other modes of artistic expression, and Kapcia notes that, unlike literature, in the fine arts the "*vanguardismo*, political commitment and the
search for *lo Cubano* fused easily, continuing patterns evident from the
1920s" (2005, 99–100). The generation that emerged in the 1920s, which
began to demonstrate the trends Kapcia mentions, including names such
as Víctor Manuel, Carlos Enríquez, and Eduardo Abela, belonged to the
Asociación de Pintores y Escultores and was staunchly defended by the
Revista de Avance. De Juan (2007, 132–133) considers that this generation posited a new way of seeing Cuba, of accurately reflecting Cuban life,
rejected the art of the Academy and focused on assimilating contemporary
trends. The following generation, that of the 1930s, continued the search
for national values, but did so in a more private manner, in part due to
the political circumstances of the time (de Juan 2007, 134). On the global
stage, the French, and US Schools of art had begun the internationaliza-
tion of informalism (*art informel*), and this had been further bolstered by
the high prices that artworks could command in the post-WW2 market (de
Juan 2007, 132). New York had become the center of the art trade and was
also a hotbed of cultural activism. Moreover, Latin American artists, lacking national art scenes, were attracted to New York and the opportunities
to sell their work presented by US organizations, such as Pan-American
Union, the agency of the Organization of American States (de Juan 2007,
132). Once Batista gained power in the 1952 coup, the search for traditional, national elements lost its significance, and abstractionism became a
way to either resist or opt out of the Batista regime (de Juan 2007, 134–35).

Thus, by the 1950s, art had become clearly politicized and artists had played an active role in political resistance in Cuba. A group that was of particular cultural and political importance during this period was Nuestro Tiempo. This society was initially formed, without a clearly defined political aim, by musicians from the Amadeo Roldán (Municipal) Conservatory. Nuestro Tiempo swiftly attracted attention from other culturally engaged individuals from the musical world, and it was decided by its founders that it should become a society that was concerned with the diffusion of art that was more Cuban (*del pueblo*)—a society with a mass involvement but within an element of exclusivity, based on quality and talent (Gramatges 2002, 282). Although the group was created in 1951, its president, Harold Gramatges, considered the real beginning of the group to be the exhibition it held of the work of twenty contemporary Cuban artists in the society's headquarters, in Calle Reina 314—previously the base of the PSP-run Radio Emisora 1010 (Gramatges 2002, 286). Nuestro Tiempo was not radical; it was interested in quality, was particularly committed to plastic arts and film, was pro-independence, anti-imperialist, anti-cosmopolitanist, and universalist (Hernández Otero 2002, 286; Gordon-Nesbitt 2015, 42). The Cuban artistic avant-garde was close to the political avant-garde, the two linked by their rejection of established values and their rebellion against situations they found intolerable (de Juan 2007, 133). Thus, some members of the society were also members of the PSP such as Nicolás Guillén, Mirta Aguirre, Carlos Rafael Rodríguez, and José Antonio Portuondo. PSP members in charge of ideology and cultural questions showed particular interest in the society and it was Luis Más Martín, the director of Radio Rebelde, who suggested to the society that they should undertake all their activities with a clearly defined political purpose (Gramatges 2002, 282). In 1953 Nuestro Tiempo was restructured and filmmakers took a prominent role; from the end of that year, the link with the PSP deepened. The PSP's Comisión del Trabajo Intelectual moved to occupy a building on Calle 23, and the corner of four in Vedado, where it also established a permanent art gallery in which works could be exhibited and sold (Gramatges 2002, 294). De Juan also considers 1953 to be a milestone year for two reasons. First, it "marked the opening of a cycle of impoverishment of Cuban art" (de Juan 2007, 138) secondly, it was the "only instance of a coming together of artists in order to confront an official imposition" (de Juan 2007, 138). This coming together began with the first exhibition of a group known as Los Once (the eleven). De Juan (2007, 137) argues that the group's name was abstractly symbolic as there were rarely eleven participants in their exhibitions.

The search for *lo cubano* had thus not ended but had begun to move in a different direction, and Los Once "rejected *tropicalismo* in favour of a more-internationalised abstraction" (Weiss 2011b, 3–4). Los Once's style has been classified as generation specific and therefore reflective of the generational shift occurring at this time—the group had all been born around 1930, coinciding with the beginning of abstractionism. Their work was characterized by the production of pieces that had no reference to the surrounding world, i.e. contemporary Cuban reality—and its artists actively rejected government initiatives aimed at producing an official culture (de Juan 1968, 93).

Throughout the 1950s the visual and plastic arts continued to be sites of resistance and dissidence. In 1954 Los Once organized an Anti-Biennial in protest against the promotion of the Franco-sponsored Spanish-American Art Biennial, which was to be held in the National Museum of Fine Arts (Mueso Nacional de Bellas Artes, MNBA) to project art as an activity that the Batista administration promoted and fostered. Sculptors, painters, and ceramicists participated in the Anti-Biennial, actively boycotting the official Biennial and organizing an activity to run in parallel (de Juan 2007, 135–136). The Anti-Biennial was held in January 1954, in the cities of Havana, Santiago de Cuba, and Camagüey. It ended in the First Festival of Contemporary Cuban Art, which had been organized by the Federation of University Students (FEU). De Juan notes that the aesthetic rebelliousness of the event was limited to new ways of seeing, rather than the incorporation of themes that directly addressed the national crisis (de Juan 2007, 136–37). Los Once then boycotted an event held in Venezuela under the authoritarian Pérez Jiménez regime, and finally dissolved itself in 1955, hoping to avoid retaliation from the Batista administration. In 1957, they resurrected the group and protested against Batista and his planned "Salón Nacional."

Aesthetically, by 1959 the visual and plastic arts in Cuba had a well-established range of surrealist, expressionist, abstract, and figurative styles (de Juan 1968, 94–95). As discussed, they also had a clear tradition of political engagement and activism, coupled with national and international aspirations. The groups, societies, and movements of the 1920s through to the 1950s prefigured many of the Revolution's subsequent aims and values: the democratization of culture (Anon 1989), education of the population to create an informed audience (Linares et al. 1989), development of a national culture and identity (Hernández Otero 2002), art and culture's engagement with society, and the creative power and value of youth.

MAKING THE DIFFICULTIES A VIRTUE

After 1959 the relationship between artists and the public fundamentally changed. Traditional elitist concepts of art and artists were dismantled and culture occupied a central role in the rebuilding of the nation. The plastic arts, and their new forms of expression that emerged within the Revolution, would prove consistently able to respond to and grow with the difficulties faced by revolutionary Cuba. ICAIC and Casa became important promoters of the plastic arts and sites of artistic innovation. Under their auspices established forms of artistic expression thrived and new forms of production emerged, such as graphic design and particularly ICAIC's specific approach toward the film poster, which dismantled the traditions of the Hollywood film poster (Chanan 1985, 133). These two institutions championed cultural dialog with other countries and also within Cuba (de Juan 2011, 197). Indeed, UNEAC's Artes Plásticas section was under the leadership of Mariano Rodríguez (de Juan 2011, 197) until 1963 when he went to work at Casa de las Américas, becoming vice-president of the institution in 1970. However, progress in the plastic arts was not limited solely to Casa and ICAIC. The MNBA also experienced a renaissance, and many exhibition galleries—temporary and permanent—were established in the capital and across the country (de Juan 2011, 197).

During this early revolutionary period, the wider population became increasingly involved in culture. This was done though the establishment of initiatives to encourage amateur involvement in culture more generally, along with movements related to specific artistic forms, such as the mobile cinema initiative or the *escuela de brigadistas de artes plásticas*. Culture, and the plastic arts in particular, was rapidly mobilized for international dissemination. On May 20, 1962 an exhibition of twenty-four Cuban painters (and members of UNEAC), organized by Pogolotti, Servando Cabrera Moreno and Raúl Oliva, opened in Prague. It then moved on to seven other socialist countries, "in accordance with cultural agreements signed between the CNC and the Ministries of Culture of the respective countries" (Pogolotti 1962, 16).[2]

Servando Cabrera Moreno was quickly hailed as an artist who had excelled in responding to the Revolution and reflecting the new reality of the country.[3] His cycle of *campesinos y milicianos* attracted particular praise for the "epic conception" given to the way the figures were sculpted and the mural-style nature of the compositions (Catá 1962, 165). In 1962 the CNC held an exhibition of Cabrera Moreno's work in the Palacio de Bellas Artes. *Unión* described the exhibition as dealing with the themes of the Revolution and celebrated Cabrera Moreno's high-quality contribution to Cuban art, citing the national character present in his work that was helping to build the new Cuba (de la Torriente 1962, 150). In the same issue of *Unión* Edmundo Desnoes reflected on the importance and value of the plastic arts in raising consciousness through ensuring a healthy, questioning relationship with reality (Desnoes 1962, 152).

At the same time as established Cuban plastic artists were being promoted abroad and at home, the art education system was being revised in 1962 (and would be again in 1974). Construction of the flagship ENA began in the appropriated site of the former elite country club, Cubanacán, in a very public display of the revolutionary government's commitment to the democratization of culture. Work began on the school in 1962, and classes started immediately, even before the renovations were complete. However, the school, in a still incomplete state, was not formally inaugurated until 1965 on the symbolic date of July 26. By then the political climate in Cuba, and the public view of art, had begun to change (Loomis 1999, 35). Loomis, in his history of this ambitious project, argues that the purpose of Cubanacán was to train artists from Latin America and the Third World in order to give socialism its aesthetic representation, and that its architecture was to be as innovative as the idea behind the school (Loomis 1999, 19–20). Loomis views the changing attitude toward the ENA as analogous to the period of Soviet history when society began to move away from the architectural and cultural experimentation of the first years of Soviet power to the repression of the avant-garde under Stalin. He locates this tendency within the wider international move toward industrialized systems (such as prefabricated housing systems) which also implied a criticism of traditional systems (Loomis 1999, 118). Loomis also suggests that the ENA's architectural homage to Cuba's African roots—arguably most evident in Ricardo Porro's design—was another significant reason for their criticism, reflective of the contradictory cultural and political policy of the Cuban Revolution (Loomis 1999, 120–21). Porro based his design for the School of Plastic Arts—the most visible of all the schools—on a "typical" African village and addressed issues of gender by combining elements of Spanish patriarchal and African matriarchal cultural expressions. He incorporated domed cupolas, using a Catalan vault technique that allowed architects and builders to overcome the limitations placed on them by the US embargo and take advantage of the naturally occurring local terracotta. A journey from the building's entrance led to a main plaza in which a papaya-shaped fountain, a fruit with a strong female sexual connotation in Cuba, is fed by drains resembling limp phalluses (Loomis 1999, 56–69) (Figure 6.1).

Before the ENA was founded, prominent Cuban artists had tended to be absent from the classrooms, limiting their influence on the younger, emerging generations. However, this changed as the ENA tried to bring practices from Abela's Estudio Libre and the Bauhaus into the classroom, principally focused on content and the creation of a Marxist-Leninist frame of reference (Camnitzer 2003, 156). The ENA initially taught ballet, music, drama, and the plastic arts. Three years later, modern and folk dance were also added to the curriculum (Puñales-Alpízar 2012, 56). Puñales-Alpízar has established

Figure 6.1   Visual Arts School of ISA, Designed by Ricardo Porro. Photo courtesy of the author.

that the ENA, and later the ISA, benefited from significant support and encouragement from the USSR, and that in these educational establishments a new aesthetic was developed in which the social and didactic values of art prevailed. This, she argues, was partially due to the fact that there were a number of active Soviet co-workers and specialists in these institutions (Puñales-Alpízar 2012, 56).

As construction continued apace on Cuba's emblematic architectural and educational project, Cuba hosted the Congress of the International Union of Architects (de Juan 2011, 197), with the theme of "Architecture in Under-developed Countries" (UIA 2016). For the Congress, the Pabellón Cuba, situated on La Rampa (the main street that leads down from Copelia to the Malecón in the Vedado area of Havana) was built and the pavements of this area were repaired. The pavement on La Rampa showcased slabs that had been designed by some of the most important Cuban artists that were active at the time, including Wilfredo Lam, Amelia Peláez, Mariano, Portocarrero, Luis Martínez Pedro, and Sandú Darié (de Juan 2011, 197). Here the plastic arts showed some of the elements that would become so sought after in the 1970s: the crossover of art and design, the integration of art with production, and previously elite art forms being brought into the public space.

In the midst of the debates surrounding the role of art, its practitioners, and the inappropriateness of approaches such as socialist realism that characterized the 1960s, a landmark exhibition was held. The exhibition, *expresionismo abstracto*, included the works of artists such as Eiriz, Rafael Blanco, Mayito, Francisco Antigua, Augstín Cardenas and Tomás Oliva (de Juan 1968, 94). The exhibition was held between January 11 and February 3, 1963 in the Galería Habana and is considered to have marked the beginning of a new phase in Cuban art that incorporated elements such as pop (EnCaribe 2016). As the Cuban abstractionism period drew to a close, there were two important developments. First, the plastic arts became a continental-wide meeting point: in 1964 Casa held the First Meeting of Latin American Engraving, an event that ran annually until 1971 when it was replaced by the Meeting of Latin American Plastic Arts (de Juan 2011, 197). Second, the CNC became autonomous from the MINED: its authority was advanced, giving it control over the organization, coordination and direction of cultural activities (Kapcia 2005, 134).

Already by 1965, a clear revolutionary art form had begun to emerge within the Revolution: graphic design. It vehicle of choice was the poster.[4] This art form was particularly supported due to the poster's rapid ability to respond to events (de Juan 1968, 99–100). De Juan hails the posters, produced in the first half of the 1960s, which used geometrical elements and short texts, and were generally limited to two colors as important developments in Cuban graphic design. In her opinion they acted as "antiseptic" and paved the way for new innovation and experimentation, converting the challenges posted by lack of resources and equipment into design virtues, such as the (Bauhaus-esque) valuing of white spaces. De Juan also considers that the austerity of the 1960s helped to force artists to rethink images and prevented quick recourse to stereotyped images (de Juan 2007, 155–56). In particular Umberto Peña's work at Casa from 1963 (Camnitzer 2003, 82), and the work of ICAIC which eschewed the use of advertising images that were imported with the film, are both hailed as fundamental in the development of Cuban graphics and of its international reputation (de Juan 2011, 206–207).

The rise of Cuban graphic design and poster art demonstrated another trait that became increasingly valued in Cuban revolutionary culture: assimilation and re-elaboration. Cuban artists assimilated international trends—the personal styles of American poster-makers, such as Saul Bass and Milton Glazer, the style of the 1960s' Czech film posters by Josef Flejar and Zdenek Chotenovsky, the *images d'Epinal*, the neo-Art Nouveau style popularized by the Fillmore and Avalon posters of the mid-1960s, the pop art of Andy Warhol, Roy Lichtenstein, and Tom Wesselman, re-elaborated into a distinctly Cuban setting (Sontag 1970, xv). Polish poster art in particular was an enduring influence on Cuban poster art, demonstrating that political work did not have to be bullish and devoid of beauty (Camnitzer 2003, 109). Moreover, the poster artists' perpetuation of the theatrical poster (Sontag 1970, xiv) demonstrated another desirable characteristic—interdisciplinarity.

Graphic design and poster art were in some ways a particularly privileged mode of artistic expression in that they did not suffer from the same limitations as other, more established, forms, such as literature, because they had no serious precedent in Cuba. They were also a mode of expression inherently suited to the government's focus on taking art to a wider audience because, as Sontag argues, "good posters cannot be an object of consumption by an elite [. . .] the space within which the genuine poster is shown is not elitist, but a public—communal—space" (Sontag 1970, xv). The needs of the Revolution could also be easily integrated into artists' identities and the medium provided an excellent platform on which to bring together two opposing views of art: that of art as an individual practice and that of art as a politically or ethically engaged service (Sontag 1970, xv–xvi). The range of styles among leading poster artists and with their individual bodies of work reflected Cuba's rich cultural history whilst echoing the raging contemporary cultural debates and the cultural practitioners' rejection of a single unitary style.

Given that problems of aesthetics were considered to be problems of politics (Garaudy 1965, 100), the Cuban Revolution's central tenet of internationalism takes on a new significance within the plastic arts. The continual rejection of cultural chauvinism and of the appropriation of Cuba's cultural heritage in the drive for internationalism was "Cuba's indigenous path to cultural revolution" (Sontag 1970, xix). This approach was particularly useful for an inherently cannibalistic medium such as graphic design, which easily fed off other cultures, assimilated them and produced something new and "Cuban." Finally, posters were an early example of the crossover of high and popular art; they created a system of mutual feedback with popular art which was subsequently used by "high culture"—epitomized by the works of Raúl Martínez, Alberto Jorge Carol and Juan García Miló's work in Teatro Escambray, and Leandro Soto (Camnitzer 2003, 112).

OSPAAAL reaffirmed Cuban art's politically engaged nature and provided one of the most public forums within which to exhibit Cuban poster art. The organization was founded in January 1966 during the midst of the Sino-Soviet split. Posters produced for the event spoke of the various liberation struggles that were taking place in the underdeveloped regions of Asia, Africa, and Latin America. The posters, which were in a smaller format so that they could be folded into the associated publication *Tricontinental* were of high quality and deeply original. They combined "dissimilar elements from Third World cultures, particularly those with the most authentic indigenous traditions," and re-contextualized symbolic images (Dopico 2009, 290). The plastic arts' connection to Latin America, and the symbolic linking of the M-26-7 to artistic promotion and diversity of expression, continued with the

1966 Moncada celebrations. The students from the ENA, under the direction of Chilean abstract painter Roberto Matta, attempted a group mural in Casa (de Juan 1968, 97). With the founding of the PCC in 1965, there was a move toward an increasingly systematic promotion of culture and cultural education. Several educational events were held to improve the country's cultural offerings. These included a round-table on the teaching of plastic arts (8–11 September 1966) (Anon 1966d), the first national congress of the *instructores de arte* (July 1967) (Rassi 1967a, 1967c, 1967b), national plans for students' cultural education, and the introduction of competitions such as the biannual Salón Nacional de Dibujo (Anon 1969a), and later the complementary Salón Nacional de Carteles 26 de Julio (Anon 1972b).

AN EDUCATED STRUGGLE

From the mid-1960s, a more systematic diffusion of culture from Cuba's socialist allies began to be developed, and from the second issue of 1966 *Unión* began introducing its readers to contemporary literature from "brother socialist countries" (Anon 1966e, 5). As part of this organization and "harnessing" of the power of culture, new cultural organs also began to proliferate to fill perceived needs. These newer publications were focused on transforming the normally passive reader into a social and historical subject and active participant in the nation's cultural construction. In 1966 *Caimán Barbudo* was founded, initially as a monthly cultural supplement to *Juventud Rebelde*, the publication of the Unión de Jovenes Comunistas. *Caimán Barbudo* was very politically committed and believed in the championing of high-quality art. From the outset *Caimán* played an important role in informing its readership about the plastic arts though interview, criticism, commentaries and reviews (Montero Méndez 2006, 16). The journal argued that genuine art was never counterrevolutionary (Anon 1966b, 1). In explaining its position, the editors pledged the journal's commitment to the development of an authentic culture for the Revolution and its fight against underdevelopment (Anon 1966b, 1–2). It also considered knowledge of previous cultures. The opening issue addressed Cuba's situation as an underdeveloped country and linked its fight for development to the development of an authentic national culture (Aloma et al. 1966). *RC*, the precursor to *Revolución y Cultura*, was founded the year after *Caimán Barbudo*. *RC* sought to build links between the artist and the *conjunto* from which they had historically been removed, and was international in its approach.

> [RyC] aims to analyze and report on the problems of our time and clarify what role the intellectual plays in this confrontation. At the same time, it wishes to

be a vehicle for the current trends in art and literature inside and outside our country. We believe, with Martí, that fighting for culture is, first and foremost, fighting for the liberation of the nation. But we do not believe that with the liberation of the nation the struggle stops and we know that the ideological debate must remain open to the stage of conquered sovereignty to overcome the burdens left by the colonial ideology. This magazine also aspires to be a means for these purposes. (Rodríguez 1967, 5)

Both *RC* and *Caimán Barbudo* (*Caimán*) were more overtly militant than existing cultural magazines. *Caimán* rejected cultural production that did not deal with "social themes," that avoided conflicts, and that hid behind words imbued with "second-hand metaphysics" (Aloma et al. 1966). *RC* took this a step further and actively rejected "decorative" typography. *RC* paid less attention to typography because the governing board—Otero in particular—felt that if the magazine continued the path of "visual sensuality," they would fall into the trap of formalism, thereby neglecting the real product of the magazine (Otero 1967, 95). In an interview about *RC,* Otero unequivocally linked the magazine to armed struggle, describing it as a combative space "this is a fighting magazine, not one to relax with leafing through it [. . .] this is a magazine for breaking mental castles" (Otero 1967, 95).

Otero positioned *RC* apart from established magazines such as: *Unión*, which was focused on artistic-literary problems; *Casa*, which was focused on the socio-economic and political problems of Latin America; *Gaceta*, which as an official organ of UNEAC had to reflect the range of opinions of its members. Otero also set *RC* apart from *Caimán*, which he claimed had a unified generational approach, but, Caimán, like the other magazines paid very little attention to works which had already been published abroad. *RC* was designed to fill the gaps that were left by these other magazines. Otero considered that this meant that *Pensamiento Crítico* was therefore *RC*'s closest competitor. It was planned that, like *Pensamiento Crítico*, *RC* would publish work that focused on socioeconomics and politics. However, *RC* hoped to distinguish itself by publishing the most representative texts of the key currents of contemporary thinking in art, literature, economics, and politics. Initially issued as a monthly or bimonthly publication, it was planned that it would increase its frequency. Finally, *RC* demonstrated the closer linking of art with industry and education as Otero emphasized that the magazine was not just for writers and artists but also for technicians and teachers in the fields that would be discussed (Otero 1967, 94–95). In 1972 *RC* became *Revolución y Cultura,* the official organ of the CNC. As with its previous iterations (*Pueblo y Cultura, RC*) *Revolución y Cultura* constantly engaged with the official cultural policy, and dedicated a substantial amount of space to the plastic arts.

RC's stridently combative tone fitted with the increasingly radicalized atmosphere and the ongoing, mounting sense that Cuba was under siege. The cultural arena's response to this was twofold. First, the focus turned increasingly inwards to the rediscovery of national forms and traditions. Second, existing cultural tropes and poles began to be questioned in the search for new centers of non-alignment. The remaining structures that reflected the systems of artistic production under capitalism were abolished and it was decided by the government that the Revolution should provide for artists rather than leave them to live off the proceeds of their work. Royalties for authors were abolished in 1967, ensuring that authors had to be employed by, and thus dependent upon, the state (Casal 1971, 457). Cultural practitioners were paid to work within the existing cultural apparatus, educational systems, media, and the diplomatic services and often the more "problematic" cultural figures found themselves posted abroad (Kumaraswami and Kapcia 2012, 26).

The plastic arts were at the forefront of the shift in cultural orientation, and its international projection. The 1967 M-26-7 celebrations were centered on the visit of the *Salón de Mayo* (Salon du Mai). The Salón had begun in 1944 and had its roots in opposition to Nazi fascism and the Nazi regime's rejection of abstract art. The 1967 visit involved 150 artists and intellectuals producing, or reporting on, cultural work based around the idea of collectiveness. Cuba was the first country in Latin America to host the event, which had previously been held in Sweden, Switzerland, Yugoslavia, and Japan (Schütz 2009, 276). The event was held on La Rampa in July, having been transferred, on the initiative of Lam, from Paris to Havana (de Juan 2011, 198). There was widespread interest in the Cuban Revolution in France, in part due to the French anti-Stalinist sentiment and subsequent search for a new socialist model, but also in part due to the positive reports of the Revolution from intellectuals, including Jean-Paul Sartre and Simone de Beauvoir (Schütz 2009, 276). A significant number of French and international critics and artists had accompanied the works to the city.

In a move that emphasized the international, interdisciplinary nature of the plastic arts, a collective artwork, *Cuba colectiva*, was planned. The piece was a large collective mural, in the shape of a spiral drawn by Eduardo Arroyo and Gilles Aillaud which divided the 55m^2 canvas into equal sections and all participating artists were allocated a space by lot. There were two exceptions: the center was reserved for Lam and lot number twenty-six was reserved for Fidel. Lisandro Otero's square read "The Revolution is the creativity of everyone, the responsibility of everyone" (Schütz 2009, 277). Lam was in charge of the central segment of the spiral and designed the rhomboid shapes that were reminiscent of the *íremes*, the masked dancers who carry out specific functions during the liturgy of Afro-Cuban religions (de Juan 2011, 198).

The delegates were aided and entertained in their efforts by dancers from the Tropicana cabaret, popular musicians, and the general public. Close to dawn the finished mural was taken to the nearby Pabellón Cuba, where it was exhibited together with the works of the *Salón de Mayo* (de Juan 2011, 198–199). The exhibition was also a chance to celebrate the prowess of the emergent young Cuban painters (particularly those from Cubanacán), who were lauded for their ability to hold their own, "shoulder to shoulder with masters of recognized international fame" (Vidal 1968). At the end of the *Salón de Mayo*, the exhibition went to the Museo Bacardí in Santiago de Cuba (Schütz 2009, 276). In his analysis of the event, Schütz points out that all significant currents of contemporary art were represented: classic modernism, surrealism, new figuration, lettrism, situationists such as the COBRA group, neo-realists, pop art, op art, and action painting. Socialist realism was the only contemporary style not represented (Schütz 2009, 279).

The event, and particularly the "total art" element of the collective mural, profoundly affected all participants (Schütz 2009, 279), and was a shining example to the international community of the value of culture in revolutionary Cuba. Gallardo Saborido considers that the *Salón de Mayo* and Cultural Congress the following year clearly corresponded to the revolutionary government's propagandistic interests. The events contributed to Cuba's prestige among the New Left at a time when Cuban-Soviet relations were on rocky ground (2009, 148). They were also fundamental in articulating the active participation of the cultural sector in the development, and defense of the nation and its cultural expression.

CHANGING ROLES, CHANGING INSTITUTIONS

The mounting sense of siege that came to characterize the late 1960s and early 1970s was partially reflected in the drive to create greater organizational coherence. This was manifested by a focus on organization at an institutional level, to allow greater contribution to the Revolution, and the search for a national identity and its constituent parts. Within these new and existing institutions, sub-groups within institutions continued to propagate, in what Kumaraswami and Kapcia see as a response to the individual and collective need for group identity. Such proliferation was aided by the formal institutional spaces that allowed individuals to develop their own way of contributing to the Revolution (2012, 101).

The 1968 Havana Cultural Congress further developed ideas on the ways in which the artist and intellectual could contribute to the Cuban Revolution and other liberation movements. It also further married the idea of culture and national defense, and, due to the split in thinking between European Marxists and Latin American Marxists that became apparent at the Congress, added further impetus to culture's development. Shortly after the Cultural Congress, the Revolutionary Offensive was launched on March 13. The Offensive was part of the government's attempts to achieve economic independence, which culminated in the 1970 *zafra*. It involved the nationalization of remaining non-agricultural enterprises, giving rise to a period of "consolidation and radicalisation" of the Cuban Revolution (Anon 1968d).

The Offensive marked a move away from material to moral incentives, reminiscent of approaches adopted in 1917 by the Bolsheviks, and sharing some features with the Chinese Great Leap Forward, including centralization (Mesa-Lago 1969). Carmelo Mesa Lago sees the Offensive as indicative of the desire to achieve rapid development and as an acceleration of the process that began when the leadership aligned itself with more orthodox Marxism-Leninism (Mesa-Lago 1969, 22–24). In the arts, the Revolutionary Offensive helped to consolidate Cuba's increasing international renown and build closer links between popular culture and "revolutionary" culture (Vázquez 1968).

Artistic innovation and diversity continued to be linked to the M-26-7 celebrations, an organizational feat that also served to confirm art's inherently revolutionary capacity. For the 1968 celebrations, one interdisciplinary team worked to organize the Third World Exhibition at the Pabellón Cuba, while another team of designers, sculptors, musicians, and lighting technicians showcased artworks that dealt with the "hundred years of struggle" (alluding to the ongoing fight for independence since the Ten Year's War in 1868) along the pavement between the Pabellón Cuba and Plaza de la Revolución in Havana. At the Plaza large-scale designs provided the backdrops to music and lighting effects. Santa Clara's Revolution Square hosted another event that involved numerous artistic disciplines, taking place near the armored train captured by Che in the fight against Bastista (de Juan 2011, 198). Culture's militant status was cemented with the beginning of the FAR's annual competitions in literature and the plastic arts.

The First National Meeting of Writers and Plastic Artists in the wake of Che's death confirmed culture's status as a form of social production, and as a defensive weapon (Isidron del Valle 1968). As the international community began to fear the rise of high Stalinist socialist realism in Cuba in the wake of the controversy surrounding the treatment of Padilla and Arrufat, a new generation of Cuban artists was beginning to emerge. The first cohort of students graduated from the ENA on 2 December 1968, which also happened to be the 10th anniversary of the landing of the yacht Granma.[5] At the ceremony, the Minister of Education, José Llanusa Gobel, described the students as the individuals who would go out and begin a revolution in the arts (Anon

1968c). He also stressed the link between culture and society, asserting that the Revolution's defining characteristic was to fight against old attitudes.

Therefore, the graduates had the task to make this a reality within culture, and remedy the "difficult" label that the older generation had assigned to culture. Llanusa Gobel also took the opportunity to reiterate that artistic freedom within the Revolution and that all forms of art were welcome, on the condition that they contributed to cultural development:

> Our Revolution defines a line. There is no discussion about the form of aesthetic expression, but rather about how art serves the people, their happiness, their cultural development. For that there is all the freedom. (Anon 1968c)

1968 was a turning point for Cuba: relations with the USSR were strained, the European left had failed to appreciate Cuba's exceptionalism, the Latin American Communist Parties were beginning to distance themselves from the Revolution, Cuba's organic revolutionary model had failed, and geopolitical pressures were increasingly hostile. By the beginning of 1969 a period of reassessment had begun which was centered on different ideas of modernity and on the nature of becoming a modern nation. This was almost by definition a contradictory period: modernity often implies simultaneously an inward and outward looking discourse. Weiss considers that the anti-imperialism and national cultural identification of the 1970s were insular, while the internationalist position was outward-looking but also chauvinist. The inward gaze acted as a type of quarantine while the outward focus helped to assert Cuba as a leader of the periphery—a concrete position rather than a nebulous "other" (Weiss 2011b, 4).

The period can also be read in terms of García Canclini's four projects of modernity: emancipation, expansion, renovation, and democratization (García Canclini 1995, 265). Each of these projects had internal tensions as well as contradictions in relation to the other projects. By the late 1970s (as alluded to by Hart in the closing speech of the UNEAC's Second Congress), the project of emancipation was widely considered to have been completed. However, in the early and mid-1970s this project was still in full swing, complete with the discrepancies between modernism and modernity. This process—including that of the *quinquenio gris*—demonstrates what García Canclini terms "hybridity" and "hybridisation": strategies that enable adoption, assimilation and re-elaboration, thereby mitigating the tensions between the modern, the traditional, the internal, and the external, and that separates culture from the socioeconomic (García Canclini 1995, 1–11).

The late 1960s and early 1970s were thus both national and international. Both of these currents had always been present in the cultural imaginary and had been expressed in the government's ten-point plan in 1961, the 1940 constitution, and the ideas of José Martí. Each of these areas of focus fed off the others. Without a strong national identity Cuba could not forcefully articulate its leadership of the international anti-imperialist movement, and yet, internationalism formed the core of Cuba's emergent national identity. The contradictions that are inherent in debates about modernity also permeated other areas of life in Cuba, and to some extent resurrected the debates around the different interpretations of the role of culture in socialism. These debates continued, but were internalized during the 1970s as part of the attempt for more institutional and organizational clarity for greater efficiency. This drive was also, in part, intended to help project a unified front in the face of external aggression. However, the debates still persisted, and particularly in the plastic arts which were less affected by the regulatory currents of the *quinquenio gris*.

The contradictions of these debates and the institutionalizing drive were reflected in the plastic arts which turned their focus inwards to an exploration of Cuba's history and cultures whilst simultaneously embracing international styles and asserting its position at the international vanguard. The *Salón 70*, held in the MNBA, was emblematic of the preoccupations of the 1970s. The event was a group exhibition that showed the work of some of the "most prominent artists of the previous ten years and a significant number of young artists" (Montero Méndez 2009, 259). The exhibition served as a point of confrontation between artistic, historic, and aesthetic values within the development and evolution of Cuban painting (Montero Méndez 2006, 76) and as an expression of the impact of the social achievements that had occurred over the decade (Montero Méndez 2006, 8).

The contradictory nature of debates about modernism was further heightened by the implicit promotion of a certain dogmatic interpretation of socialist culture that Cuba's entry to COMECON seemed to suggest, supported by the edicts of the First National Congress of Education and Culture, in the wake of the *Caso Padilla*. Art was subordinated, to some extent, to the perceived political needs of the Revolution, and a more exclusive reading of *Palabras* gained influence: this interpretation of *Palabras* did not necessarily lie in the increasingly selective interpretation of the infamous "within the Revolution, everything. Against the Revolution, not one right" (Castro 1961a). Rather, it was in the primacy of the Revolution's need to exist and the artists' commitment to this need before their own needs as creative individuals. A result of this harder line, and the subjugation of art to politics that this entailed, there was a greater focus on the historical context in art; a focus which led to the production of art that helped to consolidate the Revolution's aims.

The drive for the country to gain economic independence was behind a reassessment of Cuba's resources, one of which was the inherent creative capacity of the people. In order to make the quantitative leap forwards in terms of the quality of production, cultural levels had to be raised and the democratization of culture demanded the inculcation of popular culture into the Revolution's cultural canons. The view of art as a defensive weapon and inherently educational tool further bolstered the focus on populism. Socio-historical themes, portraiture and landscape emerged as dominant trends during this period. However, they were expressed in playful, self-reflective manners in various styles, pop art, neo-expressionism, photorealism, abstraction (Montero Méndez 2009, 258). The turn inwards to the rediscovery of national themes and patriotism reflected the emergent codes of *cubanía* and the drive to rediscover national traditions and heritage. Yet, the reassessment of the country's history and the focus on historical context also functioned as a conduit for the continued expression of the Revolution's intrinsic internationalism. New international styles were assimilated and used in the emerging sociohistorical and pastoral focus in art. This ultimately created a stylistic rupture with previous forms of expression that cleared the way for a "regeneration of thought based on individual creativity and the enrichment of the spectrum of conceptual interests" (Montero Méndez 2006, 9).

1970 was also the beginning of a period of significant international recognition for the emergent generation of Cuban artists. A particularly clear example of this was Manuel Mendive (1944–). Mendive graduated from San Alejandro in 1963 and in 1970 won an award at the second Cagnes-sur-Mer International Painting Festival in France (Ojeda Jequin 2009, 230). Mendive's work was based on his Afro-Cuban belief system and the nation's history (de Juan 2011, 207). He thus exhibited some of the central preoccupations of culture in the 1970s: the exploration of Afro-Cuban traditions and the country's past. Mendive also took art beyond the traditional confines of the gallery and encouraged popular participation in his performances (Montero Méndez 2009, 258). Thus he involved the *pueblo* in the creative process and further democratized culture. He brought new styles from Latin America into a Cuban, and subsequently international, setting (Montero Méndez 2009, 258). Mendive was fundamental to the development in Cuban art in another way—he was a "bridge" artist who marked the beginning of the transition from the internationally established older artists and the rise of younger artists, who ascended in the 1970s, in various waves while the older artists, such as Eiriz, Peña, Chago, Martínez, and Cabrera Moreno, gradually withdrew from the scene. These younger artists were "often isolated from rural areas, they were the first to be educated in a network of art schools founded, or radically transformed, by the Revolution" (Eligio 2001, 31).

The plastic arts in the 1970s were, therefore, a point of confluence for a number of different ideas about national identity, cultural history, the relationship between art and economy, and the role of art in socialism. The form was also afforded a certain level of protection against more dogmatic ideological currents, particularly during the *quinquenio gris*. This was due to several reasons: their development and democratization under the Revolution, their politicized nature, the emergence of new art forms native to the Revolution, significant international recognition, and the fact that Casa was their natural home. The plastic arts, therefore became a particularly suitable platform from which to publicly engage with cultural policy, and to pursue alternative interpretations of socialism, such as those in Latin America and the Third World. Perhaps most importantly, particularly given the focus on anti-imperialism, decolonialization and becoming a modern nation, the plastic arts were an area in which Cuba could position itself as the leader of the socialist camp.

Throughout the 1970s, the plastic arts remained a firmly established site of collectivity and internationalism and demonstrated considerable progress in the development of an authentically Cuban art form. They remained inherently political and valued for their mobilization capacity. The cultural engagement and orientation program of the 1960s had begun to be translated into a significant number of students studying the arts. In 1970 the ENA boasted 782 students in total (328 of them women), who, in addition to their artistic education received "regular" educational classes until the end of middle school (Anon 1970b, 9). The ENA had established six provincial schools in ballet, music, and plastic arts, and twenty-four art schools with forty specialties, eighteen in music, eighteen in plastic arts, eleven in ballet, nine in modern dance, and just one in drama (Anon 1970b, 10). These twenty-four art schools had a total of 3,647 students (Anon 1970b, 10). The plastic arts had become an important mobilization tool in other, diverse areas such as health, heritage, education, and production (such as the 10 million-ton *zafra* and the posters created for it by Raúl Martínez). Sculpture was particularly praised for the way sculptors linked their work to that of the community (Anon 1970b, 20).

The 1971 First National Congress of Education and Culture, like the 1968 Havana Cultural Congress, responded to emergent trends in the cultural and political arenas. Culture was celebrated in terms of its offensive/defensive qualities and its educational capacity. Camnitzer sees the conference as an event that was used to emphasize some points at the cost of others, and which blurred the interpretation of "ideological rigour" (Camnitzer 2003, 127). During this time Moisei Kagan remained a significant influence, and many institutions did not change their approach and openness, yet the primacy of different tendencies did shift (Camnitzer 2003, 127–128). Many new cultural officials with a military background subtly favored politically oriented artists for promotion and facilitated the availability of dogmatic publications in book shops. These lower level changes occurred without a shift in the beliefs of the government (Camnitzer 2003, 127).

During this more regulatory phase of the Revolution, the plastic arts took center stage in the development of an engaged culture geared toward the continental struggle for freedom. More specifically, the plastic arts responded to the process of consolidating the democratization of culture that had begun to develop concurrently with the more systematic institutionalization of the Revolution. This drive became particularly pronounced from the latter half of the 1970s. Again, the plastic arts demonstrated their inherent agitational capacity and interdisciplinarity when, in 1971 and 1972, painters joined the model of revolutionary theater: Teatro Escambray (Camnitzer 2003, 156). Painters and ENA graduates, Alberto Jorge Carol and Juan García Miló, joined the ensemble in 1971 and 1972 respectively with the aim of expanding the activities of the group to encompass the plastic arts. Carol had submitted this idea to the ensemble's leader, Corrieri, in 1971, who then invited him to join the group (Carol 1974, 24). In 1973 they began Cuadrodebate (painting debate), a programme that encouraged debates and political discussions from the audience. They organized mobile exhibits of modern figurative painting with expressive distortions that addressed specific regional problems (Camnitzer 2003, 156). The exhibits were presented with a structure that encouraged debates with the audience (Camnitzer 2003, 156). Moreover, in order to achieve the goal of political discussion, their paintings were "high in literary content" (Camnitzer 2003, 159). A painting was left behind in each community visited, to be used by the local revolutionary organizations in the way they judged to be most productive (Carol 1974, 28).

Cuadrodebate toured with Teatro Escambray and in the nights on which they were not holding the debate the painters would attend the theater ensemble's performances. During the day they would paint in their lodgings and in public, and would frequently help out with the Teatro Escambray's tasks. In April 1973, after Teatro Escambray's second seminar, Cuadrodebate carried out an independent tour around areas that had been preselected with the municipal PCC. This tour involved a stay of two days in each area. The first day was spent unpacking and then, conditions permitting, painting in public or visits and conversations with the *campesinos* and then Cuadrodebate during the evening. The following day was spent conducting interviews in houses deemed to be "representative" of the area. The group moved on to the next spot on the morning of the third day and began the cycle again (Carol 1974, 28).

Political engagement and debate at a continental level were also encouraged with the Meetings of Latin American Plastic Arts. In August 1972, the First Meeting of Latin American Plastic Art, which took over from the previous event, was held. As Gordon-Nesbitt points out, the meetings provided an alternative to the more regulatory and increasingly dogmatic application of cultural policy during the *quinquenio gris,* but also fitted with the focus of the 1971 First National Congress of Education and Culture (2012, 347). It was anticipated that meetings would "provide a forum for defining a role that all artists with a revolutionary *consciencia* could assume, emphasising the necessity of creating new values in configuring an art that would be the patrimony of all and an intimate expression of Our America" (Gordon-Nesbitt 2012, 347–48). Purely aesthetic discussions were ruled out and leading artists situated themselves within the (armed, if necessary) revolutionary struggle against cultural infiltration (Gordon-Nesbitt 2012, 349). The cultural strategies of imperialism were analyzed, and attending artists agreed upon concrete measures with which to combat its isolating mechanisms (Gordon-Nesbitt 2012, 348). These measures included the creation of a continent-wide network of information, associated coordinated information centers, and symbols that could be used in the continental struggle (Gordon-Nesbitt 2012, 349). The event was organized in collaboration with the Institute of Latin American Art at the University of Chile and culminated in an exhibition of artworks from participating countries, which featured 240 works from 147 artists (Gordon-Nesbitt 2012, 348). The second Meeting of Latin American Plastic Arts, held in October 1973, was attended by 37 artists from nine countries. The meeting discussed the work undertaken in line with the 1972 agreements and later plans, which included acts of solidarity with those fighting the Chilean coup, the incorporation of visual images into the daily struggle and the promotion of artistic activities among the working class. A complementary exhibition of 150 works was held in the MNBA and delegates also participated by painting art works on the museum patio (Gordon-Nesbitt 2012, 351–52). The Third Meeting did not take place until 1976, and with participation limited to Puerto Rico and the Dominican Republic. However, there were plans for a subsequent Meeting which included the whole Caribbean in order to help combat the fragmentation that the region had historically been subjected to (Anon 1976a).

1973 marked the 20th anniversary of the storming of the Moncada barracks. To celebrate, an exhibition—*Past and Present, Transit towards a Definitive Present*—was organized at Casa (de Juan 2007, 144). The exhibition was deliberately organized around a common theme and had the aim of "transcend[ing] the collection of individual works in order to give shape to a common endeavour and a common work from its inception to its conclusion" (de Juan 2007, 144). Initial work sessions were held to discuss the exhibition's goals, its ideological content and its artistic form. Once a blueprint for the exhibition's display and the visual form to be used had been decided upon, artists discussed the work in progress among themselves; thus, all participated in the overall plan and each of the individual sections (de Juan 2007, 144). Art works were made by individuals, collaborations, and collectives and therefore produced something that had both a common foundation that belonged to everyone: the Revolution (de Juan 2007, 148). De Juan also considers the exhibition important in demonstrating that high-quality art could be produced from few resources and—primarily because it demonstrated a unitary character (rather than style)—asserting and defining the personality of a people and a culture (de Juan 2007, 145–48). The exhibition demonstrated the value of motivated collective work and of constructive criticism and analysis in achieving goals—in this case a cohesive, engaging exhibition which involved people at all levels (de Juan 2007, 147). It also demonstrated the ongoing process of democratization of culture, which saw a shift from painting, a private activity, to design, a public activity (de Juan 2007, 153). Thus design, or cultural forms that crossed over with design, were particularly valuable.

In 1974, the CNC's annual work plan reflected the ongoing desire to equalize cultural inequalities and to continue developing culture's ability to be mobilized in the defense of the nation. The critical assimilation of world culture, study of Cuban cultural roots, promotion, and mobilization of particular modes of cultural creation—each one according to their impact—and emphasis on the promotion of young artists, were all points of action in the CNC's plan (Anon 1974e). The improvement of the quality of cultural production was closely linked to these drives, which in turn was linked to the Revolution's ongoing quest for independence. This focus on quality meant that the plastic arts were subject to the same drive to fill technical gaps, which had permeated other areas of Cuban life as part of the bid to achieve economic independence. Art students who were considered outstanding in some way were awarded scholarships and sent to the USSR to complete postgraduate study. Upon the completion of their postgraduate study, it was envisaged, they would return to ISA and replace the Soviet teaching staff, thereby ending another form of dependency brought about by technical shortcomings.

It was at this time that the curriculum of the ENA was changed, along with the planned curriculum for the ISA. Camnitzer sees the curriculum change as a reflection of the combination of the embargo, the 10-million ton *zafra* failure, isolationist tendencies, the rise of dogmatism, and consequently Soviet sectors, and the nationwide attempt to unify the country's curricula (Camnitzer 2003, 159). Camnitzer also considers the 1970s to be particularly "sovietophile" and suggests that a particular Soviet advisor, Anatole Tishenko, had input into the curricular planning of the ENA. He argues that the majority of supposedly "Soviet" contributions actually came from the Cuban artists who had already studied in the USSR, and that these "Soviet" changes were promoted by Carlos Suárez, who was in charge of art education at the time (Camnitzer 2003, 168). Educational programs of study to the USSR had been in place since the early 1960s, probably 1961 (Anon 1963b; Quesada

1972), though uptake had been limited (Quesada 1972, 26). However, children of high-ranking PSP members had also been given the opportunity to study in the USSR before the Revolution (López Oliva 2015; Pogolotti 2015). If what Camnitzer argues is true, then it goes some way toward explaining the difficulty that the later generation of Cuban artists who had studied in the USSR reportedly experienced in finding jobs and recognition upon their return to Cuba in the 1980s.

In a 1974 report outlining the new directives for the teaching of Art in Cuba, with the aim of creating ISA, it was observed that the system was to be restructured following the recommendations of Soviet advisors. Marxism-Leninism became a mandatory topic on the curriculum; MINED was made responsible for art teaching, at the basic/elementary level and had to approve the study plans for general teaching, while the CNC was put in charge of teaching methodology, technical skills and artistic specialties (Anon 1974b). The timetable at ISA was to include theoretical training in Marxism-Leninism, history, language and literature, Marxist-Leninist aesthetic principles, and Spanish language, alongside specific creative training and individual practice time (Table 6.1). Camnitzer, in discussing the content of the planned curricula, asserts that one aim was "an application of Marxist-Leninist economic theory to the interpretation of practical problems derived from the construction of socialism" (Camnitzer 2003, 169). Such an approach fits in with the greater integration of culture into the economy and production that had gained traction since the failure of the 1970 *zafra*.

The CNC's cultural aims for 1975 also demonstrated an increased focus on the Soviet input into cultural education and the exchange with socialist countries. In many respects the CNC's work plan was, as with previous years, a continuation of the revolutionary government's 1961 ten-point cultural plan. However, there was now more focus on exchange with the USSR, and particular emphasis was placed on the need to make the most of the advice from Soviet specialists, and the centrality of Marxism-Leninism to the creative process was stressed (Anon 1975b). Given this apparent shift toward the USSR's experiences and recommendations—seemingly confirmed by the First Congress of the PCC's call to also look to the experiences of the USSR, now in a period of stagnation and reactionism that has come to characterize the Brezhnev era—it would, at first sight, seem logical that a didactic, reductive approach toward the plastic arts, typified by the socialist realism of late Stalinism, was inevitable. However, my argument, in line with that of Camnitzer, is that the Congress actually endorsed the opposite approach (Camnitzer 2003, 126). The PCC's 1975 *Thesis and Resolution* on literary and artistic culture affirmed the importance of artistic innovation and experimentation, particularly regarding the assimilation and re-elaboration of cultural heritage rather than its "servile imitation" (Anon 1975c, 21). The document acknowledged the necessity for

Table 6.1 *Proposed ISA Timetable*

	Year and hours per week				
General tasks	1	2	3	4	Total hour per year
Marxism-Leninism	-	2	2	2	210
History	3	2	2		280
Language and Literature	4	3	3	3	550
Marxist-Leninist Aesthetic Principles				1	35
Pedagogic Elements				1	35
Language	2	2	2	2	280
Sub total	9	9	10	9	
Weekly total of special training	27	27	26	27	3745
Sub total	36	36	36	36	5050
Weekly total for individual work	12	12	12	12	1500
Total	48	48	48	48	6550

Source: Anon (1974a, 8–9)
Note: These work schemes were for Music, Plastic Arts, Ballet, Modern Dance and Popular Dance.

art that contributed to the education of the population but simultaneously stressed that art and literature could not be reduced to a purely didactic role. The nexus between socialist art and reality, the document argued, lay in art's comprehension of the essences of its reality and the aesthetic expression of this understanding through the most appropriate formal structures. The faithful copying of reality was not the desired result; rather, it was the recognition that the dynamic and vivid reflection of knowledge can, in art, lead to the unraveling of the inherent truth of objective processes through their specific aesthetic languages. As Camnitzer argues (2003, 10–11), this stance was far removed from the ossified approach to art that engendered the socialist realism of Late Stalinism. Instead, it sits much more comfortably with the approaches of Lenin, but particularly of Anatolii Lunacharskii during the early 1920s (Fitzpatrick 1970)—a period of great significance to the Cuban Revolution more generally.

In addition to confirming the value of multiple aesthetic approaches the focus of the PCC's First Congress on criticism and the involvement of youth sat neatly with the tendencies already developing in the plastic arts. It was during the first half of the 1970s that criticism in the plastic arts began to occupy an increasingly important role, and in *Caimán Barbudo* in particular. From its inception, the magazine had played an important role in keeping readers informed about the developments in the plastic arts and, thanks to the work of art critic Ángel Tomás González in the 1970s, it became an important organ which addressed polemics regarding artistic creation (Montero Méndez 2006, 16). The work of Tomás González (*Caimán Barbudo*), Alejandro G Alonso (*Juventud Rebelde*) José Veigas and Aldo Menédez (*Revolución y Cultura*), and Leonel López Nussa (*Bohemia*), were fundamental in shaping the artistic criticism of the 1970s (Montero Méndez 2006, 16). Their work helped to overcome the void left by the tendency to focus on the *aficionado* movement in the early 1970s, as part of the move to further democratize culture (Montero Méndez 2006, 16). Effective criticism demanded the complete and active participation of the critic and therefore complemented the emerging tendency within the plastic arts, embodied by the exhibition celebrating the Moncada attack. These two tendencies—criticism and the promotion of youth—were formally institutionalized the following year with the inauguration of the Salón Permanente de Jóvenes (SJP) in the MNBA and the parallel creation of channels for criticism in the press coverage surrounding the SJP. Montero Méndez (2006, 17) observes that the criticism of the 1970s was predominantly focused on briefs, reviews and commentaries on exhibitions, in which the critics focused on artistic production, trends and individual exhibitions. These elements were generally discussed and analyzed without questioning their validity within the emergent revolutionary canon of plastic arts. Photorealism was the exception to this rule, for which it was criticized by Ángel Tomás, as an art form "that did not defend the postulates of a revolutionary art, read under the Marxist-Leninist guidelines" (Montero Méndez 2006, 17).

This general characteristic of criticism in the 1970s has several possible interpretations that are not entirely contradictory. First is the notion that only artists who were somehow deemed "acceptable" or already firmly established were given the opportunity to present at exhibitions, hence the lack of questioning of their position in the Cuban canon to which Montero Méndez alludes. The exhibition of established artists in traditional spaces also left room for younger artists to take up the "public art" mantle, however, they saw fit. A second interpretation is that the art world was comparatively silent, compared to the heyday of public art/art in public in the 1960s (Kapcia 2005, 160), due to the focus on the *aficionado* movement and the drive to involve more and more of the population in cultural creation. As a result younger artists were studying at the ENA or "out in the field," participating in projects such as Cuadrodebate, that blended art, productivity, and mobilization, thereby promoting a crossover between "high" art and "popular" art. Thirdly, given the plastic art's international prestige, the successful development of the artistic mode in the 1960s and the determined application of an open interpretation of *Palabras* in some fields, there was little questioning of the validity of a body of work. Criticism was therefore an indispensable developmental tool, as it allowed for the neutralization of ideologies hostile to the Revolution, and the subsequent assimilation of the best of universal culture. With these neutralized, assimilated elements could then be channeled into the nation's production. The ever-deepening merging of culture and economy in the fight against underdevelopment, and the clarification of the nature of Cuba's relationship with the USSR in the new constitution, led to a very pragmatic period of appropriation in culture.

Mosquera saw the Cuban national tendency for appropriation, assimilation and re-elaboration as indicative of its underdeveloped state, and, as such, characteristic of all underdeveloped countries with aspirations of development:

> Naturally, this is not an exclusive phenomenon of Cuba. In general, it has been the peoples who fight against underdevelopment who, in a process that is not limited to the field of culture, have been able to appropriate foreign resources to transform them, put them at the service of their political and social reality, always so dramatic in the underdeveloped world. (Mosquera 1983, 359)

The SJP then, in addition to formally institutionalizing the promotion of youth and consolidating the value of criticism, also demonstrated this tendency for appropriation, assimilation and re-elaboration. The first SJP was particularly significant in that, by bringing together work produced between 1970 and 1975 for the first time, it allowed emergent trends among the new generations of artists "collectively erupting" into the art scene to be identified (Montero Méndez 2006, 63). Among the wide variety of styles two clear tendencies were identified: neo-expressionism and photorealism (Montero Méndez 2006, 63).

There are conflicting views surrounding the emergence of the photorealist trend, which has previously been interpreted as proof of Cuba's cultural dependency on the USSR (Camnitzer 2003, 9). Camnitzer considers the trend (and its name), which existed between 1973 and 1979, to have a "vague ideological reason," potentially resulting from the vogue for the testimonial in literature (itself a class of cultural production specific to the Revolution) which emphasized the "direct documentary contact with reality" (Camnitzer 2003, 9). The testimonial, which embraced the author's immediacy to the historic events of the Revolution, offered "a lively and functional alternative to socialist realism, effectively responding to some of the needs of the revolutionary process of the time" and, as an aesthetic, developed an idiosyncratic form of expression (Camnitzer 2003, 9). However, that is not to say there was no crossover between photorealism and socialist realism as direct documentary contact with reality, and the author's immediacy to revolutionary events, was central to socialist realism as it developed (Von Geldern and Stites 1995, xviii). Weiss develops Camnitzer's argument further and considers photorealism as a site of potential protest (and parody) (Weiss 2011b, 35–37). Montero Méndez concurs with Weiss's and Camnitzer's arguments but also highlights the "Cubanisation" of the approach after its critical appropriation and assimilation. She argues that photorealism became a "societal blueprint" because of what the style stood for: a move away from the "ethical function of art as an assertion of universal values" to the reaffirmation of identity "from a humanist, lyrical and intimate standpoint" (Montero Méndez 2009, 259). The approach allowed artists to remain true to history, criticize the enemy and develop a new form of revolutionary iconography that continued in the tradition of Cuban art (Montero Méndez 2009, 259).

Photography had played an important role in the early years of the Revolution, its immediate representation of reality and easy reproduction proving important tools in the dissemination of images of the victorious Revolution and its key figures in the nation's imaginary (Weiss 2011b, 36). The medium had also played an important role in the liberation movements in Latin America and Africa, and the subsequent creation of identities based around these movements (Weiss 2011b, 36). However, it also reflected the determined focus on the "faithful" representation of reality, demanded by the socialist realism of the late 1930s and 1940s, or indeed the early focus on photo documentary and photo montage in Soviet international propaganda magazines such as *SSSR na stroike* (The USSR in Construction). Finally, the style was very close (and for some, too close) to the photorealism movement that emerged in the USA toward the end of the 1960s. The medium therefore potentially assimilated the tools and techniques of socialist realism, the heroic photography of the 1960s and US photorealism and then re-elaborated them to serve the cultural expression of Cuban revolutionary society.

The movement's figurehead work, Flavio Garciandía's *Todo lo que Ud. necesita es amor* (All You Need Is Love, 1975), can be read as a product of this approach and the competing elements within it. In the painting a young Cuban woman lies on the vibrant green grass and smilingly gazes out at the viewer who is situated close to her. She is painted in high focus and the background blurs into a sea of green behind her, creating an intensely realist but also highly lyrical portrait. The work can be read in a multitude of ways and context is key in this paradigmatic work, demonstrating the enduring pragmatic and multifaceted approach toward external cultures and politics within Cuban cultural production. On the one hand, the title is a famous Beatles' lyric from the 1967 song, perhaps aligning the painting, and the artist, with the West and therefore supporting the US tactic of beaming in Western rock music to the island to foster dissent. On the other hand, the painting took ownership of the sentiment expressed in the song. Garciandía combines the title with the "fabulous, soft focus parfait" (Weiss 2011b, 35) of his coursemate, Zaída del Rio, in the context of a society that had eschewed the capitalist system (exemplified by the United States), and embraced the humanist, lyrical, and intimate aspect of art (in opposition to the USSR). In doing so the artist affirmed that happiness and success could not be measured solely in terms of capital and reasserted the value of the individual in society. Moreover, the song was performed in the first live satellite broadcast, suggesting that the painting could also be paying a tribute to the truly international. Thus, the work can be interpreted in multiple ways to suit multiple viewpoints and/or agendas. Therefore, I would argue that photorealism in Cuba was the product of multiple influences. Its varied reception was demonstrative of the ongoing debates about modernity within Cuba and ideas about the different ways in which work could be appropriated and re-elaborated (and indeed about who was the enemy).

In her analysis of the photorealism movement, Weiss highlights the discursive nature of the plastic arts in Cuba and the gradual return to public debate in the second half of the 1970s. Form, Weiss argues, had become separated from content in the 1976 Constitution, with suspicion firmly falling on content (Weiss 2011b). She considers this split to mirror the "split between political and cultural avant-gardes, and an increasingly contentious relation between them" (Weiss 2011b, xiii). The photorealists questioned this separation of form and content, making it clear that they considered the two to be inseparable. By using the objective techniques of journalism in the subjective style of the documentarists, the artists made the familiar seem strange, thereby questioning the constitution's ruling. They used photorealism as a tautology, separating the technique from the use of photography in the 1960s to establish a revolutionary hall of images in the national narrative. The polemic caused by *All you need is love* marked the first time that plastic artists were able to question the official critics' interpretations (Weiss 2011b, 37; Mosquera 2003, 219).

The new developments in the plastic arts of the Revolution, polemics included, seemed to provide conclusive evidence that the *quinquenio gris* was coming to an end, with a return to a more open cultural atmosphere akin to that of the 1960s. This was seemingly confirmed by the inauguration of two cultural institutions that promised a more tolerant atmosphere in 1976. The first was MinCult, which "caused a significant change within the institutional landscape" and created the national system of *casas de cultura* in response to the growing demand for cultural participation thanks to the rise in education levels (Gordon-Nesbitt 2012, 81). MinCult offered a new open cultural space for the promotion, organization, and discussion of culture. The second important cultural institution was the ISA, a financially independent unit of MinCult (MinCult 1981, 7). ISA offered, for the first time in Cuba, the opportunity for the study of art at a higher level while the system of scholarships for graduate and postgraduate study abroad remained in place (Anon 1975a, 2). The institute considered students who studied there to be professionals who were perfecting their technique—an approach that remains today. The students had access to exhibition spaces before they graduated, in particular during their final year of studies (Camnitzer 2003, 160). ENA graduates were ISA teachers and/or graduates, along with Soviet assessors in some technical areas where Cuban knowledge was considered lacking. From the 1980s, ISA was the "workshop where the change in Cuban [plastic] arts was forged" (Montero Méndez 2009, 259). Montero Méndez attributes this to the combination of intellectual curiosity with other aspects of spiritual and social elements, such as science, religion, politics and philosophy (Montero Méndez 2009, 259).

ISA encouraged the individual in art but also had a potentially more negative effect. In theory ISA, and the ENA, ensured employment once a student had graduated, providing a sense of security and stability to the local and national art scene. On the other hand, it also set the parameters of art produced, though its system of prizes, spaces, and training opportunities which, essentially, clarified the bounds of acceptability—particularly in the wake of the *quinquenio gris*. The relative shortage of middle art schools across the country—four in total, one in Santiago de Cuba, one in Holguín, and two in Havana—reinforced conformity among those wishing to pursue higher art education (Kapcia 2005, 160–61). ISA was also evidence that the more dogmatic interpretations of culture, and art, were not restricted to the *quinquenio gris* and did in fact rumble on until the end of the decade. A number of individuals who were perceived by some to be very pro-Soviet were put in positions of power within the new institute.[6] These individuals were alleged by some interviewees to have promoted a more "Soviet," that is dogmatic approach toward art.

There were also, reportedly, tensions among the teaching staff with regard to technique. This division was roughly between the Soviet advisors and the established Cuban artists, with recognized works, who formed part of the teaching body. In some of the interviews conducted the Soviet advisors are reported to have considered the Cuban students—and the practicing artists on the teaching staff—technically deficient. The veracity of this was confirmed by interviews with some of the Cuban artists who pursued postgraduate studies in the USSR when later recalling their experiences. This attitude was opposed to the ideas and styles of the majority of Cuban artists who were active in ISA, but was reportedly adopted by some groups within the institute—as it had been within the ENA curriculum when Mario Rodríguez Alemán was the general director of Artistic Education in the CNC (Castellanos León 2010, 34). The consensus among those interviewed is that the artists who adopted Soviet methodology were mediocre and used it as a means of social mobility and professional advancement. There is also the suggestion that the Soviet approach, and by extension socialist realism, was considered by some to be an effective antidote to the influence of the USA, in particular its movements of abstract expressionism and action painting—in the Cuban art scene (Castellanos León 2010, 34). However, the perceived net result was that some plastic artists who were against Soviet pedagogical approaches were refused posts in ISA during this perceived "pro Soviet" phase.

Attitudes had come full circle by the late 1970s/early 1980s and this in turn negatively affected some of the students returning from the USSR during this period who found themselves unable to complete their social service in the ISA due to their perceived "Sovietness." These students either went to San Alejandro (which traditionally has been considered to be more open than ISA in the late 1970s/early 1980s) or established schools outside of the capital. By the time of the first Biennial, a "revolution in teaching" at ISA in the plastic arts was under way (Montero Méndez 2009, 259). Flavio Garciandía was elected the head of the department of painting at ISA. He established educational practices that reflected his convictions as an artist (Montero Méndez 2009, 259). He embraced cosmopolitanism, a "thirst for information and a discriminating view of local and universal culture" (Montero Méndez 2009, 259).

The "sin" of these "Soviet" artists aside, the generation that had emerged by the 1970s was the first generation that had been completely shaped by the Revolution and was therefore "without a pre-revolutionary burden" (Camnitzer 2003, 4). This was the generation of "certain hope" that was promoted by cultural activities and the emergent cultural policy, and which forms the focus of Hortensia Montero Méndez's study. The generation was at the fore of cultural developments and activities, particularly from 1977, when its name was adopted by Juan Marinello at the opening of the Third SJP (Montero Méndez 2006). The promotion of this generation, and the return of public debate was reflected at all levels of society, with the founding of the *Casa de Cultura* network in 1978 which worked in parallel with the *aficionado* movement. Evening courses were provided at middle schools and ISA to allow workers to continue their art education after beginning within the system of the *casas*.

The aim of these movements was to allow the largest possible number of Cubans access to spaces that would allow them to enjoy art, to be artistically educated, and to form part of the nation's cultural production. They were the practical manifestation of the government's desire to further democratize culture, and to further integrate culture into the economy. Hart's 1978 speech at the Meeting of the Ministers of Culture of the Socialist Countries, explaining the Cuban government's view of culture as an economic stimulant and product, marked the beginning of a new phase of the relationship between art and the economy. Design became a key area of focus: it implied an element of collectivity, interdisciplinarity, technical mastery, and the ability to respond in a pragmatic and profitable way to the needs of the Revolution. Quality remained a key feature of art's incorporation into industry and there was a view that design had to be aesthetically pleasing in order to perform its functional role of promotion (de Juan 2007, 153).

REDEFINING THE POSSIBILITIES OF ART

The net result of the reassessment and recasting of the relationship between art and industry and of the new approach to culture heralded by MinCult was a flourishing of the plastic arts. A new aesthetic began to emerge at the end of the 1970s in what Mosquera argues was the artists' attempts to break free from the bureaucratic and ideological impositions of the government—in part at the Soviet government's request to curtail artistic freedom—that had ended the discursive atmosphere of the 1960s (2001, 13). These artists of the 1970s "adopted the new concepts and visuality of the Cuban renaissance that would mark the 1980s" (Montero Méndez 2009, 259). Parody, popular culture, symbols, the Americas and their constituent civilizations, Afro-Cuban religions, European cultures, and the transcultural nature of Caribbean heritage were all factors of influence for artists that were active in the 1980s. Many of them also embraced multimedia and interdisciplinary practices in their art (Montero Méndez 2009, 259).

The exhibition *Volumen Uno*, held at the Centre for International Art Centro in January 1981, marked the beginning of a new flourishing of the plastic arts. The exhibition featured eleven artists, and was seen by 8,000 visitors in just two weeks (Camnitzer 2003, 3). The exhibition is generally the point at which new Cuban art is understood to have begun (Weiss 2011b, xiii; Camnitzer 2003, 1). The new Cuban art was broad-based, appealed to a wide sector of the population, and marked both the resurgence of old trends and the beginning of new ones. The exhibition was a reaction to the "anathematising of culture and especially of its critical vocation by the Cuban leadership" (Weiss 2011b, xiii). It also marked a foray into the public sphere of a cohort of artists who had been raised entirely within the Revolution and its contradictions. As such, while it marked a rupture in some ways, it was, in others, the continuation of Cuban cultural traditions, and their contradictions. This art, like that of the 1960s and of the Cuban vanguard in the 1920s and 1930s, was both politically committed and critical of contemporary politics. It also reflected its generation's belief in the Revolution's utopian project of independence, and in the far-reaching possibilities of art (Weiss 2011b, xiv-xv). Similarly, the art of the 1980s, including *Volumen Uno*, which seemed to be such a break with what had gone before, was, in many ways, the continuation of Cuban cultural traditions. These included assimilation, debate and the commitment to the fight against underdevelopment and dependency. The latter two of these Mosquera attributed to the range of styles that Cuban artists developed (Mosquera 1983, 358). Internationalism, albeit expressed differently than it had been in the 1970s, was at the heart of art of the 1980s as artists explored the country's identity (even if it was done through the prism of the individual) and communicated their desire to insert Cuba into the international narrative.

However, the new Cuban art also seemed to break with cultural traditions, and this led to a mixed reception from the viewing public, whilst also demonstrating the plastic arts' ability to act as a litmus test for cultural policy. The sheer range of styles and proliferation of exhibitions, which tended to be restricted to small circles, in some cases created a distance between artists and audience. This was a departure from the customary responsive relationship that had developed between artists, the public, and the demands of the Revolution (Kapcia 2005, 161). Cultural democratization and the search for cultural identity seemed to have been replaced by group and individual identities and eclecticism. This was both a conscious choice of a carefully curated eclectic and a chaotic mix of individualism (Kapcia 2005, 161). Artists of the new Cuban art put forward work that expressed the complex and interrelated cultural heritages of the nation and that was in contact with global contemporary art practices (Weiss 2011a, 25). They also viewed art's revolutionary capacity in a different light, arguing that art was revolutionary in its independence of thought and its ethical foundation. Throughout the 1980s, their work became a space of struggle that firmly believed in the power of art but was aggressive and caustic at times (Weiss 2011a, 25). Parody was an important element of much of the reflexive work produced, which often alluded to political and social problems (Pogolotti 1997, 169). In this new art there was also a focus on "immediate effects, in creative forms that reflected the contingency of the moment and therefore showed a predilection for the ephemeral over the durable" (Pogolotti 1997, 170). This was a further departure from earlier art, which had focused on producing long-term results. The tendency toward parody in the plastic arts became more pronounced in the late 1980s, for example in the work of artists such as Glexis Novoa and his *Etapa Práctica* (Figure 6.2). He used "supermacho" installations that seemed to be the embodiment of communist monumentalism. His work poked fun at the system, taking advantage of the promotion of Cuban art abroad, the criticism leveled at his friends and contemporaries, and the canons of "good" art in Cuba. Thus he was able to say what other artists had not been able to, in a body of work that was deeply confrontational but completely sanctioned and beyond criticism (Weiss 2011b, 74–76).

By the late 1980s, a marked process of self-censorship had begun. This self-censorship was partially a response to polemics, occasionally initiated by the lower ranks of officials within the art world "which showed an excess of paternalism toward the public combined with a lack of artistic sophistication and an excess of dogmatic revolutionary zeal," surrounding the work produced by this younger generation (Camnitzer 2003, xxix). The work produced celebrated the new openness of cultural policy and creation, but was not always particularly accomplished in terms of communication or sufficiently tactful in addressing the myths of the Revolution, and instead focused

Figure 6.2   Detail of Orlando Suarez's mural *Dawns of the Revolution* in the National Omnibus Terminal, Havana. Courtesy of the artist.

on formal artistic accomplishment (Camnitzer 2003, xxix). This reaction to the work of the young artists—resulting in the cycles of exhibitions organized in the Castillo de la Real Fuerza in 1988—aimed at encouraging more rigorous artistic public expression from these artists. The events surrounding the Fourth Congress of the UNEAC demonstrate the disjunction between cultural policy and cultural education (cadres, *instructores de arte*, advisors). This disjunction had begun in the early 1970s and subsequently became institutionalized. This was because individuals who had been trained to administer art at a time when more "dogmatic" cultural figures were in charge of art education at a popular level had, by the late 1980s, risen to occupy more prominent positions.

In a manner analogous to the increasing division between cultural bureaucrats and cultural practitioners in the exhibition of plastic artists, sculptures became a site of debate between opposing views of culture and its role(s).

The treatment of sculpture was symptomatic of the different perceptions of art's roles, and the different spheres of art that it was unofficially believed best suited each of these unofficial constituent roles. Among cultural officials with differing views regarding culture and socialism, art was unofficially divided into sections which included art as education, art as commemoration, and art as design. Art's different roles were catered to by different institutions and different political sub-groups, which, much as in the 1960s, resulted in the propagation of different artistic styles and approaches. I therefore argue that far from being a monolithic period with the imposition of doctrine from the top down, the late 1970s and the 1980s were a period of many competing, and occasionally conflicting, views regarding cultural policy and the intellectual and cultural production in a socialist nation. Whist socialist realism did not become an official aesthetic language in Cuba at any stage during this period (or indeed ever), some of the practices adopted suggest that the style was unofficially favored for educational and informative purposes due to its clarity of message. This led to its self-imposition on artists who wished to succeed or who were unsure of the practical application of cultural policy. This uncertainty and mimesis in aesthetics and attitudes led to the circulation of multiple strains of socialist realism.

Other plastic art produced in the 1980s generated polemics in different ways to *Volumen Uno*. One emergent trend in the 1980s, which sat easily with the cultural aims of the PCC's 1980 congress, and also with any lingering dogmatic interpretations of socialist art, was the proliferation of monuments and environmental sculptural projects and the idea that art should be public. Monuments, environmental sculpture and murals were a very public linking of the work of the artist with the concerns of the people, reminiscent of the function of poster art and graphic design in the 1960s. For example, Orlando Suárez produced an informative mural celebrating the 100 years of struggle for independence in the Havana omnibus terminal in 1979 (Figure 6.3). Some consider the mural to be emblematic of didactic socialist realist art, by way of Mexico, in Cuba but also the paradoxical nature of cultural production in Cuba in the 1970s (López Olivia 2015b). Suárez, who had founded the Experimental Graphics Workshop in 1962 and later had a position of influence in ISA, had strong links with Mexican muralism (having had some training with David Alfaro Siqueiros) and who was keen to popularize the style in Cuba (López Olivia 2015a).

Similarly, the earlier murals of Carmelo González Iglesias, who had particularly strong links with Bulgaria, were considered by some artists to be reminiscent of a type of socialist realism in Cuba (López Olivia 2015a). Sculptures produced during this period demonstrated a range of styles, such as Sergio Martínez's *Quijote de América*, Sandú Darié's *árbol rojo*, and José Villa's monument to Che Guevara (de Juan 2011, 214). Alonso González argues that other works seemed to draw more obvious parallels with what he considered to be negative Soviet tendencies (i.e., the monumentalism and didacticism seen in high Stalinist socialist realism), such as Thevia Marín's sculpture to independence fighter Serafín Sánchez in the Sancti Spiritus Revolution Square (Alonso González 2015, 147). Alonso González describes the sculpture as "a freestanding socialist realist sculpture" (Alonso González 2015, 147), which may in part be a result of the greater restrictions placed on public monuments (Alonso González 2015, 140). Alonso González argues that Cuba's focus on the recovery and construction of national traditions,

Figure 6.3 *Untitled "Practical period" from 3rd Havana Biennial 1989* **Oil on Paper, Wood and Canvas, Wooden Structure, 16 × 49 Feet.** Pérez Art Museum Miami collection, Miami. Courtesy of the artist.

themes, and figures caused it to avoid replicating the Stalinist Soviet model (2017, 55). The Revolution Squares planned across the country were, however, a particular site of combat between different interpretations of the roles of art:

> The large amount of resources and time invested in the Squares turned them into contested spaces and the focus of public interest, prompting a heated debate among the cultural workers and artists, and between them and different political actors. This was because this monumental typology was new and distinctively Cuban. Although other socialist countries emphasised the construction of new civic centres, these lacked the heritage and commemorative component of Cuban Squares. (Alonso González 2017, 143)

The net result of the *plazas de la revolución* and their ideological importance was that the leadership commissioned low-profile artists to complete the tasks. These artists were unproblematic and conforming to the monumental, socialist realist mold, which meant that the government avoided public competitions or the relinquishing of power to CODEMA (Alonso González 2017, 143).

The plastic arts and monuments in particular became a battlefield for conflicting approaches toward revolutionary culture that included ideas about aesthetic freedom and continuity, breaking with the past and orthodox approaches to culture. The 1982 Third Congress of the UNEAC did not end these divisions. However, it did confirm that the heart of Cuban cultural policy was to promote a widespread, diverse popular movement around culture which would help the creation of high quality art. Thus, different strains of thought and approaches toward culture were united by a common goal. UNEAC and the PCC's assurances of inclusivity, the focus on public debate, public contact, and constructive criticism meant that "revolutionary art form(s)" functioned as a useful umbrella term that allowed cultural practitioners to pursue their own aesthetics safely within the Revolution. This approach was similar to the way that, in the USSR of the 1930s, "socialist realism" had functioned as a convenient (empty) term that would help to unify the factionalized cultural community and provide a democratic style that would ensure that culture was understood by all sectors of society, regardless of their class origin or educational level. So, by the beginning of the mid-1980s, a cultural policy that was open to multiple interpretations, the hangover of fear created by the *quinquenio gris*, the emerging canons of "good" art (thanks to the systems of prizes that had begun to emerge from the mid-1960s), the multiple roles that art could potentially now occupy, and the prevalence of different interpretations of socialism that still abounded led to the renewed circulation of different manifestations of, and attitudes toward, "official" culture.

Ever since the failed *zafra* of 1970 and the subsequent reassessment of the island's possible paths to independence, culture had become progressively linked to the economy. During this time the plastic arts had become increasingly integrated into the economy and productivity. One example is Alberto Lescay's *Figura Ecuestre de Antonio Maceo* which, having won the FAR's sculpture competition for a monument to Antonio Maceo in Santiago de Cuba's plaza in 1982, was finally inaugurated in 1991 after much delay. The project—an offshoot of Lescay's final piece during his studies in the USSR—also had a clear economic focus. The piece ultimately included the creation of a permanent workshop in Santiago de Cuba which would produce the materials needed for the sculpture in addition to providing training for sculptural technicians (Lescay 2015).

Another, more public, experiment in linking art and economy was the TELARTE project that began in 1983. TELARTE was an experiment in mass art distribution, and was organized by MinCult and the Textile Industry section of the Ministry of Light Industry (MinCult 1983, 37). Fourteen different artists contributed twenty designs and eighteen of these designs were and plastic artists contributed designs for textile painting: eighteen of these designs were then printed in four different color variations each on runs of ten thousand meters (MinCult 1983, 37). The fabric, which was appropriate for hot climates, being used to make dresses, shirts, and banners, among other things (MinCult 1983, 37). The exhibition of these fabrics attracted over 7,000 visitors and was hailed as demonstrating a "new area of vital importance for visual artists to link themselves to material production" (MinCult 1983, 37). Printing was principally done in the textile factories Combinado Textil "Desembarco del Granma," with four thousand workers, and the Textilera Ariguanabo, with five thousand workers (Camnitzer 2003, 114–15, 351). According to Camnitzer's figures the number of designs increased steadily between 1983 and 1989 and,[7] in 1989, the production of Cuban and international artists was combined, making two distinct programs (Camnitzer 2003, 351). The path had been laid for initiatives such as TELARTE in the

1960s, as school and university students participated in initiatives that gave them "first-hand experience of the productive structure of the island in all its difficulties and all the responsibilities" (Rodríguez 1967, 10). They also echo the early Cuban revolutionary projects in theater and cultural education conducted in the 1960s, as well as the integration of art and productivity, and the focus on collectivity exemplified by Teatro Escambray.

Art and economy fused in another way, with the Biennial de Habana, which began in 1984. The Biennial acted as a platform that reasserted Cuba's place in the international arena and attempted to establish a new order (Weiss 2011a, 17). The event was organized by the Centro Wilfredo Lam (now the Centro de Arte Contemporáneo Wilfredo Lam), which was also inaugurated in 1984, two years after the artist's death. The Centro had the aim of investigating and promoting the contemporary plastic arts from the areas of Africa, Asia, Middle East, Latin America and the Caribbean. It also encouraged the study and promotion of the works of Lam (CACWilfredoLam 2016). The Biennial was the institution's signature event, and was a fundamental initiative in MinCult's new political strategy and a "banner under which Cuba would broadcast the diversity of its cultural landscape to the world and, in that, its re-conquest of its own identity" (Weiss 2011a, 17). The Biennial complemented the already-established Cuban festivals for cinema, dance, jazz and the *Feria del Libro*, and was part of the drive—similar to that of the 1968 Havana Cultural Congress—to establish Cuba as the center of the Third World (Weiss 2011a, 17). The event was notable for its ambition, and brought a forum that was taken for granted in Europe and North America into the Latin American and Caribbean domain, providing a collective space for countries that did not traditionally have such forums. In creating this space the Biennial "aimed at nothing less than creating, for the art and artists of the entire Third World, a space of respect and stature equal to that granted artists in the developed West" (Weiss 2011a, 17). The ambition and scope of the Biennial was a reflection of the Revolution's resolute internationalism and anti-imperialism: cultural dependency would be replaced by a new international cultural order. In this way, the Biennial "raised important questions not only about the nature of art made outside the Western market system, but also about its relationship with that system—these are, inevitably, questions about culture and power" (Weiss 2011a, 18).

The 1984 event focused on the regions of José Martí's "Nuestra América" (Weiss 2011a, 18), and, although it came at a time of significant transformation of contemporary art in Cuba, Weiss considers the Biennial's initial ideology and rhetoric to have come from the perspective of the older generations, being "in both political and aesthetic terms, defined by an old-fashioned identity politics mixed with the strident cadences of early revolutionary rhetoric" (Weiss 2011a, 19). The event was organized by formal artistic and aesthetic criteria rather than by country and was housed in the Pabellón Cuba and the MNBA (Weiss 2011a, 20). The Biennial's director, architectural historian Llilian Llanes Godoy, considered the Biennial a meeting place not only for artists and artists, but also for artists and life of the city and built links between the Biennial and the CDRs and governmental agencies (Weiss 2011a, 20–21). Conceiving of the Biennial as a social space also complemented the continuing focus on cultural democratization and the close relationship between artists and the people. The Biennial enjoyed political benefits and produced a space in which cultural exchange was valued as much as the display of art (Weiss 2011a, 21). Perhaps because of the way the event was conceived, it had an unusual degree of independence and a direct relationship with government (Weiss 2011a, 23–27). The second Biennial (1986) expanded the geographical scope of the project and also included a special exhibition on the works of Latin American masters, acting as a type of "primer" on the plastic arts of the region—once more emphasizing art's educational capacity. This primer was supported by another, in the form of the Biennial's catalog, which included short texts about the art and art history of each of the participating shows (Weiss 2011a, 22)

INTERNATIONAL(IST) CULTURE

As we have seen, in addition to the international prestige and established educational system that the plastic arts had developed prior to the Revolution, they also had a tradition of political engagement and a long-standing preoccupation with the search for, and expression of, a coherent national identity. This led to a hybrid approach to the plastic arts throughout the period analyzed which eventually resulted in a more complete separation of the perceived roles of art in the late 1970s and 1980s.

The plastic arts quickly demonstrated an ability to respond to the political and social needs of the Revolution, whilst skillfully navigating the problems faced by the Revolution. As a result, a form of expression specific to Cuba quickly emerged, providing hope for the embedding of a much sought-after national cultural expression. The plastic arts, and these new forms of expression, were also particularly well suited to the Revolution's internationalist aims. They transcended linguistic and cultural barriers and demonstrated the value of the conscious assimilation of foreign styles and tendencies and their re-elaboration within a clearly defined national context that then resonated with national and international audiences. Early revolutionary art projects and events, the *Salón de Mayo* included, also served to demonstrate to the international community the value of culture in the fights for national liberation, and its value in Cuba. As the nation's gaze shifted inwards, international art projects such as the Meeting of Latin American Plastic Art served as a way of continuing to contribute to the Revolution, whilst avoiding the more dogmatic tendencies.

The plastic arts' privileged position—maintained due to their supporting institutions, international prestige, and variety of potential interpretations, and responsiveness—ensured they were able to constantly push the boundaries of applications of cultural policy, and, to some extent, to forge their own path in exploring alternative ideas of socialism. Concurrently a new generation of artists emerged and brought with it new approaches toward the role of art within the Revolution and new styles of assimilation—such as photorealism—which could be promoted or condemned by the different approaches toward art. However, the demarcation of this new generation and these new approaches was further complicated by the simultaneous emergence of a new generation of cultural cadres and officials. Different approaches to art had co-existed from the beginning of the Revolution, in part due to the division of labor between the CNC and UNEAC and the public nature of debates in the 1960s. However, in the 1970s they found themselves pitched against one another, as art and culture were fused with education (1971 Congress) and economy (failed 1970 *zafra*). Each of these approaches was validated by the PCC's 1975 Congress *Thesis and Resolution* on artistic and literary culture. Over the next decade this led to the circulation of multiple approaches, each of which could be classed as socialist realism. Different approaches were promoted among the constituent roles of "art" assigned by the Revolution: didacticism and verisimilitude in public educational and commemorative projects; utility and practical solutions to problems within the economy; politically engaged, high-quality, and multiple aesthetic styles within what might be considered the more institutionalized art spaces such as galleries, universities, and (inter)national exhibitions. Concomitantly, the emphasis on clarity and unity, and the continuing call for culture to reflect the Revolution's reality gave rise to different perceptions of art within the Revolution, resulting in the presence of organizational socialist realism and the beginnings of the aesthetics of a distinctly Cuban socialist realism. Such multiple, coterminous currents meant that the USSR was both a model to be emulated and a hostile force. The pragmatic assimilation of the most useful elements of Soviet culture was encouraged by the new articulations of cultural policy, as was the rejection of other Soviet cultural approaches. The plastic arts were at the forefront of this practical approach toward the culture of the USSR and the multiple interpretations of which elements to assimilate that it engendered. Thus, the plastic arts in Cuba occupied multiple roles, as a site of resistance, a means of escape, and as an essential vehicle in a deeply utopian, international project.

NOTES

1. However, Camnitzer also points out that *Origenes* regionalism (which involved the search for an authentic American expression rather than the adoption of European abstractionism and consequently bridged the gap between realism and abstractionism) acted as an alternative to the influence of Mexican muralism (2003, 107).

2. Painters included: Angel Acosta León, Adigio Benítez, Cabrera Moreno, Hugo Consuegra, Salvador Corratgé, Sandú Darié, Antonia Eiriz, Carmelo González, Fayad Jamis, Guido Llinás, Raúl Martínez, Luis Martínez Pedro, Raúl Milián, José Mijares, Pedro de Oraá, Amelia Peláez, Umberto Peña, René Portocarrero, Mariano Rodríguez, Loló Soldevilla, Juan Tapia Ruano, Antonio Vidal, and Orlando Yanes (Pogolotti 1962, 16).

3. de Juan hails Servando Cabrera Moreno as the first artist demonstrating this shift, but that it is also visible in the works of Adigio Benítez and Orlando Yanes (de Juan, 95–96).

4. Raúl Martínez, Umberto Peña, Tony Evora, Frémez (José Gómez Fresquet), Rostgaard, Korda, Mayito and Ernesto Fernández are all artists who stood out in the early years of the Revolution for their work in the area of the industrial arts (de Juan 1968, 99–100).

5. Seventy-eight students in total, twenty-seven in the plastic arts, twenty-eight in the dramatic arts, twenty-one in ballet, and two in music (Anon 1968c).

6. In ISA three very orthodox individuals were put in power and who promoted a more dogmatic approach just as the *quinquenio* ended (López Oliva 2015b).

7. In 1983, there were sixteen designs; in 1984, twenty; in 1985, twenty-one; in 1986, thirty-one; in 1987, thirty-two; in 1989, thirty-three; and, in 1989, the production of Cuban and international artists was combined, making two distinct programs.

Chapter 7

Soviet Ruins and Stylized Nostalgia

In January 1990, the Restaurante Moscú on Calle P between Humboldt and 23 in Vedado burned down. The restaurant had opened in August 1974 shortly after Cuba's full admission to COMECON and swiftly became an enduring feature in Cuban popular culture, known for its offering of Slavic foods (Figure 7.1). It was the largest restaurant in Cuba, seating up to 400 people and offering Cuban, Slavic, and International dishes, as part of an exchange agreement between the National Tourist Institute (Instituto Nacional del Turismo, INTUR) and the Soviet Ministry of Trade. The restaurant had been restored by Cuban and Soviet specialists, with all goods supplied by the Soviet Ministry of Trade, working collaboratively with INTUR (Anon 1974f, 31).

Previously the Moscú had been the Montmartre Cabaret, one of the most famous cabaret venues of pre-revolutionary Havana, along with the Tropicana and the Sans Souci. It had been a lavish, expensive venue, run by Americans, with (frequently foreign) name acts and also large-scale shows: Edith Piaf, Nat King Cole, and Olga Guillot are all reported to have performed there. The Moscú's former location today remains derelict, identifiable only though the restaurant's distinctive tiled façade on Calle P (Figure 7.2). The culinary gap left by the demise of the Moscú is today filled by two restaurants, one which claims to be Russian: TaBARish (20 between 5th and 7th, Miramar) and the other which claims to be Soviet: Nazdorovie (Malecón between Prado and Carcel, Centro Habana). Each of these restaurants is highly stylized, evoking a Russian/Soviet "chic" with strong "Eastern" aesthetics.

The Moscú and the history of the space it occupied reflects the enduring approach toward the way the Cuban-Soviet alliance is viewed.[1] The restaurant appeared during a period that is sometimes interpreted as a particularly "Soviet" phase of the Cuban Revolution and when the USSR was a frequent point of

Figure 7.1   The Moscú in 2017. Photo courtesy of the author.

discussion and investigation in the popular mass Cuban press. It replaced a symbol of the previous dominant foreign presence, the American-run Montmartre, which in turn drew on the cultural cachet of the dominant cultural hub of the time: Paris. Once established, the Moscú swiftly became a permanent fixture in Cuban everyday popular culture and is remembered with affection by Cubans who grew up while it existed. The site has been left untouched since the restaurant was destroyed by a fire. Instead it stands as a forlorn monument to an era that remains relatively unexamined by historians working on Cuba and has come to be viewed as a firmly closed darker chapter of the Revolution's history. Arguably, even this is reflected in the remains of the building: on the street corner that meets the perennially busy street of 23 (La Rampa), there is a graffiti stencil "sic semper tyrannis" (thus always to tyrants).

Figure 7.2 The Moscú in 2017. Photo courtesy of the author.

However, the former restaurant's cultural geography also speaks to other elements of the Cuban Revolution that are sometimes eclipsed by the specter of the "Soviet." It sits between the Habana Libre, and the Pabellón Cuba, two reminders of the revolutionary government's commitment to the country's independence and cultural internationalism. One block away the Casa Museo Abel Santamaría is a testament to the roots of the Revolution and its enduring ideological foundation, and Calle P eventually intersects with the street 10 de Octubre, named after the date on which the Ten Years' War began in 1868.

The rebellion that began the Cuban Revolution was popularly supported, and broadly nationalistic; it sought to redress societal inequalities and achieve economic independence and national sovereignty. The role of culture in society was particularly valued within the conceptual framework of the type of socialism eventually adopted by the Cuban revolutionaries. As a result, artists were presented with the opportunity to occupy a central role in the construction of a new revolutionary society, and the fight against imperialism. In this way, the links between politics and culture were re-prioritized.

Culture was at the heart of the unique nature of the Cuban Revolution and fundamental in the government's approach toward nation building. It was an important site of debate that had the discursive space that was not routinely available to other areas which made up the Revolution's infrastructure, such as the economy or the political apparatus. Peregrinations on these areas were restricted by the pressing demands of the Revolution and dogma. In this way culture became an increasingly important focus of debate and an important means by which the Cuban Revolution was able to assert its sovereignty on a national level, project the legitimacy of the Revolution on an international level, and provide as much of the population as possible with ownership of the revolutionary process. It was also an outlet of resistance to the normative culture propagated by the United States and CIA-funded cultural programmers, publications and events, which sought to promote pro-American cultural freedom movements. Artistic production and cultural development became indispensable components of the mobilization to defend and advance revolutionary aims. Resultantly, artists were viewed as militants and their production considered a means of resisting and subverting the damaging forces of imperialism. Cuba's colonial past was reassessed and dominant critical discourses were ideologically deconstructed in the conscious reconfiguration of cultural poles. The Revolutionary government's focus shifted toward the Third World, underdevelopment, and the role of the artist and intellectual in liberation movements.

Cultural policy was never a monolithic entity that was articulated and applied in a top-down manner. It was an ongoing, multi-layered, discursive process. It was formulated to include as many Cubans as possible at all levels and in all related sectors. The objective was to evolve a cultural policy that reflected the cultural needs of the Revolution and with which Cuban people could identify. This was achieved through debate on what and how cultural policy should be delivered and, importantly, how it could remain relevant and influential in a fast changing political, economic and social environment. Cultural policy, therefore, was constantly evolving and constantly being redefined in response to landmark political, social, and economic events and was never evenly applied.

The non-uniform nature of Cuban cultural policy was most evident in the first decade of the Revolution, when emergent cultural institutions were erratically formed and in a constant state of flux. Practitioners struggled to identify the most pressing tasks of culturally (re)constructing the nation. This led to a succession of short-term experiments and artistic license to explore new forms of delivery. Early in this era institutions were formed around particular personalities who had been active in the pre-1959 revolutionary struggle, such as Alfredo Guevara and ICAIC or Haydeé Santamaría and Casa, and their specific commitment to the development of a Cuban revolutionary culture. Other, broader, umbrella institutions, such as the CNC and the UNEAC, were created in response to the need to organize culture more generally and to recognize the quality of cultural output. Their roles were clarified in response to a perceived moment of crisis—the PM affair—and the ensuing public debate which culminated in *Palabras a los intelectuales*. Palabras remained the loadstone of cultural policy until the Special Period.

The emergence of these organizations marked the beginning of the heterogeneous interpretation and application of cultural policy. When it first existed as such, cultural policy was roughly grouped around ten central ideas that reflected the historical roots of the 1959 rebellion and assumed a certain level of support for the Revolution from practitioners unless explicitly stated otherwise. The frenetic and erratic atmosphere of the 1960s allowed for the development of multiple interpretations and applications of cultural policy based around each of the different cultural institutions and their subgroups. The multiplicity of approaches and outputs were publicly debated in the emerging cultural publications. These debates were always intimately linked to ideas about the direction, priorities, and ideology of the Cuban Revolution and were therefore also linked to ideas about which sub-group within the revolutionary apparatus was best qualified to take control of the cultural tasks facing the revolutionary government. The divisions and debates were further complicated by the need to mobilize educational programmers and cultural efforts and the pre-existing structures—of the PSP—that this favored, particularly given the recent establishment of the alliance with the USSR. The grass-roots radicalization of the population in response to events such as the Bay of Pigs and the Cuban Missile Crisis accelerated the development of a widespread political consciousness, which did not necessarily agree with Soviet ideology. Reflecting the government's focus on national sovereignty and independence, a distinctly "Cuban" interpretation of socialism began to develop. This ideological strain was codified by the creation of the PCC in which members of the guerrilla M-26-7, rather than the PSP, dominated.

Key issues for the revolutionaries were perceived in response to external threats, disillusionment with existing theoretical models, and an ever-more urgent desire to coherently articulate a national identity. Paramount to the response required was a clearer organizational structure in the Revolution's institutional apparatus and the external projection of unity. This led to the beginning of a period of institutionalization and reassessment of Cuba's past and possible alternative paths to independence. Such cultural introspection was once again complicated by the ongoing process of defining what the Revolution stood for, and the integration of culture to ideas about education, economy and development. There was a further layer of complication added to the ongoing debates about education, which was the most enduring gateway to Soviet-style ideology and attitudes. From the mid-1960s onwards generations raised, within the Revolution, on Soviet manuals of Marxism emerged. Members of these generations, such as Lisandro Otero, began to occupy positions of power within revolutionary institutions toward the mid-late 1970s and early 1980s, reflecting, to some extent, the wider population's education, and their expectations of culture. The merging of these ideological currents and the focus on economic development ultimately led to the separation of the components which constituted ideas about revolutionary "art" and "culture."

As the two case studies on theater and the plastic arts have thrown into sharp relief, culture, or cultural policy, was a conduit for examining the nation's diverse past within the framework of the new nation, which permitted for the salvaging of any element considered useful and its re-elaboration into the new national setting. The way different media were treated demonstrated attitudes toward different aspects of Cuba's past. Theater paid particular attention to the damaging effects of the country's colonial past and its resultant underdeveloped status. This meant that it became a forum in which to combat the country's history of excluding certain sectors and enduring or subsequent real and perceived isolation that may have been caused by the assimilation of an undesirable cultural element. In doing this it also became a crucible for experimentations in the creation of a new, revolutionary, inclusive, accessible, and educational art form with a rich diversity of styles. The plastic arts had attention paid to their history of independent creation and political commitment. Their diversity and originality which lay in the successful assimilation of the nation's myriad of historical cultural currents was celebrated and the artistic form became a focus for investigation into how to raise the cultural level of the population, and expressing the "Cuban" in the international. Due to its non-verbal nature it also became a valued conduit for experimenting with different approaches to educating the population. The calculated varying treatment of the different media also speaks to which different elements of the emergent national identity the government and cultural practitioners wished to emphasize. Theater was particularly suited to demonstrate the move from alienation and the individual to collectivity, while the plastic arts lent themselves to demonstrating the nation's history of resistance that had now become commitment to continental Revolution.

In the same way that cultural policy was not monolithic, nor was the Cuban perception of, and relationship with, the USSR. Culture was a key medium in which the Cuban differences with the USSR were negotiated. Ideologically the two countries had little in common, for the same reasons that some of the more orthodox members of the PSP did not support the rebellion: the country was theoretically unready for socialist Revolution. Cuba's enduring connection with the USSR was born of a pragmatic response from both parties. In an increasingly polarized geopolitical climate the rapid deterioration of Cuban-US relations made it imperative for Cuba to find a trading ally and secure military protection capable of rivaling the force of the United States: the USSR was the only viable alternative. The USSR initially turned to Cuba out of economic and then ideological practicality: it needed large amounts of sugar which it was unable to produce, and Cuba presented an unparalleled opportunity for the USSR to gain prestige on the international stage and demonstrate the vitality of the Soviet socialist movement. However, the prolonged focus on sugar production meant that the USSR came to be seen by Cubans as another imperial force, and alternative ways of developing the Cuban economy were explored.

This shifting of the Cuban government's priorities meant that the nation's richest resource, its people and their inherent creative talents, was reappraised and efforts made to harness this potentially liberating force. The perception of the USSR as another imperial power had ramifications across all aspects of the Cuban Revolution as the focus moved to maintaining the nation's independence in all spheres, including ideologically. This renewed sense of siege caused the nation's gaze to turn inwards in a bid to identify and rescue the elements of the nation's history that could be used as a protective barrier against external threats. At the same time, internationalism became the Cuban government's path to independence as the two countries had a fundamentally different opinion of the global political situation and the best method to pursue socialism at an international level. Ultimately the two countries adopted a more pragmatic approach toward each other, working together to achieve mutually beneficial goals, and the balance of influence shifted as Cuba cemented its reputation as the vanguard of Third World socialism. However, there were always multiple currents of political thought in existence within the Cuban Revolution. These currents co-existed throughout the period examined, which meant that the USSR was constantly viewed as anathema, inspiration and everything in between. Such complexity is reflected in the ongoing ambiguity about how the term "Soviet" is understood and what it actually stood for among Cubans during the period analyzed and stands for today.

The October Revolution and the early years of Bolshevik rule held a significant place in Latin American revolutionary thought, as did the early efforts to educate the Russian, and then Soviet, population and widen the boundaries of culture. Equally, the rapid industrialization of the Stalin regime was a model that spoke to individuals in countries seeking to lift themselves out of underdevelopment. However, the errors and the human cost of the USSR's variant of socialism, not least those of the Stalin regime which came to light from the mid-1950s onward, were also equally known and used to warn of the dangers of collaboration with the USSR or as impetus to search for alternative interpretations of socialism.

The international perception of the USSR became inextricably linked with the rule of Stalin and remained shaped by the legacy of this period. The events and lasting impact of this administration were slow to be addressed publicly nationally or internationally. Perhaps because of this the period in which culture in Cuba was most heavily regulated, the *quinquenio gris*, has often been described as the most "Soviet" period in Cuba's history. This label is to some extent explained by the institutionalization which took place during this period which saw the introduction of some Soviet structures, such as *Poder Popular*, which mirrored the Soviet experience in preparation for Cuba's full induction into COMECON. This was also the first peak in the discussion about the USSR and the popular press.

However, as this research has demonstrated, the 1970s, and particularly the period of 1971 to 1976, was not necessarily a "Soviet" period of the Cuban Revolution which saw the wholesale imposition of Soviet ideas about cultural organization and aesthetic styles onto the cultural production of the Cuban Revolution. Indeed, the force of the debates of the 1960s, and Ambrosio Fornet's discussion of the *quinquenio gris*, regarding revolutionary culture (of which socialist realism formed only a part) reflect the overwhelming rejection of the imposition of any model or approach. Rather, the decade of the 1970s, and the period of the *quinquenio gris* in particular, is better understood as a period of bellicose expression of emergent ideas of nationalism in response to a mounting sense of isolation and siege. From 1968 onwards, as Cuba moved away from European ideas of socialism and opposition to the Revolution mounted, artists were viewed as soldiers. Cultural administration and cultural practitioners were mobilized to defend against overt external threats, but also perceived internal threats such as alienation. The reclassification of cultural practitioners in the national imaginary gave primacy to a certain set of behavioral expectations, which coalesced with orthodox Marxist ideas about the creation and promotion of an educative culture.

As a by-product of the new emphasis on the fostering of a coherent national expression and the artist as soldier, foreign culture occupied a contentious position. From the late 1960s until the mid-1970s there was an ambiguous approach toward "good" and "bad" foreign influences, with no concrete canon against which such influence could be measured. The USSR, as the most consistent foreign presence, occupied an equally contentious position within the Cuban cultural imaginary at this stage. The continuing local power struggles and discussion about economic and political approaches further complicated the perception of the Soviet superpower.

The USSR formed part of Cuba's "Imaginary West": the perception of practices, knowledge, and aesthetics that belonged to products of imperialism. It simultaneously also formed part of Cuba's everyday reality, as the most immediate, functioning example of popular socialist culture. Such an approach is reflected in the treatment of the idea of the USSR in Cuba during this period. The move toward full membership of COMECON seemed to imply the primacy of a particular ideological approach was confirmed by the promotion of orthodox individuals, often with military background, to positions of power in culture. The proliferation of articles about the USSR in the popular mass publications and cultural publications reinforced this idea.

However, the latter phenomenon also demonstrates the ongoing focus on education, informing the population (particularly in the cultural press) about the country's closest ally and its cultural practices and history. The ambiguity regarding the Cuban relationship with the USSR, the interpretative spaces that it left for the application of policy, and the power struggles it enabled, were arguably one of the greatest contributors to the general perception of the early 1970s as "Soviet." Such uncertainty permitted multiple strains of cultural practices concerning the "Soviet," with each instance equally open to interpretation. The polemical position that the USSR, and its ill-defined presence in Cuban society, continued to occupy in revolutionary society contributed to varying perceptions of the superpower's role in the Revolution that was not clarified until the 1976 Constitution.

The period 1968–1976 does not represent an overwhelmingly "Soviet" period. Rather, as this book has revealed, it was a period of intense re-evaluation of notions of culture and internationalism in a society in the throes of a second phase of revolutionary change as the nation attempted to modernize. Moreover, in its drive for modernization, the Cuban Revolution in the 1968–1976 period demonstrates the contradictory and unequal way in which the journey to modernity unfolded in Latin America. Caught between international isolation and subordination, expressions of emergent Cuban nationalism took on a particularly strident tone as the government strove to maintain its path to independence.

The new Constitution codified Cuba's commitment to internationalism and clarified the nature of Cuba's relationship with the USSR. It also clarified the contentious position of "foreign" culture, which was deemed acceptable if it was properly critiqued, assimilated and re-elaborated in a way that was clearly Cuban. However, with the creation of MinCult the cultural infrastructure began to resemble that of the USSR more closely, a reflection of the increasingly streamlined, and controlled, interaction of the two countries. There was a renewed drive to nurture the latent creative talent in the Cuban population, as part of the linking of culture and education to the economy. This meant that the USSR was viewed as an education source that would help train Cubans in areas where a lack of technical knowledge was holding back the development of the Cuban economy and cultural expression.

Thus, the perceived best of the USSR was appropriated (at different times, and by different groups) and reinterpreted into a Cuban setting. Co-operation and collaboration with the USSR was once more embedded into cultural policy, but in terms that emphasized the equality of the relationship and the ways in which it would benefit Cuba. Within culture, Cubans were sent to study in the USSR, and Soviet advice was taken on the structuring of ISA. Even there, though, the Soviet influence was carefully controlled: ISA was located in Cubanacán, an internationally acclaimed architectural testament to the unique nature, and aesthetics, of Cuba and the Revolution, Soviet advisors were employed in the technical, skills-based classes, and the Cuban artists sent to the USSR had all already excelled in their fields and had distinctive styles.

Simultaneously, institutions that were distinctly Cuban, such as the Center for Martian Studies, began to proliferate, demonstrating the ongoing commitment to the exploration and rescue of national heritage in the construction of the new national image. During this period the Cuban-Soviet alliance began to take on a performative element, as cooperation was focused around significant dates in the history of each country. In these symbolic celebrations of solidarity and cooperation the focus was placed on the period that spanned the October Revolution until the death of Lenin, the fight against fascism, cultural traditions and folklore. For example, *Bohemia* sported an image of Lenin on its cover for the issue of the first week of November every year. Such demarcation of the alliance helped to create internal space for cultural creation and the exploration of national identity. In the 1970s, cultural history (folklore and traditions) had been used as a gateway for potential further cooperation with the "brother socialist" countries. By the 1980s it had come to be used as a protective barrier that allowed for the public affirmation of friendship and cooperation, but also performed a protective role due to its historic quality. This shift also fitted with the changing Soviet perception of the Cuban Revolution: as the revolutionary government positioned itself at the vanguard of alternative interpretations of socialism, Soviet discussion of Cuba increasingly presented the Revolution as a national liberation movement, rather than a socialist revolution, slowly following the Soviet developmental model.

In examining the multiple currents of cultural production, organization and revolutionary thought, this book has revealed that the 1980s—despite the increasingly strained relationship between Cuba and the USSR—were actually the most "Soviet" period particularly in terms of organization, the demands placed on public culture and the promotion of a certain type of artistic production. This was in part because of the ongoing dominance of Soviet-trained Cubans in institutional administration but also because some of the different currents of thought within the Revolution combined around ideas of the coalescence of education, culture, and economy. These commonly shared ideas involved assisting the crossover of elite and mass culture for educational purposes and the use of culture for international agitation. Both of these necessarily included the clear inscription of coherent national and regional identity into cultural production.

In the mid and late 1970s inspiration was taken from the October Revolution's early linking of culture to economic production, through movements such as constructivism. However, given the heterogeneous nature of interpretations of socialism within the Revolution that continued to exist, and the ongoing perceptions of the demands placed on culture, the application of the emergent cultural policy in some spheres continued to be contradictory and at times regulatory. This led to a type of organizational socialist realism though the practices of certain institutions, which was arguably then promoted by the subsequent overt rejection of Soviet ideas and models and styles in the bid for national independence.

However, the drive to further integrate culture into economic production caused the culture's educational and informative qualities to become separated from its artistic and innovative qualities as certain elements of each form of cultural expression were promoted. This selective advancement and support of certain types of cultural production led to a separation of culture into public and private. "Public" culture—murals, statues, posters, theater performances—informed and educated. "Private" culture that focused on artistic innovation—such as sculpture, painting and installations—was confined to increasingly closed artistic circles. In some cases this separation ended up alienating the artist from revolutionary society, such as the New Art of Cuba that emerged in the 1980s.

Internationalism remained the way in which cultural practitioners, and cultural institutes, were able to question this separation of culture's roles and to propose alternative interpretations of socialist culture. Cultural events aimed at an international audience, such as the Biennial and the Festival of

Teatro Nuevo, helped to begin recreating the discursive atmosphere of the 1960s. New emphasis was placed on the search for the cultural expression of a national identity but more fully inscribing Cuban culture within the Latin American and Caribbean tradition. The renewed focus on cultural internationalism was complemented by a systematic analysis of Cuban revolutionary culture to date to search for trends and ways in which to improve cultural output and its efficiency. Such analysis of cultural production included the questioning of Soviet ideas and approaches that had found a place in Cuban culture. In some areas, such as informative or performative culture, an element of "Soviet" culture remained. However, in artistic higher education institutes, particularly ISA, there was an increasing rejection of Soviet influence and presence (now seen as cultural imperialism), which also included protecting against future influence: theater quotas were restructured, artists who had studied in the USSR were not employed in the capital's landmark artistic centers, and Soviet assessors did not have their contracts renewed.

This research has revealed that culture, and the evolving cultural policy in Cuba, frequently acted as spaces in which the revolutionary government and cultural practitioners could define their differences and articulate their own definitions of Revolution and socialism and debate the developing national identity. It has highlighted the ambivalences of the Cuban-Soviet relationship within Cuba's domestic cultural policy. In doing so it has evidenced how internationalism formed the core of Cuba's emergent national identity, and how this narrative allowed revolutionary practitioners to assimilate a wide range of cultural trends whilst maintaining a clear political commitment. Among its original contributions, this monograph offers a careful re-reading of the meanings and contradictions of socialist realism in the context of the post-1959 Cuban experience, drawing on my identification of the inherent internationalist qualities of the doctrine.

This study has revealed that throughout the period 1961–1987 there were many different perceptions of the USSR within the cultural spaces of the Cuban Revolution, and indeed of what "Soviet" actually meant.[2] These impressions were constantly in flux, reacting to the needs of the Revolution and the perceived distribution of power within cultural administration. Regarding the concept of socialist realism in the Cuban context this study has demonstrated that in the same way there was never a unitary idea of "Revolution" and "Socialism" in Cuba, there was never a single notion of socialist realism. The concept was open and mutable and contingent on the individual's conception of the role of culture in a socialist society and the envisioned task of either the specific art form.

This diversity of the constantly shifting interpretations of key concepts and their impact on the role of culture, along with the tendency of cultural policy to react rather than anticipate, led to multiple strains of approaches that could be termed socialist realism. These approaches both coexisted and conflicted at times. Such strains were born out of the ongoing commitment to the creation of a socialist culture that reflected its people to a national, and international audience, and the different paths toward this goal that were considered viable.

In particular, the plastic arts were key in the revolutionary authorities' navigation of international Cold War binaries as was the theater in the exploration of Cuba's national and regional cultural traditions. The detailed analysis of these two cultural modes in chapters 4 and 5 has revealed how ideas about internationalism and traditional cultural forms were able to be harnessed by different artistic media, practitioners, and institutions to help negotiate the Cuban government's path toward a distinctly Cuban form of socialism. This socialism drew on the best of other models, including those from the USSR, but also from Latin America and the Caribbean. In the selective assimilation of Soviet elements and the skillful maneuvering around Soviet priorities, cultural policy, production and organization was always tempered by the Revolution's enduring ideological roots.

NOTES

1. Zoe García Miranda *Todo tiempo pasado fue mejor* (2008) and Jacqueline Loss (2013, 197–213) have both explored the Moscú in more detail.

2. Ongoing issues around how Soviets are viewed in Cuba are discussed by both Loss (2004, 2009, 2012, 2014) and Puñales-Alpizar (2012, 2013).

Bibliography

Abashin, Sergei. 2011. 'Sovetskaia vlast i uzbekskaia makhallia,' *Neprikosno-vennii zapas*: 70–78. http://magazines.russ.ru/nz/2011/4/a11-pr.html [accessed 3/04/2017].

Acosta, Blanca. 1982. 'Una gira de fraternidad: grupo teatro escambray en estados unidos,' *Conjunto*, 53: 115–19.

Aguirre, Mirta. 1963. 'Apuntes sobre la literatura y el arte,' *Cuba Socialista*, 3: 62–82.

———. 1981. 'Realismo, realismo socialista y la posición cubana,' in Mirta Aguirre (ed.), *Estudios Literario* (Havana: Editorial Letras Cubanas), pp. 424–67.

Alonso, Pedro Ignacio, and Hugo Palmarola. 2009. 'A Panel's Tale: The Soviet KPD System and the Politics of Assemblage,' *AA Files*, 59: 30–41.

Alonso, Pedro Ignacio, and Hugo Palmarola. 2014. *Panel* (London: Architectural Association Publications).

Andropov, Iurii. 1983. 'Rech' General'nogo sekretaria Tsentral'nogo Komiteta KPSS,' *Pravda*, June 1983, 1–2, 16.

Anon. 1946. 'O repertuare dramaticheskikh teatrov i merakh po ego uluchsheniu,' *Bol'shevik*, 16: 591–96.

———. 1949a. 'Ob odnoi antipatrioticheskoi gruppe teatral'nykh kritikov,' *Pravda*, 28 January, p. 3.

———. 1955b. 'Samodeiatel'noe iskusstvo,' in Boris A. Vvedenskii (ed.) *Bol'shaia Sovetskaia Entsikopediia*, vol. 27 (Moscow: Gosudarstvennoe nauchnoe izdatel'stvo), p. 661.

———. 1955c. 'Sotsialisticheskii realizm,' in Boris A. Vvedenskii (ed.) *Bol'shaia Sovetskaia Entsikopediia*, vol. 40 (Moscow: Gosudarstvennoe nauchnoe izdatel'stvo), pp. 180–2.

———. 1959. 'Una posición,' *Lunes de Revolución*, 23 March, 1: 2.

———. 1962a. 'Grupo Hermanos Saíz de la Unión de Escritores y Artistas de Cuba,' *Gaceta de Cuba*, 5: 16.

———. 1963b. *Anteproyecto del plan de cultura de 1963* (Havana: Consejo Nacional de Cultura).

———. 1966a. *Cultura; teatro, artes plásticas, arquitectura, música, danza, literatura, cine* (Havana: Consejo Nacional de Cultura).

———. 1966b. 'El Caimán Barbudo ha hecho acto de presencia,' *Caimán Barbudo*, 1: 1–2.

———. 1966e. 'Nota Inicial,' *Unión*, 5: 5–6.

———. 1967a. 'Los premios literarios de la UNEAC 1967,' *Granma*, 8 November, p. 6.

———. 1968c. 'Efectuada la primera graduación de la Escuela Nacional de Arte,' *Granma*, 3 December, p. 3.

———. 1969a. 'Convocatoria al Salón Nacional de Arte Plásticas de la UNEAC,' *Granma*, 16 September, p. 5.

———. 1969b. 'Soglasheniia v oblasti kul'tury,' *Kuba*, 12: 42.

———. 1970. *Política cultural de Cuba* (Havana: Consejo Nacional de Cultura).

———. 1971. El Primer Congreso Nacional. *Revista de la Biblioteca Nacional de Cuba José Martí.* http://revistas.bnjm.cu/index.php/revista-bncjm/article/view/1732.

———. 1972b. 'Convocatoria para el IV Salón nacional de Carteles 26 de Julio,' *Granma*, 15 May, p. 3.

———. 1974a. 'Declaración del Segundo Encuentro de Plástica Latinoamericana,' *Unión*, 13: 151–5.

———. 1974b. *Directivas y Resoluciones Sobre la Enseñanza del Arte* (Havana: Consejo Nacional de Cultura).

———. 1974e. *Indicaciones generales del Presidente del Consejo Nacional de Cultura para el desarrollo del trabajo en 1974* (Havana: Consejo Nacional de Cultura).

———. 1974f. 'Restoran Moskva,' *Kuba*, 11: 30–31.

———. 1975a. *Convocatoria a escuelas de arte y cultura. Dirección General de Escuelas curso 1976–77* (Havana: Consejo Nacional de Cultura).

———. 1975b. *Directiva No.1 del Consejo Nacional de Cultura para el desarrollo del trabajo en 1975* (Havana: Consejo Nacional de Cultura).

———. 1975c. Tesis No. 6, Proyecto de Plataforma Programática Del Partido Comunista de Cuba, *Bohemia*, 43 (supplement): 1–32.

———. 1976a. 'Declaración emitida en el Encuentro de Plástica Latinoamericana 1976,' *Granma*, 24 May, p. 4.

———. 1979c. 'Declaración del Simposio de Identidad Cultural Caribeña,' *Granma*, 23 July, p. 4.

———. 1979e. 'Evalúa Armando Hart de evento de gran importancia política y cultura,' *Granma*, 5 March, p. 2.

———. 1979g. 'Participarán unos 30 países caribeños en el próximo CARIFESTA '79,' *Granma*, 3 April, p. 4.

———. 1980a. 'Círculo de Bellas Artes,' in Marina García (ed.), *Diccionario de la literatura cubana*, vol. 1 (Havana: Editorial Letras Cubanas), p. 215.

———. 1981a. 'Encuentro de teatristas latinoamericanos y del caribe,' *Casa de las Américas*, 22: 134.

———. 1981b. 'Teatral'noe dvizhenie na kube segodnia,' *Latinskaia Amerika*, 13: 115–26.

———. 1982a. 'En el festival de teatro de Havana 1982,' *Tablas*, 1: 36–37.

———. 1989. 'Declaración de principios de artistas plásticos que acordaron no concurrir al VIII Salón de Pintura, Escultura y Cerámica convocado por el Instituto Nacional de Cultura,' in Ricardo Hernández Otero (ed.), *Revista Nuestro Tiempo. Complicación de trabajos* (Havana: Editorial Letras Cubanas), pp. 170–1.

———. 1996. 'Cuba,' in Don Rubin and Carlos Solorzano (eds.), *World Encyclopaedia of Contemporary Theater*, vol. 2 (New York: Routledge), pp. 215–41.

———. 2009. 'Consagración de la Sacra Catedral Ortodoxa de la Virgen de Kazán,' *Opus Habana*, 12: 1–XII.

Anon, Armando Hart Davalos, and Lupe Velez. 1979. 'Prazdnik kubinskoi kul'tury,' *Latinskaia Amerika*, 10: 138–40.

Anon, E. Radomyslenskii, and A. Okun. 1977. 'Ot Gavany do Eskambraia. Beseda s E. Radomyslenskim i A. Okunem,' *Latinskaia Amerika*, 9: 134–38.

Anreus, Alejandro. 2004. 'The Road to Dystopia: The Paintings of Antonia Eiriz,' *Art Journal*, 63: 4–17.

Antuña, Vicentina. 1963. 'Casa de cultura en Praga,' *Pueblo y Cultura*, 14: 9–14.

AP, Associated Press. 2016. 'Fidel Castro's Name Will Never Appear On a Cuba Monument, Says Brother Raúl,' *Guardian*, 4 December, https://www.theguardian.com/world/2016/dec/04/fidel-castro-name-cuba-never-on-monument-says-brother-raul [accessed 1 April 2017].

Arrufat, Antón. 2002. 'Un escritor al que le sigue latiendo el corazón,' in Leonardo Padura Fuentes and John M. Kirk (eds.), *La cultura y la revolución cubana: conversaciones en Havana* (Havana: Editorial Plaza Mayor), pp. 53–90.

Avíla, Leopoldo. 1969. 'Escrito en las Puertas,' *Verde Olivo*, 15: 13.

Azicri, Max. 2000. *Cuba Today and Tomorrow: Reinventing Socialism* (Gainesville: University Press of Florida).

Báez, Luis, and Armando Hart Davalos. 1986. *Cambiar las reglas del juego* (Havana: Editorial Letras Cubanas).

Bain, Mervyn J. 2005. 'Cuba-Soviet Relations in the Gorbachev Era,' *Journal of Latin American Studies*, 37: 769–91.

———. 2007. *Soviet-Cuban Relations, 1985 to 1991* (Lanham: Lexington Books).

———. 2008. *Russian-Cuban Relations Since 1992: Continuing Camaraderie in a Post-Soviet World* (Lanham: Lexington Books).

———. 2010. 'Havana and Moscow, 1959–2009: The Enduring Relationship?,' *Cuban Studies*, 41: 126–42.

———. 2011. 'Russia and Cuba: "Doomed" Comrades?,' *Communist and Post-Communist Studies*, 44: 111–18.

———. 2013. *From Lenin to Castro, 1917–1959: Early Encounters between Moscow and Havana* (Lanham: Lexington Books).

———. 2015. 'Review: Escrito en cirílico: el ideal Soviético en la cultura Cubana posnoventa,' *Bulletin of Latin American Research*, 35: 109–10.

———. 2016. 'Moscow, Havana and Asymmetry in International Relations.' *Cambridge Review of International Affairs*, 29 (3): 1044–60.

———. 2017. 'Havana, Moscow and Beijing: Looking to the Future in the Shadow of the Past,' *Social Research: An International Quarterly*, 84 (2): 507–26.

———. 2017. 'Russia, Cuba and Colonial Legacies in the Twenty-first Century,' *Journal of Transatlantic Studies*, 15 (1): 1–17.

———. 2018. 'Havana and Moscow in the 1970s: "Sovietization" in an Era of Détente,' in E. J. Kirk, A. Clayfield and I. Story (eds.), *Cuba's Forgotten Decade: How the 1970s Shaped the Revolution* (Lanham: Lexington), pp. 23–40.

———. 2018. 'Raúl Castro and Cuban-Russian Relations, 2008–2018,' in H. M. Erisman and J. H. Kirk (eds.), *Cuban Foreign Policy: Transformation under Raúl Castro* (Lanham: Rowman & Littlefield).

———. 2018. 'Russo–Cuban Relations in the 1990s,' *Diplomacy & Statecraft*, 29 (2): 255–73.

———. 2019. *Moscow and Havana 1917 to the Present: An Enduring Friendship in an Ever-Changing Global Context* (Lanham: Lexington Books).

Bain, M., and L. F. Mollinedo. 2016. 'Cuba: Trapped by History – Still?' *International Politics*, 53 (2): 260–76.

Barghoorn, Frederick C. 1960. *The Soviet Cultural Offensive: The Role of Cultural Diplomacy in Soviet Foreign Policy* (Princeton: Princeton University Press).

Ball, Alan. 1997. *Russia's Last Capitalists: The Nepmen 1921–29* (Berkeley: University of California Press).

Bek, Aleksandr. 1951. *Volokolamsk Highway* (Moscow: Foreign Languages Publishing House).

Bekarevich, Anatolii Danilovich, et al. (eds.). 1979. *Kul'tura Kuby* (Moscow: Nauka).

Bekarevich, Anatolii Danilovich, et al. 1977. *Velikii Oktiabr' i kubinskaia revolutsiia* (Moscow: Nauka).

Benedetti, Mario. 1971. 'Situación actual de la cultura cubana,' in Mario Benedetti (ed.), *Literatura y arte nuevo en Cuba* (Havana: Editorial Estela), pp. 7–32.

Berger, John. 1973. *Ways of Seeing* (London: Penguin Books).

Betancourt, Juan Carlos. 2012. 'The Rebel Children of the Cuban Revolution: Notes on the History of "Cuban Sots Art,"' in Jacqueline Loss and José Manuel Prieto (eds.), *Caviar with Rum: Cuba-USSR and the Post-Soviet Experience* (New York: Mamillan), pp. 69–84.

Beumers, Birgit. 1997. *Yuri Lyubimov at the Taganka Theater 1964–1994* (Amsterdam: Harwood Academic Publishers).

———. 1998. 'Performing Culture: Theater,' in Catriona Kelly and David Shepherd (eds.), *Russian Cultural Studies: An Introduction* (Oxford: Oxford University Press).

———. 1999. 'The "Thaw" and After, 1953–1986,' in Robert Leach and Victor Borovsky (eds.), *A History of Russian Theater* (Cambridge: Cambridge University Press), pp. 358–81.

Blasier, Cole. 1983. *The Giant's Rival: The USSR and Latin America* (Pittsburg: University of Pittsburgh Press).

Bonachea, Rolando, and Nelson P. Valdés. 1972b. '*Culture and Revolutionary Ideology: Introduction*,' in Bonachea, Rolando and Nelson P. Valdés (eds.), *Cuba in Revolution* (New York: Anchor Books), pp. 497–9.

Bowlt, John E. 2002. 'Stalin as Isis and Ra: Socialist Realism and the Art of Design,' *The Journal of Decorative and Propaganda Arts*, 24: 34–63.

Bown, Matthew. 2012. '1954–1964,' in Matthew Bown, Zelfira Tregulova and Evgenia Petrova (eds.), *Socialist Realisms: Soviet Painting 1920–1970* (Milan: Skira), pp. 96–113.

Brundenius, Claes. 2002. 'Whither the Cuban Economy after Recovery? The Reform Process, Upgrading Strategies and the Question of Transition,' *Journal of Latin American Studies*, 34 (2 May): 365–95.

Buckwalter-Arias, James. 2005. 'Reinscribing the Aesthetic: Cuban Narrative and Post-Soviet Cultural Politics,' *PMLA*, 120: 362–74.

Caballero, Magdalena Garrido. 2009. "Las Relaciones Culturales Hispano-soviéticas (1931–1939)." *Ayer*, 74: 191–217.

Cabrera Infante, Guillermo. 1960. 'Editorial,' *Lunes de Revolución*, 8 February, 46: 3.

CACWilfredoLam, Centro de Arte Contemporáneo Wilfredo Lam. 2016. 'Quiénes Somos,' http://www.wlam.cult.cu/index.php/quienes-somos [accessed 11/8/16].

Camacho Albert, René. 1972. 'Está Jornada es un importante eslabón cultural entre nuestros países,' *Granma*, 2 November, p. 2.

Camnitzer, Luis. 2003. *New Art of Cuba* (Austin: University of Texas Press).

Cano, Osvaldo. 2015. Interview.

Carbonell Cortina, Néstor. 1989. *And the Russians Stayed: The Sovietization of Cuba: A Personal Portrait* (New York: William Morrow and Company).

Carifesta. 2016. 'History of Carifesta,' http://en.carifesta.net/history-of-carifesta/ [accessed 16/05/2016].

Carol, Alberto Jorge. 1974. 'Cuadodebate,' *Revolución y Cultura*, 24: 24–29.

Casal, Lourdes. 1971. 'Literature and Society,' in Carmelo Mesa-Lago (ed.), *Revolutionary Change in Cuba* (Pittsburgh: University of Pittsburgh Press), pp. 447–70.

Casañas, Inés, and Jorge Fornet. 1999. *Premio Casa de las Américas: Memoria, 1960–1999* (Havana: Fondon Editorial Casa de las Américas).

Castellanos León, Israel. 2010. 'Moscú Rojo, Fijeza Visual en tr3s tiempos,' *Revolución y Cultura*, 1: 28–41.

Castro, Fidel. 1961a. 'Discurso pronunciado por el Comandante Fidel Castro Ruz, Primer Ministro del Gobierno Revolucionario y Secretario del PURSC, como conclusión de las reuniones con los intelectuales cubanos, efectuadas en la biblioteca nacional el 16, 23 y 30 de junio de 1961,' http://www.cuba.cu/gobierno/discursos/1961/esp/f300661e.html [accessed 2/04/2017].

———. 1961b. 'Discurso pronunciado por Fidel Castro Ruz, Presidente de Dobla República de Cuba, en las honras fúnebres de las víctimas del bombardeo a distintos puntos de la república, efectuado en 23 y 12, frente al cementerio de Colón, el día 16 de abril de 1961,' http://www.cuba.cu/gobierno/discursos/1961/esp/f160461e.html [accessed 2/04/2017].

Castro, Fidel. 1981. 'Discurso pronunciado en el Acto de Clausura del II Congreso de los CDR, efectuado en el Teatro "Carlos Marx," el 24 de Octubre de 1981,' http://www.cuba.cu/gobierno/discursos/1981/esp/f241081e.html [accessed 28/10/2018].

Catá, Almayda. 1962. 'Servando Cabrera: un nuevo lenguaje plástico,' *Unión*, 6: 165–66.

Chanan, Michael. 1985. *The Cuban Image: Cinema and Cultural Politics in Cuba* (London: BFI Publishing).

Cinco Colina, Ileana. 2010. 'Enseñando Ruso,' *Revolución y Cultura*, 1: 24–27.

Clark, Katerina. 1996. *Petersburg: Crucible of Cultural Revolution* (London: Harvard University Press).

———. 1997. 'Socialist Realism With Shores: The Conventions of the Positive Hero,' in Thomas Lahusen and Evgeny Dobrenko (eds.), *Socialist Realism Without Shores* (London: Duke University Press), pp. 27–50.

———. 2000. *The Soviet Novel: History as Ritual* (Bloomington: Indiana University Press).

———. 2011. *Moscow, the Fourth Rome: Stalinism, Cosmopolitanism, and the Evolution of Soviet Culture, 1931–1941* (London: Harvard University Press).

Clayfield, Anna. 2013. "An Unfinished Struggle? The Guerrilla Experience and the Shaping of Political Culture In the Cuban Revolution." PhD diss. University of Nottingham.

———. 2019. *The Guerilla Legacy of the Cuban Revolution* (Gainesville: University of Florida Press).

CNC, Dirección General de Teatro. c.1973. *Reglamento de los Grupos Teatrales* (Havana: Consejo Nacional de Cultura).

Cole, Ken. 2002. 'Cuba: The Process of Socialist Development,' *Latin American Perspectives*, 29: 40–56.

Colina, Enrique. 2008. *Los Bolos en Cuba* (Havana: ICAIC).

Condee, Nancy. 2000. 'Sots-Art, Conceptualism, and Russian Postmodernism,' in Marina Balina, Nancy Condee and Evgeny Dobrenko (eds.), *Endquote: Sots-art Literature and Soviet Grand Style* (Evanston: Northwesterns Univeristy Press), pp. vii–xv.

Conte, A. 1965. '¿Qué Opina Usted de Movimiento de Aficionados?,' *Pueblo y Cultura*, 31: 48–51.

Corrieri, Sergio, Albio Paz, Sergio González, and Rine Leal. 1978. *Teatro Escambray* (Havana: Letras Cubanas).

CTDA, Cuban Theater Digial Archive. 2017. 'Ulf Keyn,' http://ctda.library.miam i.edu/creator/266 [accessed 27/03/2017].

Cullerne Bown, Matthew. 1998. '"…the Sear, the Yellow Leaf": The Decline of Socialist Realism, 1964–1991,' in Matthew Cullerne Bown (ed.), *Socialist Realist Painting* (New York: Yale University Press), pp. 411–79.

de Juan, Adelaida. 1968. *Introducción a Cuba, las artes plásticas* (Havana: Instituto del Libro).

———. 2007. *Modern Cuban Art, Themes and Variations* (Havana: Editorial José Martí).

———. 2011. 'Half a Century of Cuban Art,' *Estudos Avançados*, 25: 197–216.

de la Torriente, Loló. 1962. 'Exposición Servando Cabrera Moreno. Dibujos de Jorge Rigol,' *Unión*, 1: 150–52.

del Pino, Amado. 2013. 'Festivales de otro siglo,' La Jiribilla, http://www.lajiribilla. cu/articulo/6116/festivales-de-otro-siglo. [accessed 1/03/2014].

Desnoes, Edmundo. 1962. 'Ver para creer,' *Unión*, 1: 149–52.

Deza, Mikhail, and Mervyn Matthews. 1975. 'Soviet Theater Audiences,' *Slavic Review*, 34: 716–30.

Díaz Sosa, Fidel. 2006. 'El proceso de difusión del Marxismo soviético en Cuba. Apuntes preliminares,' in Mely González Aróstegui and Rafael Plá León (eds.), *Marxismo y revolución: Escena del debate cubano en los sesenta* (Havana: Editorial de Ciencias Sociales), pp. 78–96.

Dimitrieva, Nina. 1958. 'K voprosu sovremennom stile,' *Tvorchestvo*, 6: 9–12.

Dobrenko, Evgeny. 2007. *Political Economy of Socialist Realism* (New Haven: Yale University Press).

Dobson, Miriam. 2009. *Khrushchev's Cold Summer: Gulag Returnees, Crime and the Fate of Reform after Stalin* (Ithaca: Cornell University Press).

Documentos. 1977. *Política Cultural de la Revolución Cubana* (Havana: Editorial de Ciencias Sociales).

Dopico, Elsa Vega. 2009. 'The Cuban Poster: Between the Rose and the Thorn,' in Nathalie Bondil (ed.), *Cuba: Art and History from 1868 to Today* (Montreal: The Montreal Museum of Fine Arts), pp. 286–354.

Duncan, W. Raymond. 1985. *The Soviet Union and Cuba: Interests and Influence* (New York: Praeger).

EcuRed. 2016. 'Luis Alberto García Hernández,' https://www.ecured.cu/index.php/Luis_Alberto_Garc%C3%ADa_Hern%C3%A1ndez [accessed 1/11/2016].

Eligio Fernández, Antonio ("Tonel"). 2001. 'Culture and Society in the Works of Cuban Artists,' in Holly Block (ed.), *Art Cuba: The New Generation* (New York: Harry N. Abrams), pp. 31–35.

Eligio Fernández, Antonio ("Tonel"). 2009. 'Ending the Century with Memories … Paper Money, Videos, and an X-Acto Knife for Cuban Art,' in Ariana Hernandez-Reguant (ed.), *Cuba in the Special Period: Culture and Ideology in the 1990s* (York: Palgrave Macmillan), pp. 179–98.

Elvira Peláez, Rosa. 1979a. 'CARIFESTA '79, en Cuba, finalizara con un carnaval caribeño en el Malecón habanero,' *Granma*, 12 March, p. 2.

———. 1979b. 'Constituida la Comisión Nacional de CARIFESTA '79,' *Granma*, 5 March, p. 2.

———. 1983. 'Comenzaron sesiones del Primer Taller Internacional del Nuevo Teatro,' *Granma*, 9 February, p. 4.

Erisman, Michael H. 2018. 'David Rising: Cuba and Its Northern Goliath in the 1970s in Cuba's Forgotten Decade,' in Emily J. Kirk and Anna Clayfield (eds.), *Isabel Story* (Lanham: Lexington), pp. 41–54.

Espinosa Domínguez, Carlos. 1983. 'Hacer de los personajes históricos seres más humanos y creíbles,' *Conjunto*, 57: 37–41.

Fay, Stephen. 2011. 'Liminal Visitors to an Island On the Edge: Sartre and Ginsberg in Revolutionary Cuba,' *Studies in Travel Writing*, 15: 407–25.

———. 2012. "Rites of Passage and Revolutions: Liminality in Cuba's Twentieth-Century Identity." PhD diss. University of Nottingham.

Fernández, José Manuel. 1964. 'Una entrevista con Otomar Kreycha. Romeo y Julieta en La Habana,' *Conjunto*, 1: 9–13.

Figueredo Cabrera, Katia. 2017. 'El Instituto de Intercambio Cultural Cubano-Soviético y su revista: una puesta por la fe,' *Espacio Laical*, 3–4: 63–74.

Fitzgerald, Frank T. 1987/88. 'The "Sovietization" of Cuba Thesis Revisited,' *Science & Society* 51 (4 Winter): 439–57.

Fitzpatrick, Sheila. 1970. *The Commissariat of Enlightenment: Soviet Organization
of Education and the Arts under Lunacharsky* (Cambridge: Cambridge University
Press).

———. 1971. 'The Emergence of Glaviskusstvo: Class War on the Cultural Front,
Moscow, 1928–29,' *Soviet Studies*, 23: 236–53.

———. 1974. 'The "Soft" Line on Culture and Its Enemies: Soviet Cultural Policy,
1922–1927,' *Slavic Review*, 33: 267–87.

———. 1976. 'Culture and Politics Under Stalin: A Reappraisal,' *Slavic Review*, 35:
211–31.

———. 1979. *Education and Social Mobility in the Soviet Union. 1921–1934* (Cambridge: Cambridge University Press).

———. 1992. *The Cultural Front: Power and Culture in Revolutionary Russia*
(Ithaca: Cornell University Press).

Ford, Katherine. 2010. 'Sounds and Silences of the Habanero Stage: Theater and the
Cuban "Quinquenio gris" (1971–1976),' *The Colorado Review of Hispanic Studies*, 8–9: 353–70.

Fore, Devin. 2006. 'Introduction,' *October Magazine*, 118: 3–10.

Fornet, Ambrosio. 1968. 'El intelectual en la revolución,' *RC*, 5: 45–47.

———. 1971. 'El intelectual en la revolución,' in Mario Benedetti (ed.), *Literatura y
arte nuevo en Cuba* (Barcelona: Editorial Estela), pp. 33–37.

———. 2007. 'El Quinquenio Gris: Revisitando el Término,' in Desiderio Navarro
(ed.) *Ciclo: La política cultural del período revolucionario: Memoria y reflexión*
(Havana: Criterios), pp. 1–22.

———. 2009. 'El Quinquenio Gris: Revisitando el Término,' in *Narrar la Nación:
Ensayos en blanco y negro* (Havana: Editorial Letras Cubanas), pp. 379–403.

Fornet, Jorge. 2013. *El 71: anatomía de una crisis* (Havana: Editorial Letras
Cubanas).

Frame, Murray. 2012. 'Cultural Mobilization: Russian Theater and the First World
War, 1914–1917,' *The Slavonic and East European Review*, 90: 288–322.

Franco, Jean. 2002. *The Decline and Fall of the Lettered City: Latin America in the
Cold War* (Cambridge, MA: Harvard University Press).

Frederik, Laurie Aleen. 2012. *Trumpets in the Mountains: Theater and the Politics of
National Culture in Cuba* (London: Duke University Press).

Frolova-Walker, Marina. 2007. *Russian Music and Nationalism: From Glinka to
Stalin* (London: Yale University Press).

———. 2016. *Stalin's Music Prize: Soviet Culture and Politics* (London: Yale University Press).

Fürst, Juliane. 2002. 'Prisoners of the Soviet Self? – Political Youth Opposition in
Late Stalinism,' *Europe-Asia Studies*, 54: 353–75.

Furtseva, Ekaterina. 1972. 'Le hemos traído el sincero sentimiento de hermandad que
experimentan los trabajadores de las repúblicas de nuestro país hacía su pueblo;

hacía la causa de la revolución cubana, primera revolución socialista del continente americano,' *Granma*, 2 November, p. 2.

Gallardo Saborido, Emilio José. 2009. *El martillo y el espejo: directrices de la política cultural cubana, 1959–1976* (Madrid: Consejo Superior de Investigaciones Científicas).

Garaudy, Roger. 1965. 'E. Fischer y el debate sobre la estética marxista,' *Unión*, 4: 90–100.

García Buchaca, Edith. 1961. 'El Primer Congreso de Escritores y Artistas Cubanos,' *Cuba Socialista*, 1: 82–91.

———. 1963a. 'El Primer Congreso Nacional de Cultura,' *Cuba Socialista*, 18: 8–29.

———. 1964. 'Las Transformaciones Culturales de la Revolución Cubana,' *Cuba Socialista*, 4: 28–54.

García Canclini, Néstor. 1995. *Hybrid Cultures: Strategies for Entering and Leaving Modernity* (Minneapolis: University of Minnesota Press).

García Espinoa Julio. 1963. 'vivir bajo lluvia,' *Gaceta de Cuba*, 2 (15) April 10: 9–13.

García Miranda, Zoe, and Ivonne Cotorruelo. 2008. *Todo tiempo pasado: fue mejor* (Bay Vista/Pastushka Films).

Gardiner, Jesse. 2014. "Reconstructing the Soviet Stage: The Discourse of Theater during the Thaw." PhD diss. University of Nottingham.

———. 2015. 'Mother Courage and Political Pragmatism: Sovietising Brecht during the Thaw,' *The Slavonic and East European Review*, 93: 626–54.

Garland Mahler, Anne. 2018. *From the Tricontinental to the Global South* (London: Duke University Press).

Garófalo, José Miguel. 1962. *Informe de la Coordinación Provincial a la Plenaria de Cultura. Intervención del comp. José Miguel Garófalo, Coordinador Provincial de la Habana* (Havana: Consejo Nacional de la Cultura).

Ginsburgs, George. 1987. *A Calendar of Soviet Treaties 1974–1980* (Lancaster: Martinus Nijhoff Publishers).

Gonçalves, João Felipe. 2013. 'Sputnik Premiers in Havana: A Historical Ethnography of the 1960 Soviet Exposition,' in Anne Gorsuch and Diane Koeneker (eds.), *The Socialist Sixties: Crossing Borders in the Second World* (Bloomington: Indiana University Press), pp. 84–120.

González, Pablo Alonso. 2015. "Nation Building and Cultural Heritage in Postcolonial Cuba (1898–2014)." PhD diss. Cambridge University.

———. 2017. *Cuban Cultural Heritage: A Rebel Past for a Revolutionary Nation* (Florida: University of Florida Press).

González Aróstegui, Mely, and Fernando Martínez Heredia. 2010. 'Cultura y Revolución en los sesenta,' in Fernando Martínez Heredia (ed.), *A viva voz* (Havana: Editorial de Ciencias Sociales), pp. 30–70.

González, Edward. 1968. 'Castro's Revolution, Cuban Communist Appeals, and the Soviet Response,' *World Politics*, 21: 39–68.

———. 1971. 'Relationship with the Soviet Union,' in Carmelo Mesa-Lago (ed.), *Revolutionary Change in Cuba* (Pittsburgh: University of Pittsburgh Press), pp. 81–104.

González Freire, Nati. 1963. 1966b. 'Taller Dramático, un grupo para teatro cubano,' *Bohemia*, 10 June, 23: 33.

———. 1977. 'Al habla con Evgueni Radomislenski,' *Bohemia*, 4 November, 44: 28.

González, Jorge Antonio. 1985. 'Fichero Teatral,' *Tablas*, 4: 64–65.

González, Jorge Antonio. 2003. *Cronología del Teatro Dramático Habanero 1936– 1960* (Havana: Centro de Investigación y Desarrollo de la Cultura Cubana Juan Marinello).

González, Reynaldo. 1963. 'Una Escuela Así,' *Pueblo y Cultura*, 17–18: 15–19.

González Rodríguez, Rafael, and Christopher Winks. 1996. 'Teatro Escambray: Towards the Cuban's Inner Being,' *TDR* (1988-), 40: 98–111.

Gordon-Nesbitt, Rebecca. 2012. 'To Defend the Revolution Is to Defend Culture: The Cultural Policy of the 1959 Cuban Revolution.' PhD diss. The University of Strathclyde.

———. 2015. *To Defend the Revolution is to Defend Culture: The Cultural Policy of the Cuban Revolution* (Oakland: PM Press).

Gor'kii, Maksim. 1977. 'Soviet Literature,' in H. G. Scott (ed.), *Soviet Writers' Congress 1934: The Debate on Socialist Realism and Modernism* (London: Lawrence and Wishart), pp. 27–69.

Gorsuch, Anne. 2003. '"There's No Place Like Home": Soviet Tourism in Late Stalinism,' *Slavic Review*, 62: 760–85.

———. 2015. '"Cuba, My Love": The Romance of Revolutionary Cuba in the Soviet Sixties,' *American Historical Review*, 120: 497–526.

———. 2002. 'La Sociedad Cultural Nuestro Tiempo,' in Ricardo Hernández Otero (ed.), *Sociedad Cultural Nuestro Tiempo: Resistencia y Acción* (Havana: Editorial Letras Cubanas), pp. 281–306.

Grigor'ev, L. 1939. 'Idustriia sotsializma,' *Pravda*, 19 March, p. 11.

Groys, Boris. 1992. *The Total Art of Stalinism: Avant-Garde, Aesthetic Dictatorship and Beyond* (Princeton: Princeton University Press).

Grutter, Virginia. 1965. 'Seminario para los dirigentes de teatro,' *Revista del Granma*, 14 November, p. 16.

Guevara, Ernesto Che. 2006. *El Socialismo y El Hombre En Cuba* (London: Pathfinder Press).

Guillén, Nicolás. 1978. 'Informe Central,' *Casa de las Américas*, 18: 35–48.

Guldberg, Jørn. 1990. 'Socialist Realism as Institutional Practice: Observations on the Interpretation of the Works of Art of the Stalin Period,' in Hans Günther (ed.), *The Culture of the Stalin Period* (London: Palgrave Macmillan), pp. 149–77.

Hammel, Claus. 1983. 'RDA. Humboldt y Bolívar o el nuevo continente,' *Conjunto*, 57: 42–104.

Hart Davalos, Armando. 1977. 'Discurso en el acto de inauguración del Centro de Estudios Martianos,' *Casa de las Américas*, 104: 56–57.

———. 1978a. 'Discurso de Clausura,' *Casa de las Américas*, 18: 60–76.

———. 1978b. 'Discurso de Clausura del II Congreso de la Unión de Escritores y Artistas de Cuba,' *Unión*, 17: 163–86.

———. 1978c. *Intervención en la IX Reunión de Ministros de Cultura de los Países Socialistas* (Havana: Editorial Letras Cubanas).

Heras León, Eduardo. 2015. Interview.

Hernández Otero, Ricardo. 2002. *Sociedad Cultural Nuestro Tiempo: resistencia y acción* (Letras Cubanas: Havana).

Horowitz, Irving Louis. 2008. *The Long Night of Dark Intent: A Half-Century of Cuban Socialism* (New Brunswick, NJ and London: Transaction Publishers).

Hosking, Gregory. 1980. *Beyond Socialist Realism: Soviet Fiction since Ivan Denisovich* (London: Granada Publishing).

Hosking, Geoffrey. 1985. *A History of the Soviet Union. 1917–1991.* (London: Harper Collins).

Hurtado, Oscar. 1966. 'Volpone y "La Rueda,"' *Bohemia*, 22 April, 16: 76.

Ivashkin, Alexander. 2014. 'Who's Afraid of Socialist Realism?,' *The Slavonic and East European Review*, 92: 430–48.

Johnson, Oliver. 2011. 'The Stalin Prize and the Soviet Artist: Status Symbol or Stigma?,' *Slavic Review*, 70: 819–43.

Jones, Polly (ed.). 2006a. *The Dilemmas of De-Stalinization: Negotiating Cultural and Social Change in the Khrushchev Era* (London: Routledge).

———. 2006b. 'Introduction: The Dilemmas of De-Stalinization,' in Polly Jones (ed.), *The Dilemmas of De-Stalinization: Negotiating Cultural and Social Change in the Khrushchev Era* (London: Routledge), pp. 1–18.

Kaier, Christina. 2005. *Imagine No Possessions: The Socialist Objects of Russian Constructivism* (London: MIT Press).

Kaier, Christina, and Eric Naiman (eds.). 2006. *Everyday Life in Early Soviet Russia: Taking the Revolution Inside* (Bloomington: Indiana University Press).

Kanellos, Nicolás. 1995. "Cuba," in Martin Banham (ed.), *The Cambridge Guide to Theater* (Cambridge: Cambridge University Press), pp. 268–71.

Kapcia, Antoni. 2000. *Cuba: Island of Dreams* (Oxford: Berg).

———. 2005. *Havana: The Making of Cuban Culture* (Oxford: Berg).

———. 2008. *Cuba in Revolution: A History since the Fifties* (London: Reaktion Books).

———. 2009. 'Lessons of the Special Period: Learning to March Again,' *Latin American Perspectives*, 36: 30–41.

———. 2014. *Leadership and the Cuban Revolution: The Unseen Story* (London: Zed Book).

Kelly, Catriona, and Robin Milner-Gulland. 1998. 'Building a New Reality: The Visual Arts, 1921–1953,' in Catriona Kelly and David Shepherd (eds.), *Russian Cultural Studies: An Introduction* (Oxford: Oxford University Press), pp. 138–53.

Kelly, Catriona, and Vadim Volkov. 1998. 'Directed Desires: Kul'turnost' and Consumption,' in Catriona Kelly and David Shepherd (eds.), *Constructing Russian Culture in the Age of the Revolution: 1881–1940* (Oxford: Oxford University Press), pp. 291–313.

Kenez, Peter, and David Shepherd. 1998. "'Revolutionary' Models for High Literature: Resisting Poetics," in Catriona Kelly and David Shepherd (eds.), *Russian Cultural Studies: An Introduction* (Oxford: Oxford University Press) pp. 21–55.

Khrushchev, Nikkita. 1960. 'Rech' tovarishcha N. S. Khrushchev na Vserossiiskom s'ezde uchitelei 9 iulia 1960 goda' Pravda, 10/06/1960, 1–3.

Kolin, Philip C. 1995. 'Tennessee Williams's A Streetcar Named Desire in Havana: Modesto Centeno's Cuban Streetcars,' *South Atlantic Review*, 60: 89–110.

Kumaraswami, Par. 2007. 'Cultural Policy, Literature and Readership in Revolutionary Cuba: The View from the 21st Century,' *Bulletin of Latin American Research*, 26: 69–87.

———. 2009. 'Cultural Policy and Cultural Politics in Revolutionary Cuba: Rereading the Palabras a los intelectuales (Words to the Intellectuals),' *Bulletin of Latin American Research*, 28: 527–41.

Kumaraswami, Par, and Antoni Kapcia. 2012. *Literary Culture in Cuba: Revolution, Nation-building and the Book* (Manchester: Manchester University Press).

Kuteischikova, Vera, and Inna Terterian. 1979. 'Literatura cubana editada en la Unión Soviética,' *Casa de las Américas*, 19: 65–68.

Kuteishchikova, V. N. 1977. 'Real'nost' narodnoi bor'by i real'nost' narodnogo soznaniia v sovremennom latinoamerikanskom romane,' in Vladimir Rodionovich Shcherbina et al. (eds.), *Sotsialisticheskii realism na sovremennom etape ego razvitiia* (Moscow: Nauka), pp. 392–412.

Lahusen, Thomas. 1997. *How Life Writes the Book* (Ithaca: Cornell University Press).

Lahusen, Thomas, and Evgeny Dobrenko (eds.). 1997. *Socialist Realism Without Shores* (London: Duke University Press).

Layera, Ramón. 1978. 'After the Coup: Four Dramatic Versions of Allende's Chile,' *Latin American Theater Review*, 12: 39–42.

Leach, Robert. 1999. 'Revolutionary Theater, 1917–1930,' in Robert Leach and Victor Borovsky (eds.), *A History of Russian Theater* (Cambridge: Cambridge University Press), pp. 302–24.

Leal, Rine. 1962. 'Primer festival del teatro hispanoamericano,' *Unión*, 1: 144–60.

Leante, César. 1979. 'Literatura del Caribe, literatura de América,' *Granma*, 25 July, p. 4.

Lent, John. 1988. 'Cuban Films and the Revolution,' *Caribbean Studies*, 20: 59–68.

Leogrande, William M., and Julie M. Thomas. 2002. 'Cuba's Quest for Economic Independence,' *Journal of Latin American Studies*, 34: 325–63.

León del Río, Yohanka, and Fernando Martínez Heredia. 2010. 'Conversación sobre los años sesenta,' in Fernando Martínez Heredia (ed.), *A viva voz* (Havana: Editorial de Ciencias Sociales), pp. 71–104.

Leonov, Nikolai. 2015 *Raúl Castro Un Hombre en Revolución* (Havana: Editorial Capitán San Luis).

Lescay, Alberto. 2015. Interview.

Lévesque, Jacques. 1978. *The USSR and the Cuban Revolution: Soviet Ideological and Strategical Perspectives, 1959–1977* (New York: Praeger).

Levin, V. 1959. 'Kuba boretsia – Kuba pobedit!,' *Pravda*, 3 January, p. 6.

Linares, Ernestina, et al. 1989. 'Manifesto,' in Ricardo Hernández Otero (ed.), *Revista Nuestro Tiempo. Complicación de trabajos* (Havana: Editorial Letras Cubanas), pp. 310–11.

Loehlin, James N (ed.). 2002. *Romeo and Juliet* (Cambridge: Cambridge University).

Loomis, John A. 1999. *Revolution of Forms: Cuba's Forgotten Art Schools* (New York: Princeton Architectural Press).

López Oliva, Manuel. 1972. 'Antecedentes del arte soviético: los pintores ambulantes,' *Granma*, 2 November, p. 4.

López Oliva, Manuel. 2015a. Interview.

López Oliva, Manuel. 2015b. Interview.

Loss, Jacqueline. 2004. "Portraitures of Institutionalization." *CR: The New Centennial Review*, 4 (2): 77–101.

Loss, Jacqueline. 2009. "Wandering in Russian," in Ariana Hernandez-Reguant (ed.), *Cuba in the Special Period: Culture and Ideology in the 1990s* (New York: Palgrave Macmillan), pp. 105–22.

Loss, Jacqueline, and José Manuel Prieto (eds.). 2012. *Caviar with Rum: Cuba-USSR and the Post-Soviet Experience* (London: Palgrave Macmillan).

Loss, Jacqueline. 2014. *Dreaming in Russian: The Cuban Soviet Imaginary* (Austin: University of Texas Press).

Lovell, Stephen, and Rosalind Marsh. 1998. 'Culture and Crisis: The Intelligentsia and Literature after 1953,' in Catriona Kelly and David Shepherd (eds.), *Russian Cultural Studies* (Oxford: Oxford University Press), pp. 56–84.

Maguire, Robert A. 1968. *Red Virgin Soil: Soviet Literature in the 1920s* (Pinceton: Princeton University Press).

Mally, Lynn. 1990. *Culture of the Future: The Proletkult Movement in Revolutionary Russia* (Berkeley: University of California Press).

———. 2000. *Revolutionary Acts: Amateur Theater and the Soviet State 1917–1938* (Ithaca: Cornell University Press).

Manuel, Peter. 1990. 'Music and Ideology in Contemporary Cuba,' *International Journal of Politics, Culture and Society*, 3: 297–313.

Manzor-Coats, Lillian, and Inés María Martiatu Terry. 1995. 'VI Festival Internacional de Teatro de La Habana: A Festival against All Odds,' *TDR (1988-)*, 39: 39–70.

Marinello, Juan. 1960. *Conversación con nuestros pintores abstractos* (Santiago de Cuba: Universidad de Oriente).

Markov, Dmitri. 1977. 'Istoricheskie otkrytaia sistema pravdvogo izobrazheniia zhizni (o novykh aspektakh obsuzhdeniia problem sotsialisticheskogo realizma v poslednie gody),' *Voprosy literatury*, 1: 26–66.

Marrero, Serafín. 1973. 'Un propósito que une a checoslovacos y cubanos,' *Revolución y Cultura*, 14: 66–68.

Martí, José. 1963. 'La exhibición de pinturas del ruso Vereschagin,' in Anon (ed.), *Obras Completas*, vol. 15 (Havana: Editorial Nacional de Cuba) pp. 429–38.

Martin, Randy. 1990. 'Cuban Theater under Rectification: The Revolution after the Revolution,' *The Dramatic Review*, 34: 38–59.

———. 1994. *Socialist Ensembles: Theater and State in Cuba and Nicaragua* (Minneapolis: University of Minnesota Press).

Martínez Heredia, Fernando. 1991. 'Cuban Socialism: Prospects and Challenges,' *Latin American Perspectives*, 18: 18–37.

———. 2017. 'Origins of Cuban Socialism,' in Antoni Kapcia (ed.), *Rethinking Past and Present in Cuba: Essays in Memory of Alistair Hennessy* (London: ILAS) pp. 42–65.

Martínez, Iván Cesar. 1974. 'El Movimiento Artístico En Las ESBEC,' *Revolución y Cultura*, 27: 28–30.

Matas, Julio. 1971. 'Theater and Cinematography,' in Carmelo Mesa-Lago (ed.), *Revolutionary Change in Cuba* (London: University of Pittsburgh Press), pp. 427–46.

Mesa, Enrique. 1977. 'Inauguró Hart en Matanzas Provincial de Comercialización y Bienes Culturales,' *Granma*, 1 June, p. 3.

Mesa-Lago, Carmelo. 1969. 'The Revolutionary Offensive,' *Trans-action*, 6: 22–29.

Mesa-Lago, Carmelo (ed.). 1971. *Revolutionary Change in Cuba* (Pittsburgh: University of Pittsburgh Press).

———. 1981. *The Economy of Socialist Cuba: A Two-Decade Appraisal* (Alburquerque: University of New Mexico Press).

Ministerstvo inostrannykh del, and Ministerio de Relaciones Exteriores. 2004. *Rossia- Kuba. 1902–2002: Dokumenty i materialy* (Moscow: Mezdunarodnaia otnoshenia).

Miller, Nicola. 1989. *Soviet Relations with Latin America, 1959–1987* (Cambridge: Cambridge University Press).

———. 2008. 'A Revolutionary Modernity: The Cultural Policy of the Cuban Revolution,' *Journal of Latin American Studies*, 40: 675–96.

MinCult. 1983. *Reunión nacional de balance del trabajo realizado en 1983* (Havana: Ministerio de Cultura).

———. 1986. *Reglamento Orgánico del Ministerio de Cultura* (Havana: Ministerio de Cultura).

———. 2016. 'Empresa Fondo Cubano de Bienes Culturales,' http://www.min.cult .cu/loader.php?sec=instituciones&cont=fcbc [accessed 12/05/2016].

Montero Méndez, Hortensia. 2006. *Los 70: puente para las rupturas* (Havana; Centro de Investigaciones de la Cultura Cubana).

———. 2009. 'The 1970s: Recovery and Contemporaneity,' in Nathalie Bondil (ed.), *Cuba: Art and History from 1868 to Today* (Montreal: The Montreal Museum of Fine Arts), pp. 258–75.

Mosquera, Gerardo. 1983. *Exploraciones en la plástica cubana* (Havana: Editorial Letras Cubanas).

———. 2001. 'New Cuban Art Y2K,' in Holly Block (ed.), *Art Cuba: The New Generation* (New York: Harry N. Abrams), pp. 13–15.

———. 2003. 'The New Cuban Art,' in Aleš Erjavec and Boris Groys (eds.), *Postmodernism and the Postsocialist Condition: Politicised Art under Late Socialism* (Berkeley: University of California Press), pp. 208–46.

Navarro, Raúl. 1985. 'La transformación estética del ambiente,' *Temas*, 1: 107–17.

Noack, Christian. 2013. 'Songs from the Wood, Love from the Fields; The Soviet Tourist Song Movement,' in Anne Gorsuch and Diane Koeneker (eds.), *The Socialist Sixties: Crossing Borders in the Second World* (Bloomington: Indiana University Press), pp. 167–92.

Nuez, Iván de la. 2013. *El Comunista manifiesto: un fantasma vuelve a recorrer el mundo* (Barcelona: Galàxia Gutenberg).

Ojeda Jequin, Aylet. 2009. 'Timeline,' in Nathalie Bondil (ed.), *Cuba: Art and History from 1868 to Today* (Montreal: The Montreal Museum of Fine Arts), pp. 228–31.

Ojito, Enrique. 2016. 'Fidel Castro: Los que dirigen son hombres y no dioses,' *Granma*, 13 December. http://www.granma.cu/cuba/2016-12-13/fidel-castro-los-que-dirigen-son-hombres-y-no-dioses-13-12-2016-23-12-43 [accessed 1/04/2017].

Okun,' Sasha. 2017. 'Sasha Okun,' https://sashaokun.com/life/ [accessed 27/03/2017].

Oramas, Joaquín. 1972a. 'Presencio Fidel en acto de inicio de la jornada de la cultura soviética en Cuba,' *Granma*, 2 November, p. 1.

———. 1972b. 'Visita el MinEd Ekaterina A. Furtseva, Ministra de Cultura de la Unión Soviética,' *Granma*, 2 November, p. 4.

Ortiz, Fernando: «Más contactos de la cultura», en Cuba y la URSS, La Habana, 1 de agosto de 1945, no. i, año i, p. 1 y p. 27.

Ortiz, Fernando. 1963. 1963. *Contrapunteo Cubano del Tabaco y el Azucar*. Introducción de Bronislaw Malinowski, Dirección de Publicaciones. Universidad Central de Las Villas. (Segunda edicion).

Otero, Lisandro. 1967. 'Tres Preguntas a Lisandro Otero,' *RC*, 1: 94–96.

———. 1971. 'Notas sobre la funcionalidad de la Cultura,' *Casa de las Américas*, 68: 94–107.

Otero, Lisandro, and Fransisco Martínez Hinojosa. 1972. *Cultural Policy in Cuba* (Paris: UNESCO [must put into chapter 3]).

Packenham, Robert. 1986. 'Capitalist Dependency and Socialist Dependency: The Case of Cuba,' *Journal of Interamerican Studies and World Affairs*, 28: 59–92.

Padura Fuentes, Leonardo. 2009. *Vientos de Cuaresma* (Barcelona: TusQuets).

Padura Fuentes, Leonardo, John M. Kirk, and Abelardo Estorino. 2002. 'Vive y escribe en una casa vieja,' in Leonardo Padura Fuentes and John M. Kirk (eds.), *La cultura y la revolución cubana: conversaciones en La Habana* (Havana: Editorial Plaza Mayor), pp. 109–32.

Palls, Terry L. 1975. 'The Theater of the Absurd in Cuba after 1959,' *Latin American Literary Review*, 4: 67–72.

Palmarola, Hugo, and Pedro Ignacio Alonso. (2014) "Tropical Assemblage: The Soviet Large Panel in Cuba." In Medina Eden, Marques Ivan Da Costa, Christina Holmes, and Marcos Cueto (eds.), *Beyond Imported Magic: Essays on Science, Technology, and Society in Latin America* (Cambridge: MIT Press), pp. 159–80.

Patterson, Thomas, G. 1994. *Contesting Castro: The United States and the Triumph of the Cuban Revolution* (New York: Oxford University Press).

Paperny, Vladimir. 2002. *Architecture in the Age of Stalin: Culture Two* (Cambridge: Cambridge University Press).

Papernyi, Vladimir. 2011. *Kul'tura Dva* (Moscow: Novoe literaturnoe obozrenie).

Pavón, Luis. 1972. 'La cultura soviética es una cultura hermana, franca, calidad. Es la cultura del socialismo, es la cultura que está por bien del hombre, que conserva el patrimonio de la humanidad y lo desarrolla,' *Granma*, 2 November, p. 2.

PCC. 1976a. *Constitución de la República de Cuba* (Havana: Partido Comunista de Cuba).

———. 1976b. *Plataforma programática del Partido Comunista de Cuba. Tesis y Resolución* (Havana: Partido Comunista de Cuba).

———. 1976c. *Tesis y resoluciones. Primer Congreso del Partido Comunista de Cuba* (Havana: Partido Comunista de Cuba).

———. 1980. *2nd Congress of the Communist Party of Cuba: Main Report* (Havana: Political Publishers).

Pérez, Fernando. 2015. Interview.

Pérez-Stable, Marifeli. 1999. *The Cuban Revolution: Origins, Course, and Legacy* (New York: Oxford University Press).

Petrov, Petre. 2011. 'The Industry of Truing: Socialist Realism, Reality, Realization,' *Slavic Review*, 70: 873–92.

Pianca, Marina. 1989. 'Postcolonial Discourse in Latin American Theater,' *Theater Journal*, 41: 515–23.

Pita Rodríguez, Francisco. 1963. 'La Graduación de los Instructores de Arte,' *Pueblo y Cultura*, 15: 22–30.

———. 1966. 'Cursos de apreciación del arte para los trabajadores,' *Bohemia*, 4 March, 9: 36–37.

Pogolotti, Graziella. 1962. 'Pintura Cubana en los Países Socialistas,' *Gaceta de Cuba*, 1: 16–19.

———. 1997. 'Art, Bubbles, and Utopia,' *South Atlantic Quarterly*, 96: 169–80.

———. (ed.). 2006. *Polémicas culturales de los sesenta* (Havana: Editorial Letras Cubanas).

Pogolotti, Graziella. 2015. Interview.

Pomerantsev, Vladimir. 1953. 'Ob iskrennosti v literature,' *Novyi Mir*, 12: 218–45.

Pozuelo, Oscar A. 2009. 'Clasicos Coleccionables,' *Abre el ojo*, 12: 178–83.

Prieto, José Manuel. 2012. 'Heberto Padilla, the First Dissident (of the Cuban Revolution),' in Jaqueline Loss and José Manuel Prieto (eds.), *Caviar with Rum: Cuba-USSR and the Post-Soviet Experience* (New York: Palgrave Macmillan), pp. 119–32.

Progress, and Editorial José Martí (eds.). 1990. *SSSR-Kuba: Al'manakh* (Moscow: Progress).

Pronskiy, Ye I. 1962. 'From the Diary of Ye. I. Pronskiy, Record of a Conversation with University of Havana Instructor, Anastacio Cruz Mancilla, 29 May 1964,' June 22, 1962, History and Public Policy Program Digital Archive, TsKhSD, f. 5, op. 49, d. 757, ll. 121–23, r. 9125. Translated for CWIHP by Gary Goldberg. http s://digitalarchive.wilsoncenter.org/document/117087 [accessed 18/06/2019].

Puñales-Alpízar, Damaris. 2012. *Escrito en cirílico: el ideal soviético en la cultura cubana* (Santiago: Editorial Cuarto Propio).

Quesada, Armando. 1972. 'un movimiento teatral sólido y coherente,' *Revolución y Cultura*, 6: 24–31.

Rafael Rodríguez, Guillermo. 2015. Interview.

Rassi, Reynold. 1967a. 'Funcionan comisiones de trabajo para tratar las tareas,' *Granma*, 1 July, p. 3.

———. 1967b. 'Llanusa ante los instructores de arte: "A los intelectuales no hay que integrarlos a la revolución, porque son la revolución misma,"' *Granma*, 3 July, p. 3.

———. 1967c. 'No hay región de Cuba que no tenga instructores de arte – Manuel Stolik,' *Granma*, 29 June, p. 3.

Reid, Susan. 2000. 'The Exhibition Art of Socialist Countries, Moscow 1958–9, and the Contemporary Style of Painting,' in Susan Reid and David Crowley (eds.), *Style and Socialism* (Oxford: Berg), pp. 101–32.

———. 2001. 'Socialist Realism in the Stalinist Terror: The Industry of Socialism Art Exhibition, 1935–41,' *Russian Review*, 60: 153–84.

———. 2009. 'The Soviet "Contemporary Style": A Socialist Modernism,' in Sirje Helme (ed.), *Different Modernisms, Different Avant-Gardes: Problems in Central and Eastern European Art After World War II* (Tallinn: KUMU Art Museum), pp. 71–112.

———. 2012. '(Socialist) Realism Unbound: The Effects of International Encounters on Soviet Art Practice and Discourse in the Khrushchev Thaw,' in Matthew Bown, Zelfira Tregulova and Evgenia Petrova (eds.), *Socialist Realisms: Soviet Paintings 1920–1970* (Milan: Skira), pp. 267–95.

Reyes, Arnoldo, and Anon. 1972. 'Sobre el Movimiento de Aficionados,' *Revolución y Cultura*, 4: 2–9.

Robin, Régine. 1992. *Socialist Realism: An Impossible Aesthetic* (Stanford: Stanford University Press).

Rodionovich Shcherbina, Vladimir, et al. (eds). 1977. *Sotsialisticheskii realizm na sovremennom etape ego razvitiia* (Mosvka: Nauka).

Rodríguez Alemán, Mario. 1977. 'La enseñanza del teatro en Cuba,' *Conjunto*, 34: 99–103.

Rodríguez, Carlos Rafael. 1967. 'Problemas del arte en la Revolución,' *RC*, 1: 6–33.

Rodríguez, Rafael. 1984. 'Símbolo de Indestructible Unidad,' *Verde Olivo*, 25: 4–7.

Rolfe, Malte. 2009. 'A Hall of Mirrors: Sovietising Culture under Stalin,' *Slavic Review*, 68: 601–30.

Rudakoff, Judith. 1996. 'R/Evolutionary Theater in Contemporary Cuba: Grupo Teatro Escambray,' *The Dramatic Review*, 40: 77–97.

Rupprecht, Tobias. 2012. "Soviet Internationalism after Stalin: The USSR and Latin America in the Cultural Cold War." PhD diss. European University Institute.

———. 2015. *Soviet Internationalism after Stalin: Interaction and Exchange between the USSR and Latin America during the Cold War* (Cambridge: Cambridge University Press).

Sala, Haydée. 1985. 'Sobre la medición de la efectividad socio-económica en la actividad teatral,' *Temas*, 1: 17–34.

Sala Santos, Haydee, and Miguel Sánchez León. 1986. 'Una encuesta sociológica: las diez mejores puestas en escena,' *Tablas*, 5: 62–72.

Salado, Minerva. 1981. 'Dom Ameriki: Vstrecha Deiatelei Teatra,' *Kuba*, 11: 5.

Sánchez León, Miguel. 1985. 'Estructura del tiempo laboral de los actores,' *Temas*, 1: 35–52.

Santana, Gilda. 1983. 'Un cuarto siglo. Teatro Estudio,' *Tablas*, 3: 11–21, 70.

Sarusky, Jaime, and Gerardo Mosquera. 1979. *The Cultural Policy of Cuba* (Paris: UNESCO).

Scarpaci, Joseph L., Roberto Segre, and Mario Coyula. 2002. *Havana: Two Faces of the Antillean Metropolis* (Chapel Hill: The University of North Carolina Press).

Schütz, Günter. 2009. 'Paris in Cuba 1967: the salón de mayo and the *cuba colectiva mura*,' in Nathalie Bondil (ed.), *Cuba: Art and History from 1868 to Today* (Montreal: The Montreal Museum of Fine Arts), pp. 276–85.

Serguera, Jorge. 1967. 'Carta del Comandante Serguera,' *RC*, 1: 93. [still as epigraph, need to change or lose].

Shatunovskaia, I. K. 1979. 'Po stranitsam zhurnala <Latinskaia Amerika>,' in Anatolii Danilovich Bekarevich, et al. (eds.), *Kul'tura Kuby* (Moscow: Nauka), pp. 306–19.

Shearman, Peter. 1987. *The Soviet Union and Cuba* (London: Routledge & Kegan Paul).

Solomon, Andrew. 1991. *The Irony Tower: Soviet Artists in a Time of Glasnost* (New York: Knopf).

Solovyova, Inna. 1999. 'The Theater and Socialist Realism, 1929–1953,' in Robert Leach and Victor Borovsky (eds.), *A History of Russian Theater* (Cambridge University Press: Cambridge), pp. 325–57.

Sontag, Susan. 1970. 'Posters: Advertisement, Art, Political Artefact, Commodity,' in Dugald Stermer (ed.), *The Art of Revolution* (London: McGraw-Hill Book Company), pp. vii–xxviii.

Soto, Leonel. 1965. 'Las Escuelas de Instrucción Revolucionaria en el ciclo político-técnico,' *Cuba Socialista*, 5: 67–82.

———. 1966. 'Los problemas sociales y culturales en la Conferencia Tricontinental,' *Cuba Socialista*, 6: 75–91.

Stalin, Iosif. 1952. 'O politicheskikh zadachakh universiteta narodov Vostoka: Rech' na sobranii studentov KUTV 18 maia 1925g,' in *Sochineniia*, vol. 7 (Moscow: Gosudarsvennoe izdatel'stvo politicheskoi literaturi), pp. 137–8.

Steinberg, Mark. 2002. *Proletarian Imagination: Self, Modernity, and the Sacred in Russia, 1910–1925* (Ithaca: Cornell University Press).

Suny, Ronald Grigor. 1998. *The Soviet Experiment: Russia, the USSR, and the Successor States* (Oxford: Oxford University Press).

Swanson, Vern Grosvenor. 1994. *Hidden Treasures: Russian and Soviet Impressionism, 1930–1970s* (Scotsdale: Fleischer Museum).

Toledano Redongo, Juan C. 2002. 'Ángel Arango's Cuban Trilogy: Rationalism, Revolution and Evolution,' *Extrapolation*, 43: 420–38.

Torres Ramírez, Blanca. 1971. *Las relaciones cubano-soviéticas (1959–1968)* (México: Colegio de México Centro de Estudios Internacionales).

Tunberg, Karl A. 1970. 'The New Cuban Theater: A Report,' *The Drama Review: TDR*, 14: 43–55.

Tupitsyn, Margarita. 1996. *The Soviet Photograph, 1924–1937* (London: Yale University Press).

UIA, International Union of Architects. 2016. 'Congresses,' http://www.uia.archi/en/s-informer/congres/tous-les-congres#.V5YH8_krKUk [accessed 25/07/2016].

UNEAC. 1978c. 'Resolución de la Unión de Escritores y Artistas de Cuba Sobre el 60 Aniversario de la Revolución Socialista de Octubre,' *Casa de las Américas*, 18: 57–58.

Valkenier, Elizabeth Kridl. 1989. *Russian Realist Art: The State and Society: The Peredvizhniki and their tradition* (New York: Columbia University Press).

Vázquez, Omar. 1968. 'La Ofensiva Revolucionaria en Artes y Espectáculos,' *Granma*, 4 June, p. 4.

Vázquez, Omar. 1972. 'Inauguran hoy exposiciones como parte de la jornada de cultura Soviética,' *Granma*, 2 November, p. 2.

Vázquez Pérez, Eduardo. 1984. 'En busca de un actor perdido,' *Tablas*, 3: 1–4, 51–55.

Vernikov, V. 1977. 'Tsennoe naslednie,' *Izvestiia*, 24 December, p. 3.

Villegas, Juan. 1989. 'Historicising Latin American Theater,' *Theater Journal*, 41: 505–14.

Vitier, Cintio. 1971. Foreword. El Primer Congreso Nacional. 1971. Revista de la Biblioteca Nacional de Cuba José Martí. http://revistas.bnjm.cu/index.php/revista-bncjm/article/view/1732.

Weiss, Judith. 1985. 'The Emergence of Popular Culture,' in Sandor Halebsky and John M. Kirk (eds.), *Cuba: Twenty-Five Years of Revolution, 1959–1984* (New York: Praeger), pp. 117–33.

Weiss, Rachel. 2011a. *Making Art Global (Part 1). The Third Havana Biennial 1989* (London: Afterall).

———. 2011b. *To and from Utopia in the New Cuban Art* (Minneapolis: University of Minnesota Press).

Weppler-Grogan, Doreen. 2010. 'Cultural Policy, the Visual Arts, and the Advance of the Cuban Revolution in the Aftermath of the Grey Years,' *Cuban Studies*, 41: 143–65.

White, Anne. 1990. *De-Stalinization and the House of Culture: Declining State Control over Leisure in the USSR, Poland and Hungary, 1953–89* (London: Routledge).

Whitney, Robert W. 2001. *State and Revolution in Cuba: Mass Mobilisation and Political Change, 1920–1940* (London: The University of North Carolina Press).

Wiles, Timothy J. 1980. *The Theater Event: Modern Theories of Performance* (Chicago: The University of Chicago Press).

Woll, Josephine. 2000. *Real Images: Soviet Cinema and the Thaw* (London: I.B Tauris).

Woodyard, George. 1983. 'Estorino's Theater: Customs and Conscience in Cuba,' *Latin American Literary Review*, 11: 57–63.

Yaffe, Helen. 2009. *Che Guevara: The Economics of Revolution* (Basingstoke: Palgrave Macmillan).

Yankovskaya, Galina, and Rebecca Mitchell. 2006. 'The Economic Dimensions of Art in the Stalinist Era: Artist's Cooperatives in the Grip of Ideology and the Plan,' *Slavic Review*, 65: 769–91.

Yoss. 2012. 'Marcianos en el platanal de Bartolo: un análisis de la historia y perspectiva de la ciencia ficción en Cuba al final del segundo milenio,' in Yoss (ed.), *La quinta dimensión de la literatura. Reflexiones sobre la ciencia ficción en Cuba y el mundo* (Havana: Editorial Letras Cubanas), pp. 61–80.

Yurchak, Alexei. 2006. *Everything Was Forever, Until It Was No More* (Princeton: Princeton University Press).

Zhdanov, Andrei Alexandrovich. 1977. 'Soviet Literature – The Richest in Ideas. The Most Advanced Literature,' in H. G. Scott (ed.), *Soviet Writers' Congress 1934: The Debate on Socialist Realism and Modernism* (London: Lawrence and Wishart), pp. 15–24.

Glossary of Terms

BNJM	Biblioteca Nacional José Martí
CDR	Comités de Defensa de la Revolución
CNC	Consejo Nacional de Cultura
CODEMA	Consejo Asesor para el Desarrollo de la Escultura Monumentaria
COMECON	Council for Mutual Economic Assistance
COMINTERN	Communist International
DRE	Directorio Revolucionario Estudiantil
EIR	Escuelas de Instrucción Revolucionaria
ENA	Escuela nacional de Arte
FAR	Fuerzas Armadas Revolucionarias
INTUR	Instituto Nacional del Turismo
ISA	Instituto Superior de Arte
KPSS	Kommunisticheskia Partia Sovetskogo Soiuza
M-26-7	Movimiento 26 de Julio
MINCULT	Ministerio de Cultura
MINED	Ministerio de Educación
MINIL	Ministerio de la Industria Ligera
MNBA	Museo Nacional de Bellas Artes
Nuestro Tiempo	Sociedad Cultural Nuestro Tiempo
ORI	Organizaciones Integradas Revolucionarias
PCC	Partido Comunista de Cuba
PSP	Partido Socialista Popular
PURS	Partido Unido de la Revolución Socialista
UNEAC	Unión Nacional de Escritores y Artistas de Cuba

RUSSIAN TRANSLITERATION SYSTEM USED

А/а	A/a
Б/б	B/b
В/в	V/v
Г/г	G/g
Д/д	D/d
Е/е	E/e
Ё/ё	E/e
Ж/ж	Zh/zh
З/з	Z/z
И/и	I/i
Й/й	I/i
К/к	K/k
Л/л	L/l
М/м	M/m
Н/н	N/n
О/о	O/o
П/п	P/p
Р/р	R/r
С/с	S/s
Т/т	T/t
У/у	U/u
Ф/ф	F/f
Х/х	Kh/kh
Ц/ц	Ts/ts
Ч/ч	Ch/ch
Ш/ш	Sh/sh
Щ/щ	Shch/shch
Ъ/ъ	"
Ы/ы	Y/y
Ь/ь	'
Э/э	E/e
Ю/ю	Iu/iu
Я/я	Ia/ia

Timelines

SOVIET TIMELINE

1917	February Revolution
	October Revolution takes power
	Proletkul't founded
1918	First National Conference of Proletkul't
1918–1921	Civil War
1919	State publishing house, Gosizdat, founded
	The Comintern (Communist International) founded
1920	All Russian Association of Proletarian Writers (VAPP) founded. Proletkul't merged into Narkompros
1921–1928	New Economic Policy
1922	Association of Artists of Revolutionary Russia (AKhRR) founded
1923	Russian Association of Proletarian Musicians (RAPM) founded
1924	Lenin dies
1925	Russian Association of Proletarian Writers (RAPP) founded
	Central committee resolution O*n the Policy of the Party in the Sphere of Artistic Literature*
1928	Cultural Revolution begins
	Gor'kii returns to the USSR
	First Five-Year Plan (*piatiletka*)
1929	The Cooperative of Artists, *Vsekhudozhnik*, founded
1931	End of Cultural Revolution
1932	Dissolution of RAPP and other proletarian artists' associations

1934	Establishment of Union of Soviet Writers
	First Congress of the Union of Soviet Writers
	Socialist Realism proclaimed
1936	Campaign against *formalizm*
1938	Committee on Artistic Affairs established
1939	The Stalin Prize (in art and literature) established
1943	Dissolution of Comintern
1944	Bek, Volokolamsk Highway
1946	Beginning of *Zhdanovshchina*
1947	Academy of Arts of the USSR (re)founded in Moscow
	Il'ia Repin Institute for Painting, Sculpture and Architecture founded
1948	Campaign against *kosmopolitizm*
1949	(Second) campaign against *formalizm*
1952	Campaign against *beskonfliktnost'*
1953	Death of Stalin
	Liquidation of *Vsekhudozhnik*
	Liquidation of All-Union Committee on Artistic Affairs of the Government of the USSR
	Ministry of Culture founded
1954	Il'ia Erenburg, *Thaw*
1956	Twentieth Congress of the Communist Party
	Khrushchev's Secret Speech
1961	Aleksandr Bek, General Panfilov's Reserve
1961	Stalin's body removed from Lenin Mausoleum
	Evgeni Evtushenko, *Babii Iar*
1964	Khrushchev's removal from power
1966	Trial of Andrei Siniavsky and Daniel
1968	Soviet intervention in "Prague Spring"
1974	Brezhnev visits Cuba
1982	Brezhnev dies. Succeeded by Andropov
1984	Andropov dies. Succeeded by Chernenko
1985	Chenenko dies. Succeeded by Gorbachev
1985–1991	*Perestroika* and *glasnost'*

CUBAN TIMELINE

| 1945 | Institute for Cuban-Soviet Cultural Exchange (IICCS) created. Beginning of publication of *Cuba y la URSS* |
| 1952 | IICCS closed down and *Cuba y la URSS* ceases publication |

1959	ICAIC founded
	Casa de las Américas founded
1960	First National Meeting of Poets and Artists
1961	CNC founded
	UNEAC founded
1962	First National Plenary for Cultural Coordinators
	First National Cultural Congress
1965	Founding of the PCC
	ENA Inaugurated
1966	Tricontinental Conference
1967	Visit of the Salón de Mayo
	Establishment of ISA
1968	Havana Cultural Congress
	First Congress of UNEAC
1969	Cuban-Soviet Friendship Society established
1970	Failure of ten million tonne *zafra*
	Salón 70
1971	First National Congress of Education and Culture
	First Meeting of Latin American Plastic Arts
1972	Cuba becomes full member of COMECON
	Days of Soviet culture begin in Cuba
1974	VI Meeting of the Ministers of Culture of the Socialist Countries held in Havana
1975	First Congress of the PCC
1976	MINCULT founded
	Unveiling of the mural *Dawns of the Revolution* by Orlando Suárez in the Havana Omnibus terminal
	ISA inaugurated
	New Constitution Ratified
1977	Instituto del Libro dismantled
	Second Congress of UNEAC
1979	Sixth Summit of the Non-Aligned conference hosted in Havana
1980	First Havana Theater Festival
	Second Congress of the PCC
1981	Volumen Uno
	First Meeting of Latin American and Caribbean Theater Workers
1982	Third Congress of UNEAC
	UNESCO declared Habana Vieja a World Heritage Site
1983	First International Festival of Teatro Nuevo
1984	First Havana Biennial
	TELARTE I

1985   Third Congress of the PCC
        TELARTE II
1986   Fourth Congress of UNEAC
        Rectification of Past Errors and Negative Tendencies begins

Index

About the Author

Isabel Story is a Lecturer/Senior Lecturer in the School of Art and Design at Nottingham Trent University. Her research focuses on aspects of Cuban and Soviet/Russian cultural policy, visual communication, soft power, socialist internationalism, and nation-building.

www.ingramcontent.com/pod-product-compliance
Lightning Source LLC
Chambersburg PA
CBHW022309280326
41932CB00010B/1033